A Treasury of
GREAT
AMERICAN
SPEECHES

The Great Speeches

Reported in the Style

of Today's Newspapers

With Descriptions of

the Circumstances, Surroundings

and Significance of Each

When It Was Delivered

And the Sequels and Repercussions

Which Made History

From

1645

to

1961

☆

With Illustrations from Various Historical Periods

A Treasury of
GREAT
AMERICAN
SPEECHES

☆

OUR COUNTRY'S LIFE
AND HISTORY
IN THE WORDS OF
ITS GREAT MEN

☆

BY CHARLES HURD

HAWTHORN BOOKS, INC.

Publishers, New York

First Edition, September, 1959
Second Printing, October, 1961
Third Printing, October, 1964

ACKNOWLEDGMENTS

The compiler of this book is indebted beyond measure to a host of individuals and publishers for cooperation in gathering the contemporary speeches included in this work. Every effort has been made to assign proper credits, both in the introductions and below, in the case of recently published works. If credits have been omitted where they are due, they will be included in subsequent editions:

Billy Sunday is quoted from *Billy Sunday, The Man and His Message*, by William T. Ellis, copyright 1941 by L. T. Myers and published by John C. Winston & Co.. Philadelphia, Pa.

Robert Benchley is quoted from *The Treasurer's Report*, by Robert Benchley, copyright 1930 by Robert C. Benchley; copyright 1958 by Gertrude Benchley and published by Harper & Brothers, New York.

Frank Lloyd Wright's speech is from *The Future of Architecture*, by Frank Lloyd Wright, published by Horizon Press, Inc., New York.

Irvin S. Cobb's speech is from *Exit Laughing*, by Irvin S. Cobb, copyright 1941, used by special permission of the publishers, The Bobbs-Merrill Co., Inc., of New York.

Fulton J. Sheen is quoted from the book *War and Guilt*, a collection of his radio broadcast talks published under the auspices of the National Catholic Welfare Conference.

The Rev. Dr. William F. (Billy) Graham is quoted from *America's Hour of Decision*, a collection of his sermons published in 1951 and copyrighted by the Van Kawpen Press, Wheaton, Illinois.

Cornelia Otis Skinner is quoted by permission of Dodd, Mead & Company, New York, from *Bottoms Up!* by Cornelia Otis Skinner, copyright 1955 by Cornelia Otis Skinner Blodgett.

Dr. Robert Oppenheimer is quoted from *The Open Mind*, copyright 1955 by J. Robert Oppenheimer, and published by Simon & Schuster, Inc., New York.

John Mason Brown is quoted with special permission from the manuscript of an unpublished speech, supplied by him.

The United States Department of State granted permission to use excerpts of speeches by President Dwight D. Eisenhower, former Secretary of State George C. Marshall and Secretary of State John Foster Dulles.

Miss Bernice Miller, secretary to former President Herbert Hoover, contributed largely to the work of selecting and reproducing the quotations from Mr. Hoover's speeches.

Former President Harry S. Truman is thanked for special permission to use his remarks.

Mrs. Eleanor Roosevelt kindly assisted in procuring her quoted speech from the Franklin D. Roosevelt Museum, at Hyde Park, N.Y., and in reviewing the edited work.

Henry Cabot Lodge Jr. supplied the manuscript from which he is quoted and contributed comments on the quotation of his grandfather, the late Senator Henry Cabot Lodge.

General Alfred M. Gruenther cooperated wholeheartedly in the presentation herein of his speech on NATO.

Adlai E. Stevenson kindly reviewed the selections used from his remarks.

Charles A. Lindbergh approved inclusion of his famous speech, with the request that it be read in the light of its time of delivery.

Miss Dorothy Thompson also cooperated graciously in the presentation of her words.

Thanks also are due to all the writers and editors of the past who have kept within easy reach the living words from the American past.

Acknowledgment is also made to the New York Public Library Picture Collection for their permission to reproduce the line drawing of Abraham Lincoln on the title page and to Bettmann Archive for their permission to reproduce their illustration entitled "Stump Speaking" on the endpapers for this book.

H-9385

FOREWORD

Here are the highlights of three centuries of our American heritage, a never-ending story merging into today and tomorrow, as told in the words of our nation's gifted speakers. Here are words that are bullets, words that are comfort, words that are exhortation, and words that make us smile or laugh at our foibles.

In time, these words span a period from 1645 to 1961; in subject matter they outline the development of the great spiritual and moral forces that combine to make us what we are. For this is the mind of America, heroic and yet homespun; the players and the lines they utter are both real.

Many other books have compiled the words of our encyclopedic "oratory." This one attempts to cut them to fit the theme of American development expressed by Daniel Webster more than 125 years ago, when he said, "Mind is the great lever of all things."

Our spoken drama divides itself naturally into five acts; the book thus is separated into five parts. While the chronology must divide past from present, nothing is here that is not living in its meaning today.

To emphasize perspective the editor has preceded each speech with a "news story," just as modern newspapers take their readers to the scenes of great events with "leads" telling the essentials of "who, what, when, where and why." Thus this book will help a reader to an understanding of the dramatic backdrop against which Patrick Henry declaimed, "Give me liberty or give me death," as it will also project him into the hushed silence of a joint session of the Congress that in 1959 heard Carl Sandburg deliver his memorable eulogy of Abraham Lincoln. In some cases out of the past, brief sequels to the speeches are recorded; but only where such sequels are significant. In half the cases, there are as yet no definitely indicated sequels, so comment is omitted.

The selections and the treatment of over 100 speeches have been made partly on the basis of straight journalistic interest, as viewed by the writer in more than 30 years of news reporting, and partly from the viewpoint of the amateur historian, because the writer has studied this art for almost as long.

Millions of words were read or re-read to choose these pages; many sources were tapped, and those sites of great speeches not already familiar to the writer were visited and studied. Invaluable aid in research and winnowing was contributed by Eleanor Hurd, and much is owed to painstaking and imaginative final editing by Whit Burnett.

There are also debts to many friends who have helped immensely by their cooperating—in response to invitations—in the selection of their own included words. Among these, in alphabetical listing, are the following:

John Mason Brown, General Alfred M. Gruenther, Herbert Hoover, Charles A. Lindbergh, Henry Cabot Lodge, Jr., Dr. Robert Oppenheimer, Mrs. Franklin D. Roosevelt, Adlai E. Stevenson, Dorothy Thompson and Harry S. Truman.

—CHARLES HURD

CONTENTS

II. GROWING PAINS

III. NEW HORIZONS

IV. DEPRESSION, WAR AND RECONVERSION

V. LOOKING FORWARD

A Treasury of
GREAT
AMERICAN
SPEECHES

I

FOUNDATIONS

JOHN WINTHROP

"Liberty is the proper end and object of authority."

PLYMOUTH COLONY, 1645—Governor John Winthrop defined the duty of "magistrates," or elected governing officials, as that of preserving the liberties of those they govern within all possible limits of human capacities, in a speech concluding a grave court dispute carried to Boston from the town of Hingham.

Simple as the judgment may seem to be, it constitutes a new definition added to the slim archives of precedent being constructed as part of the colonial legal structure.

The case began at Hingham when a militia company, or "train-band," deposed its elected lieutenant. When the lieutenant appealed to Boston for assistance in regaining his position, he won a commendation but the town refused to abide by the senior decision. A group of townsmen carried the case to court by suing Governor Winthrop.

After winning the case, the governor demanded the right to spread upon the record his own views.

THE GREAT questions that have troubled the country are about the authority of the magistrates and the liberty of the people. It is yourselves who have called us to this office, and, being called by you, we have our authority from God, in way of an ordinance, such as hath the image of God eminently stamped upon it, the contempt and violation whereof hath been vindicated with examples of divine vengeance. I entreat you to consider that, when you choose magistrates, you take them from among yourselves, men subject to like passions as you are. Therefore when you see infirmities in us, you should reflect upon your own, and that would make you bear the more with us, and not be severe censurers of the failings of your magistrates, when you have continual experience of the like infirm-

17

ities in yourselves and others. We account him a good servant
who breaks not his covenant. The covenant between you and us is
the oath you have taken of us, which is to this purpose, that we
shall govern you and judge your causes by the rules of God's laws
and our own, according to our best skill. When you agree with a
workman to build you a ship or house, etc., he undertakes as well
for his skill as for his faithfulness, for it is his profession, and you
pay him for both. But when you call one to be a magistrate, he doth
not profess nor undertake to have sufficient skill for that office, nor
can you furnish him with gifts, etc., therefore you must run the
hazard of his skill and ability. But if he fails in faithfulness, which by
his oath he is bound unto, that he must answer for. If it fall out
that the case be clear to common apprehension, and the rule clear
also, if he transgress here, the error is not in the skill, but in the evil
of the will: it must be required of him. But if the case be doubtful,
or the rule doubtful, to men of such understanding and parts as
your magistrates are, if your magistrates should err here, yourselves
must bear it.

For the other point concerning liberty, I observe a great mistake in the country about that. There is a twofold liberty, natural
(I mean as our nature is now corrupt) and civil or federal. The first
is common to man with beasts and other creatures. By this, man,
as he stands in relation to man simply, hath liberty to do what he
lists; it is a liberty to evil as well as to good. This liberty is incom-
patible and inconsistent with authority, and cannot endure the
least restraint of the most just authority. The exercise and maintaining of this liberty makes men grow more evil, and in time to be
worse than brute beasts: *omnes sumus licentia deteriores*. This is
that great enemy of truth and peace, that wild beast, which all the
ordinances of God are bent against, to restrain and subdue it. The
other kind of liberty I call civil or federal; it may also be termed
moral, in reference to the covenant between God and man, in the
moral law, and the politic covenants and constitutions, amongst
men themselves. This liberty is the proper end and object of authority, and cannot subsist without it; and it is a liberty to that
only which is good, just, and honest. This liberty you are to stand
for, with the hazard (not only of your good, but) of your lives, if

need be. Whatsoever crosseth this is not authority, but a distemper thereof. This liberty is maintained and exercised in a way of subjection to authority; it is of the same kind of liberty wherewith Christ hath made us free. The woman's own choice makes such a man her husband; yet, being so chosen, he is her lord, and she is to be subject to him, yet in a way of liberty, not of bondage; and a true wife accounts her subjection her honor and freedom, and would not think her condition safe and free but in her subjection to her husband's authority. Such is the liberty of the church under the authority of Christ, her king and husband; his yoke is so easy and sweet to her as a bride's ornaments; and if through forwardness or wantonness etc. she shake it off, at any time, she is at no rest in her spirit until she take it up again; and whether her lord smiles upon her, and embraceth her in his arms, or whether he frowns, or rebukes, or smites her, she apprehends the sweetness of his love in all, and is refreshed, supported, and instructed by every such dispensation of his authority over her. On the other side, ye know who they are that complain of this yoke and say, let us break their bands etc. we will not have this man to rule over us. Even so, brethren, it will be between you and your magistrates. If you stand for your natural corrupt liberties, and will do what is good in your own eyes, you will not endure the least weight of authority, but will murmur, and oppose, and be always striving to shake off that yoke; but if you will be satisfied to enjoy such civil and lawful liberties, such as Christ allows you, then will you quietly and cheerfully submit unto that authority which is set over you, in all the administrations of it, for your good. Wherein, if we fail at any time, we hope we shall be willing (by God's assistance) to hearken to good advice from any of you, or in any other way of God; so shall your liberties be preserved, in upholding the honor and power of authority amongst you.

The deputy governor having ended his speech, the court arose, and the magistrates and deputies retired to attend their other affairs.

The sequel:

Governor Winthrop's legal victory, more than three centuries ago and his subsequent speech, became important precedents that carried through debates during the next two centuries. In a country founded upon the basis of individual liberty, but yet one faced with the necessity to live within the bounds of legal order, this statement served as a foundation for the development of Republican and Whig arguments against the growth of over-riding central authority vested in individuals.

EDWARD RAWSON

". . . that the Lord may behold us as a people,
offering praise and thereby glorifying Him . . ."

CHARLESTOWN, Mass., June 20, 1676—The American tradition of Thanksgiving, first celebrated by our Pilgrim Fathers more than half a century ago, was proclaimed today in formal statement for the first time from the steps of the Council House.

It was on December 20, 1620, that Governor John Carver gathered around him the small band at Plymouth, to thank God in the midst of overwhelming adversities for the great gift of life itself, in the wilderness of the first colony.

Today a more secure people, through a meeting in council, issued a formal proclamation, declaimed by Edward Rawson, secretary, and ordered to be published in all the towns, for observance on June 29 by "Solemn Thanksgiving and praise to God."

Lest too much credit be arrogated to ourselves for the idea, however, it should be recorded here that the idea of a "thanksgiving" is not original with this colony; it is indeed one of the reflections of the kindnesses of the Dutch who sheltered our fathers before the voyage to America. For it was the people of the Holland states who in 1597 held the first "Prayer of Thanksgiving," to thank God for the victories by Prince Nassau over the armies of Spain.

Here is out first native proclamation of praise:

THE HOLY GOD having by a long and Continual Series of his Afflictive dispensations in and by the present Warr with the Heathen Natives of this land, written and brought to pass bitter things against his own Covenant people in this wilderness, yet so that we evidently discern that in the midst of his judgments he hath remembered mercy, having remembered his Footstool in the day of his sore displeasure against us for our sins, with many singular Intimations of his Fatherly Compassion, and regard; reserving many of our Towns from Desolation Threatened, and attempted by the Enemy, and giving us especially of late with our Confederates many signal Advantages against them, without such Disadvantage to our selves as formerly we have been sensible of, if it be the Lords mercy that we are not consumed, It certainly bespeaks our positive Thankfulness, when our Enemies are in any measure disappointed or destroyed: and fearing the Lord should take notice under so many Intimations of his returning mercy, we should be found an Insensible people, as not standing before Him with Thanksgiving, as well as lading him with our Complaints in the time of pressing Afflictions:

The Council has thought meet to appoint and set apart the 29th day of this instant June, as a day of Solemn Thanksgiving and praise to God for such his goodness and Favour, many Particulars of which mercy might be Instanced, but we doubt not those who are sensible of Gods Afflictions, have been as diligent to espy him returning to us; and that the Lord may behold us as a People offering praise and thereby glorifying Him; the Council doth commend it to the Respective Ministers, Elders and people of this Jurisdiction; Solemnly and seriously to keep the same Beseeching that being perswaded by the mercies of God we may all, even this whole people offer up our bodies and souls as a living and Acceptable Service unto God by Jesus Christ.

By the Council, Edward Rawson, Sect.

JONATHAN EDWARDS

"You are thus in the hands of an angry God."

ENFIELD, Conn., July 8, 1741— The highest-flaming reach of Calvinist orthodoxy, aimed at frightening materialistic-minded New Englanders into a renewal of faith, already termed the Great Awakening, inspired Jonathan Edwards to deliver here today a notable sermon.

Soaring above even his own famous levels of eloquence, he exhorted his congregation, and all within reach of his thoughts, to look upon themselves as instruments of sin, saved from perdition only by the grace of a God whose patience they are taxing, and whose pity they are straining.

The 38-year-old theologian is forceful in exhortation and uncompromising in his doctrine of man as an earthly sinner. In some quarters his strong denunciation of sin-filled mankind already is making theological enemies, while unquestionably awakening laymen to a renewed interest in religious matters.

Dr. Edwards was graduated from Yale College in 1720, at the age of 17, studied theology and for a while tutored at Yale. In his studies he has been a notable disciple of John Locke. In 1727 he became the colleague of his grandfather, John Stoddard, in the ministry at Northampton, Mass., and in 1729 succeeded to that parish, upon the death of the Rev. Stoddard.

Excerpts from this sermon follow:

THE WRATH of God is like great waters that are dammed for the present; they increase more and more, and rise higher and higher, till an outlet is given; and the longer the stream is stopped, the more rapid and mighty is its course, when once it is let loose. 'Tis true, that judgment against your evil work has not been executed hitherto; the floods of God's vengeance have been withheld; but your guilt in the meantime is constantly increasing, and you are every day treasuring up more wrath; the waters are continually rising, and waxing more and more mighty; and there is nothing but the mere pleasure of God that holds the waters back, that are unwilling to be stopped, and press hard to go forward.

If God should only withdraw his hand from the floodgate, it would immediately fly open, and the fiery floods of the fierceness and wrath of God would rush forth with inconceivable fury, and would come upon you with omnipotent power; and if your strength were ten thousand times greater than it is, yea, ten thousand times greater than the strength of the stoutest, sturdiest devil in hell, it would be nothing to withstand or endure it.

The bow of God's wrath is bent, and the arrow made ready on the string, and justice bends the arrow at your heart, and strains the bow, and it is nothing but the mere pleasure of God, and that of an angry God, without any promise or obligation at all, that keeps the arrow one moment from being made drunk with your blood.

Thus are all you that never passed under a great change of heart by the mighty power of the Spirit of God upon your souls; all that were never born again, and made new creatures, and raised from being dead in sin to a state of new and before altogether unexperienced light and life (however you may have reformed your life in many things, and may have had religious affections, and may keep up a form or religion in your families and closets, and in the house of God, and may be strict in it), you are thus in the hands of an angry God; 'tis nothing but his mere pleasure that keeps you from being this moment swallowed up in everlasting destruction.

The God that holds you over the pit of hell, much as one holds a spider or some loathsome insect over the fire, abhors you, and is dreadfully provoked; his wrath towards you burns like fire; he looks upon you as worthy of nothing else, but to be cast into the fire; he is of purer eyes than to bear to have you in his sight; you are ten thousand times so abominable in his eyes, as the most hateful and venomous serpent is in ours. You have offended him infinitely more than ever a stubborn rebel did his prince: and yet it is nothing but his hand that holds you from falling into the fire every moment. 'Tis ascribed to nothing else, that you did not go to hell the last night; that you were suffered to awake again in this world after you closed your eyes to sleep; and there is no other reason to be given why you have not dropped into hell since you arose in the morning, but that God's hand has held you up. There is no other reason to be given why you haven't gone to hell since you have sat here in the house of God, provoking his pure eyes by your sinful wicked manner of attending his solemn worship. Yea, there is nothing else that is to be given as a reason why you don't this very moment drop down into hell. . . .

And let every one that is yet out of Christ and hanging over the pit of hell, whether they be old men and women or middle-aged or young people or little children, now hearken to the loud calls of God's word and providence. This acceptable year of the Lord that is a day of such great favor to some will doubtless be a day of as remarkable vengeance to others. Now undoubtedly it is as it was in the days of John the Baptist, the ax is in an extraordinary manner laid at the root of the trees, that very tree that bringeth not forth good fruit may be hewn down and cast into the fire.

Therefore let every one that is out of Christ now awake and fly from the wrath to come. The wrath of Almighty God is now undoubtedly hanging over a great part of his congregation. Let every one fly out of Sodom. "Haste and escape for your lives, look not behind you, escape to the mountain, lest ye be consumed."

The sequel:

Jonathan Edwards died in 1758, the last of the great New England Calvinists. Ironically he lived in a period when great preaching was awakening new religious consciousness in men and women, but he himself was a martyr to his own uncompromising orthodoxy.

The concept of an "angry God" was being questioned more and more by men equally as devout as Dr. Edwards, who came to lay more stress on the divine qualities of mercy as preached by St. John in his writings based on the simple premise that, "God is love."

In 1750, Northampton Parish could no longer agree with the Edwards philosophy and he was dismissed. In his depression he went to Stockbridge, Mass., where he ministered to a small, mixed congregation of Indians and whites. But there he used his free time to complete the notable introspective work, "The Freedom of the Will."

Mellowing with maturity, Dr. Edwards was called in 1757 to the presidency of the College of New Jersey, later known as Princeton. However, within a year he died.

JOHN HANCOCK

"We fear not death."

BOSTON, Mass., March 5, 1774— John Hancock, as fearless in his patriotism as he is eloquent in arguing the fine points of law, today told a cheering crowd on the Commons here that Americans stand as ready to die for liberty today as were the gallant victims of the Massacre of 1770.

In the midst of rising tensions between England and the American Colonies, Mr. Hancock memorialized the Massacre, as chief speaker on the fourth anniversary of the despicable event, when British troops fired pointblank into massed demonstrators who themselves were unarmed.

Far from frightening patriots into submission to oppression, Mr. Hancock said, the martyrdom of the victims of 1770 stands as a signal warning to the British crown that, come what may, "We fear not death."

Excerpts from the speaker's eulogy of the dead and lesson for the living follow:

IT WAS easy to foresee the consequences which so naturally followed upon sending troops into America, to enforce obedience to acts of the British Parliament which neither God nor man ever empowered them to make. It was reasonable to expect that troops, who knew the errand they were sent upon, would treat the people whom they were to subjugate with a cruelty and haughtiness which too often buried the honorable character of the soldier in the disgraceful name of an unfeeling ruffian.

The troops, upon their first arrival, took possession of our senate house, and pointed their cannon against the judgment hall, and even continued them there whilst the supreme court of juridicature for this province was actually sitting to decide upon the lives and fortunes of the king's subjects. Our streets nightly resounded with the noise of riot and debauchery; our peaceful citizens were hourly exposed to shameful insults, and often felt the effects of their violence and outrage. But this was not all; as though they thought it not enough to violate our civil rights, they endeavored to deprive us of the enjoyment of our religious privileges, to vitiate our morals, and thereby render us deserving of destruction.

I come reluctantly to the transactions of that dismal night, when in such quick succession we felt the extremes of grief, astonishment, and rage; when Heaven in anger, for a dreadful moment, suffered hell to take the reins; when Satan with his chosen band opened the sluices of New England's blood, and sacrilegiously polluted our land with the dead bodies of her guiltless sons.

Let this sad tale of death never be told without a tear; let not the heaving bosom cease to burn with a manly indignation at the barbarous story through the long tracts of future time; let every parent tell the shameful story to his listening children until tears of pity glisten in their eyes, and boiling passion shake their tender frames; and whilst the anniversary of that ill-fated night is kept a jubilee in the grim court of pandemonium let all America join in one common prayer to Heaven, that the inhuman, unprovoked murders of the fifth of March, 1770, planned by Hillsborough, and a knot of treacherous knaves in Boston, and executed by the cruel hand of Preston and his sanguinary coadjutors, may ever stand in history without parallel.

But what, my countrymen, withheld the ready arm of vengeance from executing instant justice on the vile assassins? May that magnificence of spirit which scorns the low pursuits of malice, may that generous compassion which often preserves from ruin, even a guilty villain, forever actuate the noble bosoms of Americans. But let not the miscreant host vainly imagine that we feared their arms. No, them we despised; we dread nothing but slavery. Death is the creature of a poltroon's brain; 'tis immortality to sacrifice ourselves for the salvation of our country.

We fear not death. That gloomy night, the pale-faced moon, and the affrighted stars that hurried through the sky, can witness that we fear not death. Our hearts which, at the recollection, glow with rage that four revolving years have scarcely taught us to restrain, can witness that we fear not death; and happy it is for those who dared to insult us, that their naked bones are not now piled up an everlasting monument of Massachusetts' bravery.

The sequel:

Like many of his southern compatriots, John Hancock's leadership in the fight against suppressive measures involved hazarding far more than his liberty; he was a wealthy man by virtue of inheritance of the leading trading firm in Boston. Already, in 1768, his ship the *Liberty* had been confiscated by the British on charges of smuggling. In a subsequent riot it was burned.

In 1769, Massachusetts patriots had elected Hancock a member of the General Court.

A year after this speech reported here, Hancock was elected a member of the Continental Congress, and in turn chosen as its president.

When the Declaration of Independence was written, he signed it first with a bold flourish and so prominently that ever since signatures have been referred to colloquially as "John Hancocks."

Hancock died in 1793, while holding office as Governor of Massachusetts.

PATRICK HENRY

". . . as for me, give me liberty, or give me death."

RICHMOND, Va., March 23, 1775 —A 39-year-old lawyer, with hair as red as the Virginia clay—Patrick Henry—today stepped across the irrevocable boundary line of rebellion against the Hanoverian Crown in an impassioned speech before the Virginia provincial convention, meeting in St. John's Episcopal Church here.

Already noted for his angry speeches against the Stamp Act, Mr. Henry threw the convention into an uproar when he ended his talk with the stark words:

"I know not what course others may take; but as for me, give me liberty, or give me death."

Delegates to the convention immediately compared Mr. Henry's speech with the outcry by Samuel Adams after the Boston Massacre five years ago this very month, and with John Hancock's speech in Boston just a year ago memorializing that tragedy. However, Mr. Henry passed from the area of deprecation of British misrule into a call to arms.

If a single spark were needed to turn into action the plans already laid by the Continental Congress, this could easily be it. And it likewise was noted here that while Governor John Murray (Earl of Dunsmore) had been well aware of the stand to be taken by this convention —a stand bespoken by Mr. Henry—

he sent no redcoats to intervene. Truly, this convention is Virginia's body of spokesmen, rather than the House of Burgesses at Williamsburg and, noisy as he may seem to the more refined ears of his colleagues such as Peyton Randolph, Thomas Jefferson and John Mason, they are well content to let him speak for all.

Because of Virginia's unique position of leadership in the contest with the British Cabinet at London, this speech ranks almost equally in importance with any delivered in the Continental Congress at Philadelphia in September and October of last year.

The convention must choose, Mr. Henry said, between the beguiling arguments of the "siren" of hope, and "the lamp of experience." A decade of experience, he went on, had shown nothing in the conduct of the British ministry "to justify those hopes with which gentlemen have been pleased to solace themselves."

Pointing figuratively to the eastern seaports, where British forces are constantly being reinforced; toward Boston, where four regiments of troops are encamped in that city; toward New York and Chesapeake Bay, where squadrons of British vessels lie at anchor, the speaker exclaimed:

"I ask gentlemen, sir, what means

this martial array, if its purpose be not to force us to submission? . . . They are meant for us; they can be meant for no other."

Raising a warning finger, as he stood ramrod straight and faced the delegates, Mr. Henry spoke in the voice already noted for its hypnotic sway over juries in court trials:

"It is in vain, sir, to extenuate the matter. Gentlemen may cry peace, peace—but there is no peace. The war has actually begun. The next gale that sweeps from the north will bring to our ears the clash of resounding arms!"

Despite varying opinions among those attending this convention, it is generally agreed that—hothead though Mr. Henry may sometimes seem to be—his speech today was no exaggeration.

MR. PRESIDENT: No man thinks more highly than I do of the patriotism, as well as abilities of the very worthy gentlemen who have just addressed the House. But different men often see the same subject in different lights; and, therefore, I hope that it will not be thought disrespectful to those gentlemen, if, entertaining as I do, opinions of a character very opposite to theirs, I shall speak forth my sentiments freely and without reserve. This is no time for ceremony. The question before the House is one of awful moment to this country. For my own part I consider it as nothing less than a question of freedom or slavery; and in proportion to the magnitude of the subject ought to be the freedom of the debate. It is only in this way that we can hope to arrive at truth, and fulfill the great responsibility which we hold to God and our country. Should I keep back my opinions at such a time, through fear of giving offence, I should consider myself as guilty of treason towards my country, and of an act of disloyalty towards the majesty of heaven, which I revere above all earthly kings.

Mr. President, it is natural to man to indulge in the illusions of hope. We are apt to shut our eyes against a painful truth, and listen to the song of that siren, till she transforms us into beasts. Is this the part of wise men, engaged in a great and arduous struggle for liberty? Are we disposed to be of the number of those who, having eyes, see not, and having ears, hear not, the things which so nearly concern their temporal salvation? For my part, whatever anguish of spirit it may cost, I am willing to know the whole truth; to know the worst and to provide for it.

I have but one lamp by which my feet are guided; and that is the lamp of experience. I know of no way of judging of the future but by the past. And judging by the past, I wish to know what there has been in the conduct of the British ministry for the last ten years, to justify those hopes with which gentlemen have been pleased to solace themselves and the House? Is it that insidious smile with which our petition has been lately received? Trust it not, sir; it will prove a snare to your feet. Suffer not yourselves to be betrayed with a kiss. Ask yourselves how this gracious reception of our petition comports with these war-like preparations which cover our waters and darken our land. Are fleets and armies necessary to a work of love and reconciliation? Have we shown ourselves so unwilling to be reconciled, that force must be called in to win back our love? Let us not deceive ourselves, sir. These are the implements of war and subjugation; the last arguments to which kings resort.

I ask gentlemen, sir, what means this martial array, if its purpose be not to force us to submission? Can gentlemen assign any other possible motives for it? Has Great Britain any enemy, in this quarter of the world, to call for all this accumulation of navies and armies? No, sir, she has none. They are meant for us; they can be meant for no other. They are sent over to bind and rivet upon us those chains which the British ministry have been so long forging. And what have we to oppose to them? Shall we try argument? Sir, we have been trying that for the last ten years. Have we anything new to offer on the subject? Nothing. We have held the subject up in every light of which it is capable; but it has been all in vain. Shall we resort to entreaty and humble supplication? What terms shall we find which have not been already exhausted? Let us not, I beseech you, sir, deceive ourselves longer. Sir, we have done everything that could be done, to avert the storm which is now coming on. We have petitioned; we have remonstrated; we have supplicated; we have prostrated ourselves before the throne, and have implored its interposition to arrest the tyrannical hands of the ministry and Parliament. Our petitions have been slighted; our remonstrances have produced additional violence and insult; our supplications have been disregarded; and we have been spurned, with contempt, from the foot of the throne. In vain, after these things, may we indulge the fond hope of peace and reconciliation. There is no longer any room for hope. If we wish to be free—if we mean to preserve inviolate those inestimable privileges for which we have been so long contending—if we mean not basely to abandon the noble struggle in which we have been so long engaged, and which we have pledged ourselves never to abandon until the glorious object of our contest shall be obtained, we must fight! I repeat it, sir, we must fight! An appeal to arms and to the God of Hosts is all that is left us!

They tell us, sir, that we are weak; unable to cope with so formidable an adversary. But when shall we be stronger? Will it be the next week, or the next year? Will it be when we are totally disarmed, and when a British guard shall be stationed in every house? Shall we gather strength by irresolution and inaction? Shall we acquire the means of effectual resistance, by lying supinely on our backs, and hugging the delusive phantom of hope, until our enemies shall have bound us hand and foot? Sir, we are not weak, if we make proper use of the means which the God of nature hath placed in our power. Three millions of people, armed in the holy cause of liberty, and in such a country as that which we possess, are invincible by any force which our enemy can send against us. Besides, sir, we shall not fight our battles alone. There is a just God who presides over the destinies of nations; and who will raise up friends to fight our battles for us. The battle, sir, is not to the strong alone; it is to the vigilant, the active, the brave. Besides, sir, we have no election. If we were base enough to desire it, it is now too late to retire from the contest. There is no retreat, but in submission and slavery! Our chains are forged! Their clanking may be heard on the plains of Boston! The war is inevitable—and let it come! I repeat it, sir, let it come!

It is in vain, sir, to extenuate the matter. Gentlemen may cry peace, peace—but there is no peace. The war is actually begun! The next gale that sweeps from the north will bring to our ears the clash of resounding arms! Our brethren are already in the field! Why stand we here idle? What is it that gentlemen wish? What would they have? Is life so dear, or peace so sweet, as to be purchased at the price of chains and slavery? Forbid it, Almighty God!

I know not what course others may take; but as for me, give me liberty, or give me death!

The sequel:

Even Patrick Henry probably was surprised with the almost instantaneous manner in which his predictions were fulfilled.

Within less than a month, on April 19, tension exploded in Boston, with the resultant battles of Lexington and Concord.

The second Continental Congress met on May 10. By then Boston was under siege, but Ethan Allen and his Green Mountain Boys on this very date captured Fort Ticonderoga, aided by a force under the then loyal Benedict Arnold.

By June 15 the Continental Congress had "formalized the revolution" by authorizing formation of an army under General George Washington.

When the Declaration of Independence finally was forged into shape by Thomas Jefferson and adopted on July 4, 1776, Benjamin Franklin must have thought back to Henry's words when he declared, with his wry sense of humor, "We must all hang together, or assuredly we will all hang separately."

For Patrick Henry personally this was virtually his "exit line" from the national stage. In the following year he became Virginia's first elected governor, serving through 1779. As a lawyer he increased his wealth and prominence, but a military role in the Revolution—the one sure path to prominence—was denied to him, or even a role on the national political or diplomatic stages.

The destiny for the United States that he foresaw passed into other hands, and its interpretation to other orators.

SAMUEL ADAMS

"We have no other alternative than independence."

PHILADELPHIA, Pa., August 1, 1776—The veteran revolutionary, Samuel Adams, from Massachusetts, today interpreted the Declaration of Independence, in a speech before the Continental Congress, as a step from which there is no retreat; that unless victory is won slavery will be the price paid for failure

With the same undiminished fervor that has marked his leadership in the rebellion against British misrule, first displayed in his opposal more than a decade ago to the Stamp Act, Mr.

Adams said "our union is now complete," and that victory is assured.

But he cautioned that with victory, when it comes, must also come a peace that will make further wars for independence unnecessary. Considering his fiery background, this speech by Mr. Adams, second cousin of his more famous relative John Adams, and chief lieutenant of John Hancock, was moderate and perhaps memorable for the high idealism it set forth.

WE ARE now on this continent, to the astonishment of the world, three millions of souls united in one cause. We have large armies, well disciplined and appointed, with commanders inferior to none in military skill, and superior in activity and zeal. We are furnished with arsenals and stores beyond our most sanguine expectations, and foreign nations are waiting to crown our success by their alliances. There are instances of, I would say, an almost astonishing Providence in our favor; our success has staggered our enemies, and almost given faith to infidels; so we may truly say it is not our own arm which has saved us.

The hand of Heaven appears to have led us on to be, perhaps, humble instruments and means in the great providential dispensation which is completing. We have fled from the political Sodom; let us not look back, lest we perish and become a monument of infamy and derision to the world. For can we ever expect more unanimity and a better preparation for defense; more infatuation of counsel among our enemies, and more valor and zeal among ourselves? The same force and resistance which are sufficient to procure us our liberties will secure us a glorious independence and support us in the dignity of free, imperial states. We cannot suppose that our opposition has made a corrupt and dissipated nation more friendly to America, or created in them a greater respect for the rights of mankind. We can therefore expect a restoration and establishment of our privileges, and a compensation for the injuries we have received, from their want of power, from their fears, and not from their virtues. The unanimity and valor which will effect an honorable peace can render a future contest for our liberties unnecessary. He who has strength to chain down the wolf is a madman if he let him loose without drawing his teeth and paring his nails.

We have no other alternative than independence, or the most ignominious and galling servitude. The legions of our enemies thicken on our plains; desolation and death mark their bloody career; whilst the mangled corpses of our countrymen seem to cry out to us as a voice from Heaven.

Our union is now complete; our constitution composed, established, and approved. You are now the guardians of your own liberties. We may justly address you, as the *decemviri* did the Romans, and say: "Nothing that we propose can pass into a law without your consent. Be yourselves, O Americans, the authors of those laws on which your happiness depends."

You have now in the field armies sufficient to repel the whole force of your enemies and their base and mercenary auxiliaries. The hearts of your soldiers beat high with the spirit of freedom; they are animated with the justice of their cause, and while they grasp their swords can look up to Heaven for assistance. Your adversaries are composed of wretches who laugh at the rights of humanity, who turn religion into derision, and would, for higher wages, direct their swords against their leaders or their country. Go on, then, in your generous enterprise, with gratitude to Heaven for past success, and confidence of it in the future. For my own part, I ask no greater blessing than to share with you the common danger and common glory. If I have a wish dearer to my soul than that my ashes may be mingled with those of a Warren and a Montgomery, it is that these American States may never cease to be free and independent.

The sequel:

Throughout the War of the Revolution Samuel Adams continued to serve as a member of the Continental Congress from Massachusetts. But with victory in 1781, his popularity fell and he was denied a place in the Congress of the new United States because of the growing feeling that he was too radical.

Like Patrick Henry, he was forced to retreat from the national stage, but Massachusetts chose him as Governor from 1794 to 1797, again making a parallel with the career of the Virginia firebrand.

BENJAMIN FRANKLIN

"The older I grow, the more apt I am to doubt my own judgment of others."

PHILADELPHIA, Pa., 1787—In a speech on the newly written Constitution, before the Convention here at which he is the eldest sage among sages, 81-year-old Benjamin Franklin did much toward assuring adoption of this notable document by his injection of homely philosophy into the oft-times heated debate.

The diplomatic editor of *Poor Richard's Almanack* frankly told his colleagues that he is not satisfied with the Constitution drafted for submission to the States, and yet he expressed doubt that he ever would be satisfied.

More than that, however, he counseled his fellow members of the Convention against such a predisposition toward personal feelings about it as to break the unanimity of support that it must have among its authors.

The Constitution, he emphasized, represents a compromise among many ideas . . . . compromise and agreement among prejudices, passions, local interest and selfishness of views.

I CONFESS that I do not entirely approve of this Constitution at present; but, sir, I am not sure I shall never approve of it, for, having lived long, I have experienced many instances of being obliged, by better information or fuller consideration, to change opinions even on important subjects, which I once thought right, but found to be otherwise. It is therefore that, the older I grow, the more apt I am to doubt my own judgment of others. Most men, indeed, as well as most sects in religion, think themselves in possession of all truth, and that wherever others differ from them, it is so far error. Steele, a Protestant, in a dedication, tells the pope that the only difference between our two churches in their opinions of the certainty of their doctrine is, the Romish Church is infallible, and the Church of England is never in the wrong. But, though many private persons think almost as highly of their own infallibility as of that of their sect, few express it so naturally as a certain French lady, who, in a little dispute with her sister, said: "But I meet with nobody but myself that is always in the right."

In these sentiments, sir, I agree to this Constitution with all its faults—if they are such—because I think a general government necessary for us, and there is no form of government but what may be a blessing to the people if well administered; and I believe, further, that this is likely to be well administered for a course of years, and can only end in despotism, as other forms have done before it, when the people shall become so corrupted as to need despotic government, being incapable of any other. I doubt, too, whether any other convention we can obtain may be able to make a better Constitution; for, when you assemble a number of men, to have the advantage of their joint wisdom, you inevitably assemble with those men all their prejudices, their passions, their errors of opinion, their local interests, and their selfish views. From such an assembly can a perfect production be expected?

It therefore astonishes me, sir, to find this system approaching so near to perfection as it does; and I think it will astonish our enemies, who are waiting with confidence to hear that our counsels are confounded.

ALEXANDER HAMILTON

"The states can never lose their powers until the whole people of the United States are robbed of their liberties."

POUGHKEEPSIE, N. Y., 1787—The youngest of the vital young men who hammered into form the Federal Constitution derided the fears of conservative New Yorkers that establishment of the national government would mean the extinction of State sovereignty—a fear so strong among the older New York hierarchy that it still threatened ratification of the Constitution.

Alexander Hamilton, alien born in the Barbadoes, and this year only 30 years old, drew his bow in a personal contest of debate with Governor George Clinton, at the New York Constitutional Convention called to meet under Governor Clinton's chairmanship. The site itself is significant —this city settled exactly 100 years ago, unofficial center of the up-river patroons and far removed from the more cosmopolitan environs of New York City.

The stage already has been set for this debate through an exchange of letters published in the New York *Journal.* Governor Clinton is well known as the author signing himself "Cato," opposing ratification, and Hamilton as the writer of the "Caesar" replies. Here Hamilton must make up in legal and oratorical skill Governor Clinton's advantage of 18 years of seniority and political experience. However, on his side in debate are the month-in and month-out sessions with Thomas Jefferson and James Madison in drafting this experimental Constitution, and long forays into arguments embodied in articles in the *Federalist.*

It was the consensus here that Mr. Hamilton had delivered one of his greatest speeches, lifting the foundation he undoubtedly is building for great future influence and reputation. Among his auditors were those who applauded him, not the least being his own coterie of up-river friends who have been enchanted by him since this dashing young soldier and lawyer married Elizabeth Schuyler, daughter of General Schuyler and an aristocrat.

But results are what count, in politics as in battles, and at this point it is by no means certain that Mr. Hamilton has carried the field. The State Convention will not be stampeded into action, and delay now is the same as an adverse vote.

GENTLEMEN indulge too many unreasonable apprehensions of danger to the state governments; they seem to suppose that the moment you put men into a national council they become corrupt and tyrannical, and lose all their affection for their fellow citizens. . . .

The state governments are essentially necessary to the form and spirit of the general system. As long, therefore, as Congress has a full conviction of this necessity, they must, even upon principles purely national, have as firm an attachment to the one as to the other. This conviction can never leave them, unless they become madmen. While the Constitution continues to be read and its principle known, the states must, by every rational man, be considered as essential, component parts of the Union; and therefore the idea of sacrificing the former to the latter is wholly inadmissible.

The objectors do not advert to the natural strength and resources of state governments, which will ever give them an important superiority over the general government. If we compare the nature of their different powers, or the means of popular influence which each possesses, we shall find the advantage entirely on the side of the states. This consideration, important as it is, seems to have been little attended to. The aggregate number of representatives throughout the states may be two thousand. Their personal influence will, therefore, be proportionably more extensive than that of one or two hundred men in Congress. The state establishments of civil and military officers of every description, infinitely surpassing in number any possible correspondent establishments in the general government, will create such an extent and complication of attachments as will ever secure the predilection and support of the people. Whenever, therefore, Congress shall meditate any infringement of the state constitutions, the great body of the people will naturally take part with their domestic representatives. Can the general government withstand such a united opposition? Will the people suffer themselves to be stripped of their privileges? Will they suffer their legislatures to be reduced to a shadow and a name? The idea is shocking to common sense.

From the circumstances already explained, and many others which might be mentioned, results a complicated, irresistible check, which must ever support the existence and importance of the state governments. The danger, if any exists, flows from an opposite source. The probable evil is, that the general government will be too dependent on the state legislatures, too much governed by their prejudices, and too obsequious to their humors; that the states, with every power in their hands, will make encroachments on the national authority, till the Union is weakened and dissolved.

There are certain social principles in human nature from which we may draw the most solid conclusions with respect to the conduct of individuals and of communities. We love our families more than our neighbors; we love our neighbors more than our countrymen in general. The human affections, like the solar heat, lose their intensity as they depart from the center, and become languid in proportion to the expansion of the circle on which they act. On these principles, the attachment of the individual will be first and forever secured by the state governments; they will be a mutual protection and support. Another source of influence, which has already been pointed out, is the various official connections in the states. Gentlemen endeavor to evade the force of this by saying that these offices will be insignificant. This is by no means true.

The state officers will ever be important, because they are necessary and useful. Their powers are such as are extremely interesting to the people; such as affect their property, their liberty, and life.

What is more important than the administration of justice and the execution of the civil and criminal laws? Can the state governments become insignificant while they have the power of raising money independently and without control? If they are really useful, if they are calculated to promote the essential interests of the people, they must have their confidence and support. The states can never lose their powers till the whole people of America are robbed of their liberties. These must go together; they must support each other, or meet one common fate. . . .

With regard to the jurisdiction of the two governments, I shall certainly admit that the Constitution ought to be so formed as not to prevent the states from providing for their own existence; and I maintain that it is so formed, and that their power of providing for themselves is sufficiently established. . . .

That two supreme powers cannot act together is false. They are inconsistent only when they are aimed at each other or at one indivisible object. The laws of the United States are supreme as to all their proper, constitutional objects; the laws of the states are supreme in the same way. These supreme laws may act on different objects without clashing; or they may operate on different parts of the same common object with perfect harmony. Suppose both governments should lay a tax of a penny on a certain article; has not each an independent and uncontrollable power to collect its own tax? The meaning of the maxim, there cannot be two supremes, is simply this—two powers cannot be supreme over each other. . . .

Sir, we cannot reason from probabilities alone. When we leave common sense, and give ourselves up to conjecture, there can be no certainty, no security in our reasonings.

The sequel:

Without ratification of the Constitution by New York, it is doubtful if there ever could have been a Federal Government. A loose confederation of states—as Jefferson, Madison and Hamilton and the major statesmen who had joined in the Constitutional Convention well knew—could never be a power in the world. It would more likely become, like the Germanic states, a breeding ground for internecine wars.

New York as a state was ambitious. It was wealthy. Trade was making New York the shipping and financial center of the New World, at a time when soil depletion already was robbing the South of its earlier massive wealth built on cultivation of cotton and tobacco.

In New York, Governor Clinton exerted a leadership that carried him seven times into the Governorship. New York felt that already it was a power on its own, bigger in many ways than the Federal establishment to which it was asked to delegate so much.

Had not the state by its own resources made its economy great, despite occupation of the city by the British throughout the Revolution? Had it not settled its own Indian wars in the western reaches with its own resources? Had not Governor Clinton personally led the fight that already has established New York's expansionist claims to the so-called New Hampshire grants, later to become the State of Vermont?

No, Hamilton, unlike Patrick Henry, had not found in this State Convention his moment to sweep up a victory with words. Rather, he must content himself with stimulating anew men's thoughts.

Ratification of the Constitution by New York must wait another year, until a majority of the other states had acted favorably.

As for Hamilton, he wasted no time in moping. Already he was preoccupied with plans to run the Federal Government on a sound business system; it was inevitable that he would add to his legal stature great political honors—the Secretaryship of the Treasury, establishment of New York's first chartered bank.

It was equally inevitable in the hard, competitive society in which he chose to become a harsh competitive individual that he would make enemies. But as yet his path, that led almost to the Presidency itself, had not yet been permanently halted by Aaron Burr.

Even in a country as small as the United States of 1787, there was room for vast contrasts, such as those marking the difference between Hamilton's adopted northern career and the softer but sturdy accents of Virginia, where James Madison was nominated by his seniors to present the case for the Federal Constitution to the Virginia Constitutional Assembly.

JAMES MADISON

"Would it be possible for government to have credit, without having the power of raising money?"

RICHMOND, Va., June 6, 1788— James Madison, second only to Thomas Jefferson as architect of the new Federal Constitution, today urged ratification of that document in most compelling terms, as he addressed the Convention of Virginia on the need for a responsible, powerful central government but one to be held in check by a carefully contrived diversification of protections for the individual states.

His speech pointed up the vagaries of arguments mustered against the Constitution since its completion by the Philadelphia Convention a year ago. As he spoke here, the principal argument to be overcome was the fear that Virginia, already having assumed responsibility for its debts incurred in the Revolution, would be made the tax dupe of other and less provident states in future tax laws by the Federal Government. This fear was not unlike the arguments advanced in the New York Convention one year ago, when Alexander Hamilton was attempting to allay similar fears on the part of New York's vested interests.

Mr. Madison, at 33 years of age the "baby of the Virginia leaders," has few of the arts of oratory, but he already has shown by his writings his capacity to muster argument with cogent words, as when he stated, "Direct taxes will only be recurred to for great purposes."

Mr. Jefferson, for reasons of politics, has assumed the role of elder statesman and left the carrying of debate to others. General George Washington, himself the chairman of the Constitutional Convention in Philadelphia, has remained aloof and silent at Mt. Vernon.

Thus the field of political argument on behalf of the great document has been left mainly in the hands of a younger group headed by Mr. Madison and lesser known figures such as John Marshall, who has yet to make his own appeal.

GIVE ME leave to say something of the nature of the government, and to show that it is perfectly safe and just to vest it with the power of taxation. There are a number of opinions; but the principal question is, whether it be a federal or a consolidated government. . . . I myself conceive that it is of a mixed nature; it is, in a manner, unprecedented. We cannot find one express prototype in the experience of the world: it stands by itself. In some respects, it is a government of a federal nature; in others, it is of a consolidated nature.

Were it . . . a consolidated government, the assent of a majority of the people would be sufficient for its establishment, and as a majority have adopted it already, the remaining States would be bound by the act of the majority, even if they unanimously reprobated it . . . but, sir, no State is bound by it, as it is, without its own consent. Should all the States adopt it, it will be then a government established by the thirteen States of America, not through the intervention of the Legislature, but by the people at large. In this particular respect, the distinction between the existing and proposed governments is very material.

The existing system has been derived from the dependent, derivative authority of the Legislatures of the States; whereas this is derived from the superior power of the people. If we look at the manner in which alterations are to be made in it, the same idea is in some degree attended to. By the new system, a majority of the States cannot introduce amendments; nor are all the States required for that purpose; three-fourths of them must concur in alterations; in this there is a departure from the federal idea. The members to the national House of Representatives are to be chosen by the people at large, in proportion to the numbers in the respective districts. When we come to the Senate, its members are elected by the States in their equal and political capacity; but had the government been completely consolidated, the Senate would have been chosen by the people, in their individual capacity, in the same manner as the members of the other House. Thus it is of complicated nature, and this complication, I trust, will be found to exclude the evils of absolute consolidation, as well as of a mere confederacy. If Virginia were separated from all the States, her power and authority would extend to all cases; in like manner, were all powers vested in the general government, it would be a consolidated government; but the powers of the Federal government are enumerated; it can only operate in certain cases: it has legislative powers on defined and limited objects, beyond which it cannot extend its jurisdiction.

But the honorable member has satirized, with peculiar acrimony, the power given to the general government by this Constitution. I conceive that the first question on this subject is, whether these powers be necessary; if they be, we are reduced to the dilemma of either submitting to the inconvenience, or losing the Union. Let us consider the most important of these reprobated powers; that of direct taxation is most generally objected to. With respect to the exigencies of government, there is no question but the most easy mode of providing for them will be adopted. When, therefore, direct taxes are not necessary, they will not be recurred to. It can be of little advantage to those in power to raise money in a manner oppressive to the people. To consult the conveniences of the people will cost them nothing, and in many respects will be advantageous to them. Direct taxes will only be recurred to for great purposes.

What has brought on other nations those immense debts, under the pressure of which many of them labor? Not the expenses of their governments, but war. . . . How is it possible a war could be supported without money or credit? And would it be possible for government to have credit, without having the power of raising money? No, it would be impossible for any government, in such a case, to defend itself. Then, I say, sir, that it is necessary to establish funds for extraordinary exigencies, and give this power to the general government; for the utter inutility of previous requisitions on the States is too well known. Would it be possible for those countries, whose finances and revenues are carried to the highest perfection, to carry on the operations of government on great emergencies, such as the maintenance of a war, without an uncontrolled power of raising money? Has it not been necessary for Great Britain, notwithstanding the facility of the collection of her taxes, to have recourse very often to this and other extraordinary methods of procuring money? Would not her public credit have been ruined, if it was known that her power to raise money was limited? Has not France been obliged, on great occasions, to recur to unusual means, in order to raise funds? It has been the case in many countries, and no government can exist unless its powers extend to make provisions for every contingency.

If we were actually attacked by a powerful nation, and our general government had not the power of raising money, but depended solely on requisitions, our condition would be truly deplorable: if the revenues of this commonwealth were to depend on twenty distinct authorities, it would be impossible for it to carry on its operations. This must be obvious to every member here: I think, therefore, that it is necessary for the preservation of the Union that this power should be given to the general government.

The sequel:

On June 26, the Convention of Virginia ratified the Constitution by a majority vote, but protracted debate prior to that vote robbed this proud State of the opportunity to become the historic ninth state to ratify, thereby rounding out the necessary two-thirds favorable actions by those States that comprised the original thirteen.

Five days earlier, small New Hampshire had become the ninth state to act favorably. New York followed Virginia by thirty additional days, with its convention bowing to popular will on July 26, 1788.

What a year it had been—this year of searching debate, argument and counter-argument that went so far to elucidate the climate of political opinion in which the future Federal status of the United States was germinating!

Out of that debate, Madison would go forward, in the order of seniority, to occupy the White House as President, third in line after Washington, and preceded by John Adams and Thomas Jefferson.

Another Virginian, John Marshall, who delivered his own impassioned plea for ratification by Virginia four days after Madison spoke, would live to become Chief Justice of the Supreme Court and there spend 35 years writing and guiding the decisions that would arm with irrevocable legal force even today the points of law imbedded in the Constitution now under such debate.

Within a year, in the meantime, the Constitution would be translated into political form as Government and law, weak at first in structure but lusty in growth under the benevolent despotism of its first President, George Washington.

GEORGE WASHINGTON

" 'Tis our true policy to steer clear of permanent alliances with any portion of the foreign world."

PHILADELPHIA, Pa., September 19, 1796—President Washington today announced his unequivocal decision to relinquish the high office in which he set the course of the country whose freedom he won and over the writing of whose Constitution he presided, when his second term ends next March.

In a farewell address which must rank among the world's great testaments, the vigorous but aging First Citizen culled from his vast experience a set of maxims that, as he said, summarized his deep "solicitude for your welfare," embracing all the sections and peoples of the country that have burgeoned from the original thirteen colonies.

The President's address was not delivered as a set speech but was released for publication in time to make its mark, it is hoped, upon the various groups now arranging their campaigns for the election of Electors who will meet early next year to choose the successor to Mr. Washington.

It now appears that Mr. John Adams, the Vice President, will be selected as the second President of the United States, but already the murmurings of party politics are rising to a notable pitch. Chief among those who are entirely loyal to the country, to the administration and particularly to President Washington, but who feel that there should be a more open contest for high office, is Thomas Jefferson. In New York and New Jersey there is open conflict within the Federal Party between Secretary of the Treasury Hamilton and Mr. Aaron Burr, due in part to Mr. Hamilton's adroit maneuverings in achieving an exclusive charter for the Bank of New York, and closing the field, temporarily at least, to Mr. Burr's group.

There also is a notably rising tide of division between three major areas of the country, a situation to which President Washington pointed vigorously in his address. While the North Atlantic States prosper vigorously through world trade as shippers and enterprisers, rising costs and lower prices have squeezed the cotton and tobacco planters of the South. In the western reaches, loud voices are raised for legislation favoring the newly opened territories, in particular taxation benefits that will encourage development.

FRIENDS AND fellow-citizens: The period for a new election of a citizen, to administer the executive government of the United

States, being not far distant, and the time actually arrived when your thoughts must be employed in designating the person who is to be clothed with that important trust, it appears to me proper, especially as it may conduce to a more distinct impression of the public voice, that I should now apprise you of the resolution I have formed, to decline being considered among the number of those of whom a choice is to be made. . . .

The impressions with which I first undertook this arduous trust were explained on the proper occasion. In the discharge of this trust I will only say, that I have with good intentions contributed towards the organization and administration of the government, the best exertions of which a very fallible judgment was capable. . . .

Here, perhaps I ought to stop. But a solicitude for your welfare, which cannot end but with my life, and the apprehension of danger, natural to that solicitude, urge me, on an occasion like the present, to offer to your solemn contemplation, and to recommend to your frequent review, some sentiments, which are the result of much reflection, of no inconsiderable observation, and which appear to me all-important to the permanency of your felicity as a people. . . .

While, then, every part of our country thus feels an immediate and particular interest in union, all the parts combined cannot fail to find, in the united mass of means and efforts, greater strength, greater resource, proportionably greater security from external danger, a less frequent interruption of their peace from foreign nations; and what is of inestimable value, they must derive from union an exemption from those broils and wars between themselves which so frequently afflict neighboring countries, not tied together by the same government, which their own rivalships would be sufficient to produce, but which opposite foreign alliances, attachments and intrigues, would stimulate and embitter.

Hence, likewise, they will avoid the necessity of those overgrown military establishments, which, under any form of government, are inauspicious to liberty, and which are to be regarded as particularly hostile to republican liberty. . . .

In contemplating the causes which may disturb our union, it occurs, as a matter of serious concern, that any ground should have been furnished for characterizing parties by geographical discriminations—Northern and Southern, Atlantic and Western— whence designing men may endeavor to excite a belief that there is a real difference of local interests and views. One of the expedients of party to acquire influence within particular districts is to misrepresent the opinions and aims of other districts. You cannot shield yourselves too much against the jealousies and heart-burnings which spring from these misrepresentations; they tend to render alien to each other those who ought to be bound together by fraternal affection. . . .

The basis of our political systems is the right of the people to make and to alter the constitutions of government. But the constitution, which at any time exists, until changed by explicit and authentic act of the whole people, is sacredly obligatory upon all. The very idea of the power and the right of the people to establish a government presupposes the duty of every individual to obey the established government. . . .

Toward the preservation of your government and the permanency of your present happy state, it is requisite, not only that you speedily discountenance irregular opposition to its acknowledged authority, but also that you resist with care the spirit of innovation upon its principles, however specious the pretexts. . . . It is substantially true, that virtue and morality is a necessary spring of popular government. The rule, indeed, extends with more or less force to every species of free government. Who, that is a sincere friend of it, can look with indifference upon attempts to shake the foundation of the fabric? . . .

Observe good faith and justice toward all nations; cultivate peace and harmony with all; religion and morality enjoin this conduct; and can it be that good policy does not equally enjoin it? It will be worthy of a free, enlightened, and, at no distant period, a great nation, to give to mankind the magnanimous and too novel example of a people always guided by an exalted justice and benevolence. . . .

In the execution of such a plan, nothing is more essential than that permanent, inveterate antipathies against particular nations, and passionate attachments for others, should be excluded; and that in place of them, just and amicable feelings toward all should be cultivated. The nation, which indulges toward another an habitual fondness, is in some degree a slave. . . . The great rule of hatred, or an habitual conduct for us, in regard to foreign nations, is, in extending our commercial relations, to have with them as little political connection as possible.

Tis our true policy to steer clear of permanent alliances with any portion of the foreign world; so far, I mean, as we are now at liberty to do it; for let me not be understood as capable of patronizing infidelity to existing engagements. I hold the maxim no less applicable to public than to private affairs, that honesty is always the best policy. I repeat it, therefore, let those engagements be observed in their genuine sense. But, in my opinion, it is unnecessary, and would be unwise to extend them.

Taking care always to keep ourselves, by suitable establishments, in a respectable defensive posture, we may safely trust to temporary alliances for extraordinary emergencies.

Harmony, and a liberal intercourse with all nations, are recommended by policy, humanity, and interest. But even our commercial policy should hold an equal and impartial hand; neither seeking nor granting exclusive favors or preferences; consulting the natural course of things; diffusing and diversifying, by gentle means the streams of commerce, but forcing nothing. . . . There can be no greater error than to expect to calculate upon real favors from nation to nation. It is an illusion, which experience must cure, which a just pride ought to discard.

In offering to you, my countrymen, these counsels of an old and affectionate friend, I dare not hope they will make the strong and lasting impression I could wish; that they will control the usual current of passions, or prevent our nation from running the course which has hitherto marked the destiny of nations! But, if I may even flatter myself, that they may be productive of some partial benefit, some occasional good; that they may now and then recur to moderate the fury of party spirit; to warn against the mischiefs of foreign intrigues; to guard against the imposture of pretended patriotism; this hope will be a full recompense for the solicitude of your welfare, by which they have been dictated.

The sequel:

While often honored in the breach of its good advice, the Farewell Address stands as one of the great statements of principles of all time, well through the second century after its delivery.

In recurring debates, isolationists have made it seem that Washington gave all his strength to a solemn warning against "foreign alliances." The clearer view in restatement is that he warned against *"permanent"* organizations of such a nature.

No document save the Constitution has been quoted more often in political debate. And whether the arguments from it are used *pro* or *con* in the heat of political controversies, one thing stands out as time passes:

As a political testament it stands alone.

THOMAS JEFFERSON

"We are all Republicans; we are all Federalists."

WASHINGTON, D. C., March 4, 1801—Thomas Jefferson took the oath of office as President of the United States in an atmosphere which prompted him to devote all of his eloquence to restoring unity among the country's leaders lest they fall into the divisions of parties against which President Washington warned.

The words of his Inaugural Address were hopeful expressions of unity. The facts were greatly different, for John Adams today sulked in anger against the open revolt led by Mr. Jefferson himself which started the movement called popularly the Republicans, that won the majority of the electoral vote for Mr. Jefferson and robbed Mr. Adams of a second term.

In fact, until the very hour of the clock arrived last night that ended the administration of President Adams, he occupied himself in filling vacancies in public offices with hardshell Federalists who might be expected to thwart the more radical tendencies of the new men following Mr. Jefferson under the Republican banner.

Chief among these appointees is Mr. John Marshall, who within the past twenty-four hours was named

Chief Justice of the Supreme Court— a conservative Virginian counted upon to check, at the bench of ultimate appeal for all laws, such radicalism as may be written by the new Administration into the country's laws.

DURING THE contest of opinion through which we have passed, the animation of discussions and of exertions has sometimes worn an aspect which might impose on strangers unused to think freely, and to speak and to write what they think; but this being now decided by the voice of the nation, announced according to the rules of the Constitution, all will of course arrange themselves under the will of the law, and unite in common efforts for the common good. All too will bear in mind this sacred principle, that though the will of the majority is in all cases to prevail, that will, to be rightful, must be reasonable; that the minority possess their equal rights, which equal laws must protect, and to violate which would be oppression.

Let us then, fellow-citizens, unite with one heart and one mind, let us restore to social intercourse that harmony and affection without which liberty and even life itself are but dreary things. And let us reflect, that having banished from our land that religious intolerance under which mankind so long bled and suffered, we have yet gained little, if we countenance a political intolerance, as despotic, as wicked, and as capable of as bitter and bloody persecutions. During the throes and convulsions of the ancient world, during the agonizing spasms of infuriated man, seeking through blood and slaughter his long-lost liberty, it was not wonderful that the agitation of the billows should reach even this distant and peaceful shore; that this should be more felt and feared by some, and less by others, and should divide opinions as to measures of safety; but every difference of opinion is not a difference of principle. We have called by different names brethren of the same principle. We are all Republicans; we are all Federalists.

If there be any among us who wish to dissolve this Union, or to change its republican form, let them stand undisturbed as monuments of the safety with which error of opinion may be tolerated, where reason is left free to combat it. I know, indeed, that some honest men fear that a republican government cannot be strong; that this government is not strong enough. But would the honest patriot, in the full tide of successful experiment, abandon a government which has so far kept us free and firm, on the theoretic and visionary fear, that this government, the world's best hope, may, by possibility, want energy to preserve itself? I trust not. I believe this, on the contrary, the strongest government on earth. I believe it the only one where every man, at the call of the law, would fly to the standard of the law, and would meet invasions of the public order as his own personal concern. Sometimes it is said that man cannot be trusted with the government of himself. Can he then be trusted with the government of others? Or, have we found angels in the form of kings, to govern him? Let history answer this question.

Let us then, with courage and confidence, pursue our own federal and republican principles; our attachment to union and representative government. Kindly separated by nature and a wide ocean from the exterminating havoc of one quarter of the globe; too high-minded to endure the degradation of the others, possessing a chosen country, with room enough for our descendants to the thousandth and thousandth generation, entertaining a due sense of our equal right to the use of our own faculties, to the acquisition of our own industry, to honor and confidence from our fellow-citizens, resulting not from birth, but from our actions and their sense of them, enlightened by a benign religion, professed in deed and practised in various forms, yet all of them inculcating honesty, truth, temperance, gratitude, and the love of man, acknowledging and adoring an overruling Providence, which, by all its dispensations, proves that it delights in the happiness of man here, and his greater happiness hereafter; with all these blessings, what more is necessary to make us a happy and prosperous people? Still one thing more, fellow-citizens, a wise and frugal government, which shall restrain men from injuring one another, shall leave them otherwise free to regulate their own pursuits of industry and improvement, and shall not take from the mouth of labor the bread it has earned. This is the sum of good government; and this is necessary to close the circle of our felicities.

The sequel:

This Inaugural Address by President Jefferson did not close the gap in political ranks. In fact, his election marked the birth of the two-party system which, while he could not know it and despite Washington's warnings against such a decision, has become one of the great strengths of the American form of politics. For more than a century and a half, American politics have been planted upon the basic idea of responsible leadership by a majority party and the exercise of checks and balances by a responsible minority party; never a plurality of parties that make possible grasp of leadership by a minority spokesmen on the basis of deals with a host of minor parties. Such a system wrecked the French Fourth Republic.

As an echo of the Adams-Jefferson division, the United States won the service of John Marshall as Chief Justice for 35 years, in which time he made the reputation of probably the greatest man to hold that office.

His appointment as a result of John Adams' temporary spite became perhaps the most notable action by that stern old New Englander.

JOHN QUINCY ADAMS

"Think of your forefathers and of your posterity."

PLYMOUTH, Mass., Dec. 22, 1802 —"Man lives his highest destiny in the continuity of his interests as a unit within his family, his community and his country," said Senator-elect John Quincy Adams in an oration marking the anniversary of the landing of the Pilgrims here almost two centuries ago.

It seemed as though Mr. Adams, from his vantage point of political privilege as son of the incumbent President, was voicing alarm at a general tone of self-seeking among our States and ourselves as individuals. He indicated strongly that perhaps we are falling into the pit of older societies, of using our great heritage for individual gain. Instead, he constrained his hearers to make their present activities a mark of devotion to the past and a foundation for the future of the whole of America.

He took as his text the rallying cry of an ancient British chieftain, who when hard pressed by Roman conquerors cried out, "Think of your forefathers and of your posterity."

"Man, therefore, was not made for himself alone—no! He was made for his country by the obligations of the social compact; he was made for his species, by the Christian duties of universal charity; he was made for all ages past by the sentiment of reverence for his forefathers, and he was made for all future times by the impulse of affection for his progeny."

A familiar of the courts of Europe by virtue of his father's earlier missions, the Senator-elect was sent to Europe while in his teens to study. In 1781, when only fourteen years of age, he was taken by Francis Dana to Russia, where he remained for two years as a semi-official member of Dana's mission. Despite these separations from formal schooling, he was graduated from Harvard College in 1788 at the age of 21. Since then he has been Minister to The Netherlands, appointed by President Washington and serving in 1794, and for the four years ending in 1801 Minister to Prussia.

AMONG THE sentiments of most principal operation upon the human heart, and most highly honorable to the human character are those of veneration for our forefathers, and of love of our posterity. They form the connecting links between the selfish and the social passions. By the fundamental principles of Christianity the happiness of the individual is interwoven by innumerable and imperceptible ties with that of his contemporaries; by the power of filial reverence and parental affection, individual existence is extended beyond the limits of individual life, and the happiness of every age is chained in mutual dependence upon that of every other.

Respect for his ancestors excites in the breast of man interest in their history, attachment to their character, concern for their errors, involuntary pride in their virtues. Love for his posterity spurs him to exertion for their support, stimulates him to virtue for their example, and fills him with the tenderest solicitude for their welfare. Man, therefore, was not made for himself alone—no! He was made for his country by the obligations of the social compact; he was made for his species, by the Christian duties of universal charity; he was made for all ages past by the sentiment of reverence for his forefathers, and he was made for all future times by the impulse of affection for his progeny.

Under the influence of these principles, "existence sees him spurn her bounded reign." They redeem nature from the subjection of time and space: he is no longer a "puny insect shivering in a breeze"; he is the glory of creation—formed to occupy all time and all extent; bounded, during his residence upon earth, only by the boundaries of the world and destined to life and immortality in brighter regions, when the fabric of nature itself shall dissolve and perish.

The voice of history has not in all its compass a note but answers in unison with these sentiments. The barbarian chieftain* who defended his country against the Roman invasion, driven to the remotest extremity of Britain, and stimulating his followers to battle by all his power of persuasion upon the human heart, concludes his exhortation by an appeal to these irresistible feelings—"Think of your forefathers and of your posterity."

The revolutions of time furnish no previous examples of a nation, shooting up to maturity and expanding into greatness with the rapidity which has characterized the growth of the American people. In the luxuriance of youth and in the vigor of manhood it is pleasing and instructive to look backward upon the helpless days of infancy, but with continual changes of a growing subject the transactions of that early period would soon be obliterated from the memory, but for some periodical call to aid the silent records of the historian. Such celebrations arouse and gratify the kindliest emotions of the bosom. They are faithful pledges of the respect we have to the memory of our ancestors and the tenderness with which we cherish the rising generation . . .

These sentiments are wise—they are honorable—they are virtuous—their cultivation is not only innocent pleasure, it is incumbent duty. Obedient to these dictates, you, my fellow-citizens, have instituted and paid frequent observance to their annual solemnity. And what event of weightier intrinsic importance or of more extensive consequences was ever selected for this honorary distinction?

* Galgacus

The sequel:

It was in the realm of thought rather than of political administration that John Quincy Adams made his mark. He shone most brilliantly when carving out ideas, rather than in political hassling.

He did become President in 1825, but only after an indecisive struggle between Andrew Jackson and Henry Clay which threw the choice of a President in 1824 into the House of Representatives. As a result of the deal, Adams became President without a party behind him, a disillusioned man who somewhat like his father sat out a single term in the White House and was not offered a repeat performance.

But as a diplomat, John Quincy Adams became a historic figure. As an author of the Treaty of Ghent he helped to compromise the quarrels with Great Britain that had brought about the War of 1812, and when James Monroe became President he served as Secretary of State—the most distinguished period of his career.

When James Monroe rounded out the "foundation policies" of the Republic with promulgation of the Monroe Doctrine—one of the great and enduring acts recognizing the position of the United States in the Western Hemisphere—it was Adams who did the drafting, mustered the arguments, and to a large degree inserted the force of declamation in that paper.

GOUVERNEUR MORRIS

"I charge you to protect his fame. It is all that he has left."

NEW YORK, New York, July 14, 1804—All that Alexander Hamilton might have wished to have said of him in life was poured forth today in a moving funeral oration by Gouverneur Morris, diplomat and former colleague of Mr. Hamilton both in the Continental Congress and on the Committee that framed the Constitution.

He spoke over the open coffin holding the body that collapsed in sudden death only four days ago on the Weehawken Heights, across the Hudson River in New Jersey, when Mr. Hamilton engaged in a duel with Aaron Burr.

Today no words were spoken of the controversies over politics and finance that culminated in this tragic event. Neither did Mr. Morris mention the fugitive Burr.

IF ON this sad, this solemn occasion, I should endeavor to move your commiseration, it would be doing injustice to that sensibility which has been so generally and so justly manifested. Far from attempting to excite your emotions, I must try to repress my own; and yet, I fear, that, instead of the language of a public speaker, you will hear only the lamentations of a wailing friend. But I will struggle with my bursting heart, to portray that heroic spirit, which has flown to the mansions of bliss.

Students of Columbia—he was in the ardent pursuit of knowledge in your academic shades when the first sound of the American war called him to the field. A young and unprotected volunteer, such was his zeal, and so brilliant his service, that we heard his name before we knew his person. It seemed as if God had called him suddenly into existence, that he might assist to save a world! The penetrating eye of Washington soon perceived the manly spirit which animated his youthful bosom. By this excellent judge of men he was selected as an aid, and thus he became early acquainted with, and was a principal actor in the more important scenes of our Revolution. At the siege of York, he pertinaciously insisted on and he obtained the command of a Forlorn Hope. He stormed the redoubt; but let it be recorded that not one single man of the enemy perished. His gallant troops, emulating the heroism of their chief, checked the uplifted arm, and spared a foe no longer resisting. Here closed his military career.

Shortly after the war, your favor—no, your discernment, called him to public office. You sent him to the convention at Philadelphia; he there assisted in forming that Constitution which is now the bond of our union, the shield of our defense, and the source of our prosperity. In signing the compact, he expressed his apprehension that it did not contain sufficient means of strength for its own preservation; and that in consequence we should share the fate of many other republics, and pass through anarchy to despotism. We hoped better things. We confided in the good sense of the American people; and, above all, we trusted in the protecting providence of the Almighty. On this important subject he never concealed his opinion. He disdained concealment. . . .

At the time when our government was organized, we were without funds, though not without resources. To call them into action, and establish order in the finances, Washington sought for splendid talents, for extensive information, and above all, he sought for sterling, incorruptible integrity. All these he found in Hamilton. The system then adopted, has been the subject of much animadversion. If it be not without a fault, let it be remembered that nothing human is perfect. Recollect the circumstances of the moment—recollect the conflict of opinion—and, above all, remember that a minister of a republic must bend to the will of the people. The administration which Washington formed was one of the most efficient, one of the best that any country was ever blessed with. And the result was a rapid advance in power and prosperity, of which there is no example in any other age or nation. The part which Hamilton bore is universally known.

Brethren of the Cincinnati—there lies our chief! Let him still be our model. Like him, after long and faithful public services, let us cheerfully perform the social duties of private life. Oh! he was mild and gentle. In him there was no offense; no guile. His generous hand and heart were open to all.

Gentlemen of the bar—you have lost your brightest ornament. Cherish and imitate his example. While, like him, with justifiable and with laudable zeal, you pursue the interests of your clients, remember, like him, the eternal principle of justice.

Fellow citizens—you have long witnessed his professional conduct, and felt his unrivaled eloquence. You know how well he performed the duties of a citizen—you know that he never courted your favor by adulation or the sacrifice of his own judgment. You have seen him contending against you, and saving your dearest interests, as it were, in spite of yourselves. And you now feel and enjoy the benefits resulting from the firm energy of his conduct. Bear this testimony to the memory of my departed friend. I charge you to protect his fame. It is all he has left—all that these poor orphan children will inherit from their father. But, my countrymen, that fame may be a rich treasure to you also. Let it be the test by which to examine those who solicit your favor. Disregarding professions, view their conduct, and on a doubtful occasion ask, Would Hamilton have done this thing?

You all know how he perished. On this last scene I cannot, I must not dwell. It might excite emotions too strong for your better judgment. Suffer not your indignation to lead to an act which might again offend the insulted majesty of the laws. On his part, as from his lips, though with my voice—for his voice you will hear no more—let me entreat you to respect yourselves.

And now, ye ministers of the everlasting God, perform your holy office, and commit these ashes of our departed brother to the bosom of the grave.

RED JACKET

"You have got our country . . . you want to force your religion upon us."

SENECA, N. Y., 1805—Red Jacket Chief, of the Seneca Tribe and dominant spokesman for the Six Nations, eloquently challenged the ablest spokesmen among the Christian missionaries in an address here, replying to appeals to the Indians to be baptized and thereby take one more step toward integration into the American community.

To the surprise of these spokesmen for the Christian church, the eloquent warrior and friend of the late General George Washington, told the junior race that in his view the Indians have a better religion and one with less division than the white man. For good measure, using quotations that might well have been taken from the Bible itself, he cited actions by the white man in encroachment upon Indian rights, in self-divisions over doctrine and in other matters, that constituted an indictment comparable with those spoken in earlier days by the great Reform leaders within the church itself.

For these reasons, as well as the simplicity of expression used by this warrior of warriors—whose name itself came from the wearing of a scarlet coat given to him long ago by British troops—his words are memorable. In his own language his given name is far more euphonious, being Otetiani, and his title as chieftain even more picturesque—Sagoyewatha. But as Red Jacket he must be known to posterity.

FRIEND AND Brother: It was the will of the Great Spirit that we should meet together this day. He orders all things and has given us a fine day for our council. He has taken His garment from before the sun and caused it to shine with brightness upon us. Our eyes are opened that we see clearly; our ears are unstopped that we have been able to hear distinctly the words you have spoken. For all these favors we thank the Great Spirit, and Him only.

Brother, this council fire was kindled by you. It was at your request that we came together at this time. We have listened with attention to what you have said. You requested us to speak our minds freely. This gives us great joy; for we now consider that we stand upright before you and can speak what we think. All have heard your voice and all speak to you now as one man. Our minds are agreed. . . .

Brother, listen to what we say. There was a time when our forefathers owned this great island. Their seats extended from the rising to the setting sun. The Great Spirit had made it for the use of Indians. He had created the buffalo, the deer, and other animals for food. He had made the bear and the beaver. Their skins served us for clothing. He had scattered them over the country and taught us how to take them. He had caused the earth to produce corn for bread. All this He had done for His red children because He loved them. If we had some disputes about our hunting-ground they were generally settled without the shedding of much blood.

But an evil day came upon us. Your forefathers crossed the great water and landed on this island. Their numbers were small. They found friends and not enemies. They told us they had fled from their own country for fear of wicked men and had come here to enjoy their religion. They asked for a small seat. We took pity on them, granted their request, and they sat down among us. We gave them corn and meat; they gave us poison in return.

Brother, our seats were once large and yours were small. You have now become a great people, and we have scarcely a place left to spread our blankets. You have got our country, but are not satisfied; you want to force your religion upon us.

Brother, continue to listen. You say that you are sent to instruct us how to worship the Great Spirit agreeably to His mind; and, if we do not take hold of the religion which you white people teach we shall be unhappy hereafter. You say that you are right and we are lost. How do we know this to be true? We understand that your religion is written in a Book. If it was intended for us, as well as you, why has not the Great Spirit given to us, and not only to us, but why did He not give to our forefathers the knowledge of that Book, with the means of understanding it rightly. We only know what you tell us about it. How shall we know when to believe, being so often deceived by the white people?

Brother, you say there is but one way to worship and serve the Great Spirit. If there is but one religion, why do you white people differ so much about it? Why do not all agree, as you can all read the Book?

Brother, we do not understand these things. We are told that your religion was given to your forefathers and has been handed down from father to son. We also have a religion which was given to our forefathers and has been handed down to us, their children. We worship in that way. It teaches us to be thankful for all the favors we receive, to love each other, and to be united. We never quarrel about religion. . . .

Brother, we do not wish to destroy your religion or take it from you. We only want to enjoy our own.

JAMES MONROE

> *". . . we should consider any attempt on their part to extend their system to any portion of this hemisphere, as dangerous to our peace and safety."*

WASHINGTON, D. C., Dec. 2, 1823—In the greatest step to date by the United States, acting as a world power to assure the peace and security of those other nations in the Western Hemisphere which are our friendly neighbors, President Monroe today declared all of the Americas as "out of bounds" to would-be European conquerors.

A few paragraphs in a message to the newly assembled Congress, read on behalf of the President to a joint assembly of the Senate and the House of Representatives laid down a policy from which no avenue of retreat was left. In an eloquent silence after the reading, a formal motion to receive and to print the Message was adopted without debate.

One must reach back for precedent to the Pax Romana for as drastic a step taken to enclose a great portion of the world within a wall of freedom.

President Monroe declared that the United States has neither a quarrel nor a wish to interfere with or participate in any of the myriad intrigues criss-crossing the international politics of Europe. He declared further that this government accepts the status quo of all colonies or dependencies of European powers as they exist at this date in the Americas.

While President Monroe speaks as a party politician for the solidly mustered strength of the Southern States, his collaborator in framing this policy is known universally to have been John Quincy Adams, the canny New Englander and the Secretary of State. The western groupings led by Mr. Henry Clay, of Kentucky, and General Andrew Jackson, of Tennessee, both bitter political enemies of President Monroe on many domestic policies, are unanimous in support of this new "doctrine."

If one asks the questions, Why?, there need only be cited the great sweep of freedom's fire through the southern half of the Western Hemisphere in the past score of years, coincident with an unholy consolidation of monarchies in Europe—Russia, Prussia, Austria, France. These monarchial governments have joined in the so-called "Holy Alliance" for the sole purpose of defending and restoring a predatory form of self-perpetuation in Europe and whatever other reaches of the world they can redeem for their benefit.

Our immediate southern border, where we adjoin Mexico, became secure and peaceful only a year ago, when Mexico declared its freedom from Spain. Coincident with Mexican independence, Brazil, largest of the southern countries, threw off the Portuguese yoke, thereby joining Argentina, which won its freedom from Spain in 1810.

Four other major Latin countries today are struggling to coordinate their governments in freedom under the sometimes harsh but benevolent leadership of General Simón Bolívar. These are Peru, where he rules in uncontested leadership, and Venezuela, Colombia and Ecuador, where his rule is carried out by deputies.

The Spanish and Portuguese pattern of revolution is not necessarily our kind, but the freedom of these countries has been bought as dearly, and to them is just as precious as our own.

IN THE wars of European powers, in matters relating to themselves, we have never taken any part, nor does it comport with our policy to do so. It is only when our rights are invaded, or seriously menaced, that we resent injuries, or make preparations for our defence. With the movements in this hemisphere, we are, of necessity, more immediately connected, and by causes which must be obvious to all enlightened and impartial observers.

The political system of the allied Powers is essentially different in this respect from that of America.

The difference proceeds from that which exists in our respective governments. And to the defence of our own, which has been achieved by the loss of much blood and treasure, and matured by the wisdom of their most enlightened citizens, and under which we have enjoyed unexampled felicity, this whole nation is devoted. We owe it, therefore, to candor and to the amicable relations existing between the United States and those Powers, to declare, that we should consider any attempt on their part to extend their system to any portion of this hemisphere, as dangerous to our peace and safety.

With the existing colonies or dependencies of any European Power, we have not interfered and shall not interfere. But, with the Governments who have declared their independence, and maintained it . . . circumstances are evidently and conspicuously different.

It is impossible that the allied Powers should extend their political systems to any portion of either (American) Continent, without endangering our peace and happiness; nor can any one believe that our Southern brethren, if left to themselves, would adopt it of their own accord. It is equally impossible, therefore, that we should behold such interposition, in any form, with indifference.

It is still the true policy of the United States to leave all parties to themselves, in the hope that other Powers will pursue the same course.

The sequel:

The Monroe Doctrine never was seriously challenged, due in some measure to support by the British Government. On one later occasion Germany threatened to intervene in the affairs of Venezuela, using the security of nationals there as an excuse, but only a warning from the United States was necessary to stop this venture.

DANIEL WEBSTER

"Mind is the great lever of all things."

BOSTON, Mass., June 17, 1825— The power of ideas, of minds communicating grand thoughts to be later translated into the tangibles of action, inspired Daniel Webster to soar today to rare heights of inspiration as the "orator" at the laying of the corner-stone of Bunker Hill Monument, exactly 50 years after Bunker and nearby Breed's Hill were baptized in patriots' blood as an early sacrifice to our freedom.

"Mind is the great lever of all things," exclaimed this stentorian spokesman of liberty from the green hills of New Hampshire; "human thought is the process by which human ends are ultimately answered."

And those who heard him—the thousands of holiday makers who had come to picnic and to celebrate this vital anniversary in the history of liberty—received for a fleeting instant a glimpse of the inner mind of this man who by words alone is becoming a giant among giants in this growing period of our nation.

The thoughts expressed by Congressman Webster, and the inspiring and thought-provoking theme he erected upon what otherwise might have been a sentimental and mawkish occasion, were particularly gratifying to the sponsors of his talk, who had passed over numerous natives of Massachusetts to award this honor to a transplanted statesman resident in Boston only since 1816. The choice, however, was not an accident: in Washington, Mr. Webster's voice and thought stand as high or higher than those of Mr. Henry Clay and Mr. John C. Calhoun and the coterie of other great speakers. Some think it a pity that our own John Quincy Adams, although now President, is not numbered among them, but his feebleness of delivery diminishes his power of thought and action.

Nevertheless, whether Boston's greatness as an intellectual cradle be founded upon native progeny or adoptive sons, there is no minimizing the power of the intellect as it today strides out to round and refine these days of our country's years.

It is high time.

We are at peace, and no enemy of national security threatens from outside our borders. The Doctrine by President Monroe defining the interests of all of the Americas as our special interest has not been seriously challenged in the almost two years since it was proclaimed. Our western boundaries have been extended to the towering rocky Sierras in the West. Our population has grown from less than 4,000,000 in the first census of 1790 to more than 10,000,000 souls, and tides of immigration are helping to swell our own fecund birth rate.

Mr. Webster indeed is right when he cautions us that it is time to turn from these visible symbols of physical welfare to a nurturing of the mental growth so essential to well rounded development as a country.

His talk will soon be available in published form from the presses of Cummings, Hillard & Co.

THE LEADING reflection to which the occasion seems to invite us respects the great changes which have occurred in the fifty years since the battle of Bunker Hill was fought. . . . In looking at these changes, and in estimating their effect on our condition, we are obliged to consider not what has been done in our own country only, but in others also. In these interesting times, while nations are making separate and individual advances in improvement, they make, too, a common progress. . . .

A chief distinction of the present day is a community of opinions, and knowledge, amongst men, in different nations, existing in a degree heretofore unknown. Knowledge has, in our time, triumphed and is triumphing over distance, over differences of language, over diversity of habits, over prejudice and over bigotry. . . . The whole world is becoming a common field of intellect to act in. Energy of mind, genius, power, wherever it exists, may speak out in any tongue, and the world will hear it.

There is a vast commerce of ideas. There are marts and exchanges for intellectual discoveries, and a wonderful fellowship of these individual intelligences which make up the mind and opinion of the age.

Mind is the great lever of all things; human thought is the process by which human ends are ultimately answered; and the diffusion of knowledge, so astounding in the last half century, has rendered innumerable minds, variously gifted by nature, competent to be competitors, or fellow-workers, on the theatre of intellectual operation.

From these causes important improvements have taken place in the personal condition of individuals. Generally speaking, mankind are not only better fed and better clothed, but they are able also to enjoy more leisure; they possess more refinement and self-respect. . . . This remark, most true in its application to our own country, is also partly true when applied elsewhere.

Under the influence of this rapidly increasing knowledge, the people have begun, in all forms of government, to think, and to reason, on affairs of state. Regarding government as an institution for the public good, they demand a knowledge of its operation, and a participation in its existence.

A call for the representative system, wherever it is not enjoyed, and where there is already intelligence enough to estimate its value, is perseveringly made.

Where men speak out, they demand it; where the bayonet is at their throats, they pray for it.

The sequel:

This oration by Daniel Webster, here cut to the sinews of pure expression and freed of the verbiage that to modern eyes sometimes obscures his finest thoughts, ranks high in the eloquence of great thinkers who sparked the genius of expression through the next hundred years.

A Plymouth Address by Webster in 1820 had served as a trial effort for this oration. A year later he would wrap many more ideas into an epochal address on the lives of Thomas Jefferson and John Adams, and in 1843 he would return to Bunker Hill to re-state his old thesis.

As a lawyer and politician, Webster needs little description here. And this talk has been chosen rather than his great speeches in the slavery debates of later years.

The thoughts that developed in the granite convictions of his mind, the words that poured forth from his craggy face—these were his heritage to us.

EDWARD EVERETT

"The fabric of American freedom . . . may crumble into dust. But the cause in which these our fathers shone is immortal."

CHARLESTOWN, Mass., August 1, 1826—Edward Everett, who retired last year from the Greek professorship at Harvard College to pit his oratorical skill against Congressional veterans as a Representative from this District, today embellished his own bright reputation by a memorial address honoring the late John Adams and Thomas Jefferson. Both died on July 4.

Dr. Everett, in eulogizing these two highly different but grandly patriotic leaders, put into a perspective seldom realized the fantastic achievements of what is sometimes called the American ideal. By using the two heroes as a joint symbol, he separated cause from debate, principle from personality, and continuity of great ideas from the controversies of the moment.

Among the Congressman's auditors, who included a generous sprinkling of illustrious thinkers, the impression seemed quite general that the speaker not only was eulogizing men who, in death, have passed beyond controversy, but was using his speech as a lever to raise much of the current political debate above the issues of sectionalism. Indeed, as a moderate conservative, he already has felt the sting of northern opinion that oftentimes thinks his attitude toward slavery too moderate and his desire for universal political harmony too lenient toward economic threats aimed at New England from both the South and the fast-growing West.

But these taunts, and whatever degree of apprehension they raise in the mind of Dr. Everett, seemed far away as he spoke today. Instead, his voice was that of the scholar, whose eloquence has developed during his four years of editing the *North American Review*.

THE JUBILEE of America is turned into mourning. Its joy is mingled with sadness; its silver trumpet breathes a mingled strain. Henceforward, while America exists among the nations of the earth, the first emotion of the fourth of July will be of joy and triumph in the great event which immortalizes the day; the second will be one of chastened and tender recollection of the venerable men who departed on the morning of the jubilee. This mingled emotion of triumph and sadness has sealed the beauty and sublimity of our great anniversary. . . .

Friends, fellow-citizens, free, prosperous, happy Americans! The men who did so much to make you so are no more. The men who gave nothing to pleasure in youth, nothing to repose in age, but all to that country, whose beloved name filled their hearts, as it does ours, with joy, can now do no more for us; nor we for them. But their memory remains, we will cherish it; their bright example remains, we will strive to imitate it; the fruit of their wise counsels and noble acts remains, we will gratefully enjoy it.

They have gone to the companions of their cares, of their dan-

gers, and their toils. It is well with them. The treasures of America
are now in heaven. How long the list of our good, and wise, and
brave, assembled there! How few remain with us! There is our
Washington; and those who followed him in their country's confidence are now met together with him, and all their illustrious company.

The faithful marble may preserve their image; the engraven
brass may proclaim their worth; but the humblest sod of Independent America, with nothing but the dew-drops of the morning
to gild it, is a prouder mausoleum than kings or conquerors can
boast. The country is their monument. Its independence is their
epitaph. But not to their country is their praise limited. The whole
earth is the monument of illustrious men. Wherever an agonizing
people shall perish, in a generous convulsion, for want of a valiant
arm and a fearless heart, they will cry, in the last accents of despair,
O for a Washington, an Adams, a Jefferson! Wherever a regener-
ated nation, starting up in its might, shall burst the links of steel
that enchain it, the praise of our venerated fathers shall be remembered in their triumphal song!

The contemporary and successive generations of men will disappear, and in the long lapse of ages, the races of America, like
those of Greece and Rome, may pass away. The fabric of American
freedom, like all things human, however firm and fair, may
crumble into dust. But the cause in which these our fathers shone
is immortal. They did that to which no age, no people of civilized
men, can be indifferent. Their eulogy will be uttered in other languages, when those we speak, like us who speak them, shall be all
forgotten. And when the great account of humanity shall be closed,
in the bright list of those who have best adorned and served it,
shall be found the names of our Adams and our Jefferson!

The sequel:

Everett's speech this day was a landmark in his on-going career as an orator in the ancient sense of the word. He was an orator whose de-livery often overshadowed the sub-ject about which he talked, in much the same manner that, in the 1950s, some television commentators would achieve reputations that for a time left their listeners not quite certain as to what they had been talking about, but charmed by their personalities.

His gifts carried Everett into the Governorship of Massachusetts, to a brief career as Secretary of State (succeeding his friend, Daniel Webster), and on into the Senate, to which he was elected while serving in the Cabinet post.

Everett resigned his Senate seat in the second year of his term, because in 1860 his moderate attitude toward slavery embarrassed his fellow members of the Whig party. But if there was any question of his loyalty to the Union, which was beyond question, it evaporated during the Civil War when he stumped the North, addressing vast audiences, with inspirational appeals to patriots.

But even as Everett was a great orator, so he stands as the classic example that oratory may, in some circumstances, leave something lacking.

It was Everett who was chosen to deliver, and who did deliver, the great "oration" of the day at the consecration of a portion of the Gettysburg Battlefield, as a perpetual cemetery and memorial to the men who died there.

The "oration" of that day has been forgotten. It was overshadowed by some 400 words of extemporaneous remarks delivered by one of the least gifted of speakers—Abraham Lincoln.

II

GROWING PAINS

ANDREW JACKSON

"Without union, our independence and liberty would never have been achieved; without union they never can be maintained."

WASHINGTON, D. C., March 4, 1833—Any division of the United States through secession of individual States from the Union inevitably must lead to civil wars, President Andrew Jackson stated today in the Address marking his second inauguration as President.

President Jackson's exhortation served to draw attention to—and it was hoped to check—a rising tide of debate rooted fundamentally in the question of slavery. It is on this issue that the South feels that its rights are being traduced, and that the North feels equally strongly that the freedoms promised under the Constitution apply equally to all men within our borders.

Increasingly in the past decade, there have been political maneuverings designed to bring into the Union additional States whose Senators and Representatives oppose slavery, with the hope that eventually the over- whelming force of their voting strength will bring about laws forcing the South to bow to the freedom party. The reply from the South, through its greatest orators, principally Senator John C. Calhoun of South Carolina, and Senator Henry Clay of Kentucky, has been a barrage of arguments that in sum uphold the presumed rights of individual States to oppose Federal laws either through nullification or, at the extreme, secession.

General Jackson finds himself in the unenviable position of being a slave-holding Tennessee planter, and therefore one whose financial interests are those of a Southerner. Yet as President and a military leader, his convictions and actions are bound to the oaths of loyalty to the Constitution and the Government representing it as paramount above all other interests. There is no middle road for him.

71

THE WILL of the American people, expressed through their un-
solicited suffrages, calls me before you to pass through the solem-
nities preparatory to taking upon myself the duties of President of
the United States for another term. For their approbation of my
public conduct through a period which has not been without its
difficulties, and for this renewed expression of their confidence in
my good intentions, I am at a loss for terms adequate to the expression of my gratitude.

It shall be displayed to the extent of my humble abilities in continued efforts so to administer the government as to preserve their
liberty and promote their happiness. . . .

In the domestic policy of this government, there are two objects
which especially deserve the attention of the people and their representatives, and which have been and will continue to be the subjects of my increasing solicitude. They are the preservation of the
rights of the several States and the integrity of the Union.

These great objects are necessarily connected, and can only be
attained by an enlightened exercise of the powers of each within its
appropriate sphere, in conformity with the public will constitutionally expressed. To this end it becomes the duty of all to yield a
ready and patriotic submission to the laws constitutionally enacted,
and thereby promote and strengthen a proper confidence in those
institutions of the several States and of the United States which the
people themselves have ordained for their own government.

My experience in public concerns and the observation of a life
somewhat advanced confirm the opinions long since imbibed by me,
that the destruction of our State governments or the annihilation
of their control over the local concerns of the people would lead
directly to revolution and anarchy, and finally to despotism and
military domination. In proportion, therefore, as the general government encroaches upon the rights of the States, in the same proportion does it impair its own power and detract from its ability to
fulfil the purposes of its creation. . . .

But of equal, and, indeed, of incalculable importance is the
union of these States, and the sacred duty of all to contribute to its
preservation by a liberal support of the general government in the
exercise of its just powers. . . . Without union our independence

and liberty would never have been achieved; without union they never can be maintained. Divided into twenty-four, or even a smaller number, of separate communities, we shall see our internal trade burdened with numberless restraints and exactions; communication between distant points and sections obstructed or cut off; our sons made soldiers to deluge with blood the fields they now till in peace; the mass of our people borne down and impoverished by taxes to support armies and navies, and military leaders at the head of their victorious legions becoming our lawgivers and judges.

The loss of liberty, of all good government, of peace, plenty, and happiness, must inevitably follow a dissolution of the Union. In supporting it, therefore, we support all that is dear to the freeman and the philanthropist.

The time at which I stand before you is full of interest. The eyes of all nations are fixed on our Republic. The event of the existing crisis will be decisive in the opinion of mankind of the practicability of our federal system of government. Great is the stake placed in our hands; great is the responsibility which must rest upon the people of the United States. Let us realize the importance of the attitude in which we stand before the world. Let us exercise forbearance and firmness. Let us extricate our country from the dangers which surround it, and learn wisdom from the lessons they inculcate.

The sequel:

Perhaps the warning issued by President Jackson would have had greater force if his personality had been more malleable, and other factors had not intervened to create bitter enmity between him and his fellow Southerners.

As unskilled in politics as he had been supreme as a field commander, the doughty old warrior failed completely in his efforts at compromise. Only as a prophet of the blood bath that would eventually be required to purge the differences over Secession was he distinguished by this speech. But it is a notable landmark in the efforts to compromise the inevitable results of Secession.

Clay's enmity already was buried deeply in his opposition to Jackson over the establishment of an all-powerful Central Bank, and over the issue of tariffs, in which Clay had supported South Carolina's threats to secede, and Jackson had replied with a threat to send Federal soldiers into that state if it tried.

Calhoun firmly believed that a

State had the right to nullify any Federal legislation inimical to its interests. Only in the preceding December, 1832, he had resigned as Vice President, with the Senatorial election safely in his pocket.

Senator Clay would go on in his massive effort as the "Great Compromiser," but in the end he would fail, as Jackson failed in this effort at compromise. Their failures were, however, magnificent ones.

Calhoun's voice, while proved by history to be on the losing, as well as the wrong, side would become more and more powerful, as conversely Jackson's force and leadership diminished to the vanishing point even before he served out his second term.

WENDELL PHILLIPS

"When he fell, civil authority was trampled under foot."

BOSTON, Mass., Dec. 8, 1837—A 26-year-old man, with oratorical powers far beyond his age, tonight soared nearer to leadership of the Abolitionist movement, with a stirring speech on the recent murder of Elijah Lovejoy which held spellbound an audience that filled Faneuil Hall.

The speaker was Wendell Phillips. His subject was the crusading editor who was murdered by a mob at Alton, Illinois, on November 7. Lovejoy, who had been driven from city to city by opponents of his Abolitionist crusade in the West, had suffered the destruction of three newspaper presses. Finally, arming himself with the consent of the authorities, he resisted what was to be the final attack upon him.

The point that particularly aroused Mr. Phillips, as it has a wide section of opinion throughout the North, is that pro-slavery spokesmen, including at least one clergyman, have blamed Lovejoy as responsible for his own death by persistence in acting contrary to public opinion, comparing the mob that killed him to the participants in the Boston Tea Party.

ELIJAH LOVEJOY was not only defending the freedom of the press, but he was under his own roof, in arms with the sanction of civil authority. The men who assailed him went against and over the laws. The *mob,* as the gentleman terms it—mob, forsooth; certainly we sons of the teaspillers are a marvelously patient generation;—the "orderly mob" which assembled in the Old South to destroy the tea, were met to resist, not the laws, but illegal enactions. Shame on the American who calls the tea tax and stamp tax laws.

Our fathers resisted, not the King's prerogative, but the King's usurpation. To find any other account you must read our Revolutionary history upside down. Our state archives are loaded with arguments of John Adams to prove the taxes laid by the British Parliament unconstitutional—beyond its powers. It was not until this was made out that the men of New England rushed to arms. The arguments of the Council Chamber and the House of Representatives preceded and sanctioned the contest. To draw the conduct of our ancestors into a precedent for mobs, for a right to resist laws we ourselves have enacted, is an insult to their memory.

The difference between the excitements of those days and our own, which the gentleman in kindness to the latter has overlooked, is simply this: the men of that day went for the right, as secured by the laws. They were the people rising to sustain the laws and Constitution of the province. The rioters of our day go for their own wills, right or wrong.

Sir, when I heard the gentleman lay down principles which place the murderers of Alton side by side with Otis and Hancock, with Quincy and Adams, I thought those pictured lips (pointing to portraits in the hall) would have broken into voice to rebuke the recreant American—the slanderer of the dead. The gentleman said he should shrink into insignificance if he dared to gainsay the principles of these resolutions. Sir, for the sentiments he has uttered, on soil consecrated by the prayers of Puritans and the blood of patriots, the earth should have yawned and swallowed him up.

Some persons seem to imagine that anarchy existed at Alton from the commencement of these disputes. Not at all. "No one of us," says an eye-witness and a comrade of Lovejoy, "has taken up arms during these disturbances but at the command of the mayor." Anarchy did not settle down on that devoted city till Lovejoy breathed his last. Till then the law, represented in his person, sustained itself against its foes. When he fell, civil authority was trampled underfoot. He had "planted himself on his constitutional rights, appealed to the laws, claimed the protection of civil authority, taken refuge under the broad shield of the Constitution; when through that he was pierced and fell, he fell but one sufferer in a common catastrophe." He took refuge under the banner of liberty—amid its folds; and when he fell, its glorious stars and stripes, the emblem of free institutions, around which cluster so many heart-stirring memories, were blotted out in the martyr's blood.

It has been stated, perhaps inadvertently, that Lovejoy or his comrades fired first. This is denied by those who have the best means of knowing. Guns were first fired by the mob. After being twice fired on, those within the building consulted together and deliberately returned the fire. But suppose they did fire first. They had a right to do so; not only the right which every citizen has to defend himself, but the further right which every civil officer has to resist violence. Even if Lovejoy fired the first gun, it would not lessen our claim to his sympathy, or destroy his title to be considered a martyr in defense of a free press. The question now is, Did he act within the Constitution and the laws?

Throughout that terrible night I find nothing to regret but this, that, within the limits of our country, civil authority should have been so prostrate as to oblige a citizen to arm in his own defense, and to arm in vain.

Mr. Chairman, from the bottom of my heart I thank that brave little band in Alton for resisting. We must remember that Lovejoy had fled from city to city—suffered the destruction of three presses patiently. At length he took counsel with friends, men of character, of tried integrity, of wide views, of Christian principle. They thought the crisis had come; it was full time to assert the laws. They saw around them, not a community like our own, of fixed habits, of character molded and settled, but one "in the gristle, not yet hardened into the bone of manhood." The people there, children of our older States, seem to have forgotten the blood-tried principles of their fathers the moment they lost sight of their New England hills. Something was to be done to show them the priceless value of the freedom of the press, to bring back and set right their wandering and confused ideas. He and his advisers looked out on a community, staggering like a drunken man, indifferent to their right and confused in their feelings. Deaf to argument, haply they might be stunned into sobriety. They saw that of which we cannot judge— the necessity of resistance. Insulted law called for it. Public opinion, fast hastening on the downward course, must be arrested.

Does not the event show they judged rightly? Absorbed in a thousand trifles, how has the nation all at once come to a stand? Men begin, as in 1776 and 1640, to discuss principles, to weigh characters, to find out where they are. Haply, we may awake before we are borne over the precipice.

JOHN C. CALHOUN

". . . the greatest and gravest question that ever can come under your consideration: How can the Union be preserved?"

WASHINGTON, D. C., March, 1850—The South's most eloquent voice in Congress, albeit the voice of a dying man, was raised in the Senate in warning that the country below the Potomac will have no choice but to secede if current political trends—specifically admission of California as a "free" state—continue to increase the balance of national power held by the Northern states.

So spoke John C. Calhoun, 68-year-old spokesman for South Carolina, who 18 years ago led South Carolina's unsuccessful fight for nullification over the issue of tariffs, and iron-willed foe alike of the Northern freedom viewpoint and of Henry Clay's monumental efforts to compromise the feelings between North and South.

In the end the fight for perpetuation of slavery as an American institution may fail, but the voices of the Calhouns will stand always as warnings that the rooting out of such evils must be done carefully, lest with the evils also are rooted out essential liberties of minorities.

Senator Calhoun spoke on the subject of slavery, but his arguments were those of a defender of constitutional government. He warned that the agitation over slavery "has been permitted to proceed, with almost no attempt to resist it, until it has reached a period when it can no longer be disguised or denied that the Union is in danger."

Senator Calhoun's principal arguments rested upon his oft-repeated declaration that slavery is an essen-

tial element of the economic life of
the South; that it was so regarded by
the men who framed the Constitution; that the South alone must determine the position of slavery in its
affairs, and—most forcefully—that
the admission of new states as "free
states" has reached a point where the
position of the South in the Federal
government is untenable.

The answer, he warned, must
eventually be Secession, or a change
in this attitude, and he indicated
scant hope for the latter.

When Senator Calhoun rose to
speak today, he undoubtedly was
conscious of the bitter enmities he
has made in a long career, of oratorical triumphs and of deep frustrations, especially his loss of the chance
at the Presidency which he coveted.
But the old warrior did not show
rancor or bitterness.

I HAVE, Senators, believed from the first that the agitation of the
subject of slavery would, if not prevented by some timely and effective measure, end in disunion. . . . You have thus forced upon
you the greatest and the gravest question that ever can come under
your consideration: How can the Union be preserved?

To this question there can be but one answer: that the immediate
cause is, the almost universal discontent which pervades all the
states composing the southern section of the Union. This widely
extended discontent is not of recent origin. It commenced with the
agitation of the slavery question, and has been increasing ever
since. . . .

There is another, lying back of it, but with which this is intimately connected, that may be regarded as the great and primary
cause. It is to be found in the fact that the equilibrium between the
two sections in the government, as it stood when the Constitution
was ratified, and the government put in action, has been destroyed.
At that time there was nearly a perfect equilibrium between the
two, which afforded ample means to each to protect itself against
the aggression of the other; but as it now stands, one section has
exclusive power of controlling the government, which leaves the
other without any adequate means of protecting itself against its
encroachment and oppression.

The cry of Union! Union! the glorious Union! can no more prevent disunion, than the cry of Health! health! glorious health! on
the part of the physician can save a patient lying dangerously ill.
So long as the Union, instead of being regarded as a protector, is

regarded in the opposite character by not much less than a majority of the states, it will be in vain to attempt to conciliate them by pronouncing eulogies on it.

Besides, this cry of Union comes commonly from those whom we cannot believe to be sincere. It usually comes from our assailants; but we cannot believe them to be sincere, for if they loved the Union, they would necessarily be devoted to the Constitution. It made the Union, and to destroy the Constitution would be to destroy the Union. But the only reliable and certain evidence of devotion to the Constitution is, to abstain, on the one hand, from violating it, and to repel, on the other, all attempts to violate it. It is only by faithfully performing those high duties that the Constitution can be preserved, and with it the Union.

Nor can we regard the profession of devotion to the Union, on the part of those who are not our assailants, as sincere, when they pronounce eulogies upon the Union evidently with the intent of charging us with disunion, without uttering one word of denunciation against our assailants. . . .

Nor can the Union be saved by invoking the name of the illustrious Southerner, whose mortal remains repose on the western bank of the Potomac. He was one of us—a slave-holder and a planter. We have studied his history, and find nothing in it to justify submission to wrong. On the contrary, his great fame rests on the solid foundation that, while he was careful to avoid doing wrong to others, he was prompt and decided in repelling wrong. I trust that, in this respect, we profited by his example.

Nor can we find anything in his history to deter us from seceding from the Union, should it fail to fulfill the objects for which it was instituted, by being permanently and hopelessly converted into the means of oppression instead of protection. On the contrary, we find much in his example to encourage us, should we be forced to the extremity of deciding between submission and disunion.

The sequel:

Calhoun lost in the face of an unbeatable coalition—Henry Clay's famous Compromise, which won the support of Daniel Webster, even though in taking this stand the old lion from Massachusetts forfeited most of the support he had enjoyed from abolitionists.

Under this Compromise, California was admitted as a "free" state, largely to balance—from the Northern standpoint—the admission two years earlier of Texas as a "slave" state with the promised right to divide itself into as many as seven states in the future.

As a sop to the South, New Mexico and Utah were created Territories without determination as to slavery, this subject being left to their own choice when statehood might be given them in the indefinite future.

Other minor stipulations of the Compromise forbade slave-trading thereafter in the District of Columbia and promised, on paper, that Southern constables might go into northern states to retrieve escaped slaves.

The Compromise was hailed, at its adoption in September, as the great action to preserve the Union.

In actual results, the dispute broke out with renewed vigor in 1854, and in 1861 the North and South became locked in the Civil War.

RUFUS CHOATE

"There are influences that never sleep."

BOSTON, Mass., 1850—Rufus Choate, former Senator now returned to private life in the practice of the law that has made him a national figure, spoke tonight with all the eloquence for which he is noted in favor of the Compromise efforts being led in the Congress by the southern Senator Henry Clay, of Kentucky.

Before an audience that packed Fanueil Hall, Mr. Choate argued that however meritorious the effort to force the South to free its slaves may be, the cause is not sufficient to invite a civil war.

He warned that the public should beware of attempts to mold public opinion to such an extreme action that "this Union may melt as frost-work in the sun."

It is impossible at this point to assay the effect that the speech will have, but it is noteworthy that at this date in New England Mr. Choate certainly speaks for a majority opinion that—in its confusion—favors abolition of slavery as a moral principal but is utterly opposed to the attempts of the Abolitionists to carry the issue to one of war itself.

I KNOW very well that to sound a false alarm is a shallow and contemptible thing. But I know, also, that too much precaution is safer than too little, and I believe that less than the utmost is too little now. Better, it is said, to be ridiculed for too much care than to be ruined by too confident a security. I have, then, a profound conviction that the Union is in danger. I will tell you where I think the danger lies.

It is, that while the people sleep, politicians and philanthropists of the legislative hall, the stump, and the press, will talk and write us out of our Union. Yes, while you sleep, while the merchant is loading his ships, and the farmer is gathering his harvests, and the music of the hammer and shuttle wake around, and we are all steeped in the enjoyment of that vast and various good which a common government places within our reach. There are influences that never sleep, and which are creating and diffusing a *public opinion* in whose hot and poisoned breath, before we yet perceive our evil plight, this Union may melt as frostwork in the sun.

Do we sufficiently appreciate how omnipotent is opinion in the matter of all government? Do we consider especially in how true a sense it is the creator, must be the upholder, and may be the destroyer of our united government? . . .

And now, charged with the trust of holding together such a nation as this, what have we seen? What do we see today? Exactly this. It has been for many months—years, I may say, but assuredly for a long season—the peculiar infelicity, say, rather, terrible misfortune of this country, that the attention of the people has been fixed, without the respite of a moment, exclusively on one of those subjects—the only one on which we disagree precisely according to geographical lines. And not so only, but this subject has been one—unlike tariff, or internal improvements, or the disbursement of the public money, on which the dispute cannot be maintained for an hour without heat of blood, mutual loss of respect, alienation of regard—menacing to end in hate and cruel as the grave.

I call this only a terrible misfortune. I blame here and now no man and no policy for it. Circumstances have forced it upon us all; and down to the hour that the series of compromise measures was completed and presented to the country, or certainly to Congress, I will not here and now say that it was the fault of one man, or one region of country, or one party more than another.

They tell us that slavery is so wicked a thing that they must pursue it, by agitation, to its home in the states, and that if there is an implied engagement to abstain from doing so, it is an engagement to neglect an opportunity of doing good, and void in the forum of conscience. But was it ever heard of that one may not formally bind himself to abstain from what he thinks a particular opportunity of doing good? A contract in general restraint of philanthropy or any other useful calling is void; but a contract to abstain from a specific sphere of exertion is not void, and may be wise and right. . . . To win the opportunity of achieving the mighty good summed up in the pregnant language of the preamble to the Constitution, such good as man has not on this earth been many times permitted to do or dream of, we might well surrender the privilege of reviling the masters of slaves, with whom we must "either live or bear no life."

Fellow citizens, the first of men are the builders of empires. . . . Let the grandeur of such duties, let the splendor of such rewards, suffice us. Let them reconcile and constrain us to turn from that equivocal philanthropy which violates contracts, which tramples on law, which confounds the whole subordination of virtues, which counts it a light thing that a nation is rent asunder, and the swords of brothers sheathed in the bosoms of brothers, if thus the chains of one slave may be violently and prematurely broken.

HENRY CLAY

"Let us look to our country and our cause, elevate ourselves to the dignity of pure and disinterested patriots."

WASHINGTON, D. C., 1850— Henry Clay, senator from Kentucky, has appealed to the Congress, and over its head to the public, to adopt compromises on the slavery issue in constitutional form which, he conceded, will not wholly please anyone but promise to save the Union.

His speech was made in connection with the introduction of a Senate Resolution worked out in a committee of which he was chairman. But while the resolution bears the imprimatur of a committee, the whole argument is more precisely the work of this western Senator who already has won the unofficial title of "The Great Compromiser."

Rather than apologizing for such a stand, Senator Clay reiterated today that compromise must be "the nature of the government and its operations" in all spheres of major debate; that concessions mutually made —which do not violate the basic tenets of government—are honorable gestures.

IT HAS been objected against this measure that it is a compromise. It has been said that it is a compromise of principle, or of a principle. Mr. President, what is a compromise? It is a work of mutual concession—an agreement in which there are reciprocal stipulations—a work in which, for the sake of peace and concord, one party abates his extreme demands in consideration of an abatement of extreme demands by the other party: it is a measure of mutual concession—a measure of mutual sacrifice. Undoubtedly, Mr. President, in all such measures of compromise, one party would be very glad to get what he wants, and reject what he does not desire but which the other party wants. But when he comes to reflect that, from the nature of the government and its operations, and from those with whom he is dealing, it is necessary upon his part, in order to secure what he wants, to grant something to the other side, he should be reconciled to the concession which he has made in consequence of the concession which he is to receive, if there is no great principle involved, such as a violation of the Constitution of the United States. I admit that such a compromise as that ought never to be sanctioned or adopted. But I now call upon any senator in his place to point out from the beginning to the end, from California to New Mexico, a solitary provision in this bill which is violative of the Constitution of the United States.

The responsibility of this great measure passes from the hands of the committee, and from my hands. They know, and I know, that it is an awful and tremendous responsibility. I hope that you will meet it with a just conception and a true appreciation of its magnitude, and the magnitude of the consequences that may ensue from your decision one way or the other. The alternatives, I fear,

which the measure presents, are concord and increased discord
. . . I believe from the bottom of my soul that the measure is
the reunion of this Union. I believe it is the dove of peace, which,
taking its aerial flight from the dome of the Capitol, carries the
glad tidings of assured peace and restored harmony to all the
remotest extremities of this distracted land. I believe that it will
be attended with all these beneficent effects. And now let us discard
all resentment, all passions, all petty jealousies, all personal desires,
all love of place, all hankerings after the gilded crumbs which fall
from the table of power. Let us forget popular fears, from whatever quarter they may spring. Let us go to the limpid fountain
of unadulterated patriotism, and, performing a solemn lustration,
return divested of all selfish, sinister, and sordid impurities, and
think alone of our God, our country, our consciences, and our
glorious Union—that Union without which we shall be torn into
hostile fragments, and sooner or later become the victims of
military despotism or foreign domination. . . .

Let us look to our country and our cause, elevate ourselves to
the dignity of pure and disinterested patriots, and save our country
from all impending dangers. What if, in the march of this nation
to greatness and power, we should be buried beneath the wheels
that propel it onward! . . .

I call upon all the South. Sir, we have had hard words, bitter
words, bitter thoughts, unpleasant feelings toward each other in
the progress of this great measure. Let us forget them. Let us
sacrifice these feelings. Let us go to the altar of our country and
swear, as the oath was taken of old, that we will stand by her;
that we will support her; that we will uphold her Constitution; that
we will preserve her union; and that we will pass this great, comprehensive, and healing system of measures, which will hush all
the jarring elements and bring peace and tranquillity to our homes.

Let me, Mr. President, in conclusion, say that the most disastrous consequences would occur, in my opinion, were we to go
home, doing nothing to satisfy and tranquillize the country upon
these great questions. What will be the judgment of mankind, what
the judgment of that portion of mankind who are looking upon the

progress of this scheme of self-government as being that which holds the highest hopes and expectations of ameliorating the condition of mankind—what will their judgment be? Will not all the monarchs of the Old World pronounce our glorious republic a disgraceful failure? Will you go home and leave all in disorder and confusion—all unsettled—all open? The contentions and agitations of the past will be increased and augmented by the agitations resulting from our neglect to decide them.

Sir, we shall stand condemned by all human judgment below, and of that above it is not for me to speak. We shall stand condemned in our own consciences, by our own constituents, and by our own country. The measure may be defeated. I have been aware that its passage for many days was not absolutely certain. . . . But, if defeated, it will be a triumph of ultraism and impracticability—a triumph of a most extraordinary conjunction of extremes; a victory won by abolitionism; a victory achieved by free-soilism; a victory of discord and agitation over peace and tranquillity; and I pray to Almighty God that it may not, in consequence of the inauspicious result, lead to the most unhappy and disastrous consequences to our beloved country.

CHARLES SUMNER

"An essential wickedness that makes other public crimes seem like public virtues."

WASHINGTON, D. C., May, 1856 —As this month draws to a close, lowering the curtain on perhaps the most heated debates yet held in Congress over the question of slavery, the steamy atmosphere of the nation's capital seems to quiver in echoes to words said and deeds done without precedent in the history of Capitol Hill.

Senator Charles Sumner, of Massachusetts, lies grievously hurt* in his bed as a result of a beating administered to him on May 22 by Mr.

* Senator Sumner was three years in recovering from these injuries and never made a complete recovery.

Preston S. Brooks, nephew of Senator Andrew Pickens Butler, of South Carolina. Yet while Senator Sumner suffers physically, Senator Butler and Senator Stephen A. Douglas, of Illinois, carry the unseen but colorful bruises of such a tongue-lashing as never has been heard here in public debate.

The Massachusetts Senator, already noted for his mastery of invective, went beyond propriety in a two-day oration on the floor of the Senate, in which he denounced with all his abolitionist fervor what he termed "The Crime Against Kansas" —the compromise measure by which admission of Kansas as a State of the Union was predicated upon recognition of the right of perpetuation of slavery by the Southern states and within certain other territories yet to be admitted as States.

Senator Sumner's speech, has further clouded the slavery issue with bitter personal animosities.

THE WICKEDNESS which I now begin to expose is immeasurably aggravated by the motive which prompted it. Not in any common lust for power did this uncommon tragedy have its origin. It is the rape of a virgin Territory, compelling it to the hateful embrace of slavery; and it may be clearly traced to a depraved longing for a new slave State, the hideous offspring of such a crime, in the hope of adding to the power of slavery in the National Government. Yes, sir; when the whole world, alike Christian and Turk, is rising up to condemn this wrong, and to make it a hissing to the nations, here in our Republic, force—ay, sir, force—has been openly employed in compelling Kansas to this pollution, and all for the sake of political power. There is the simple fact, which you will in vain attempt to deny, but which in itself presents an essential wickedness that makes other public crimes seem like public virtues. . . .

But, before entering upon the argument, I must say something of a general character, particularly in response to what has fallen from Senators who have raised themselves to eminence on this floor in championship of human wrongs. I mean the Senator from South Carolina (Mr. Butler), and the Senator from Illinois (Mr. Douglas), who, though unlike as Don Quixote and Sancho Panza, yet, like this couple, sally forth together in the same adventure. I regret much to miss the elder Senator from his seat; but the cause, against which he has run a tilt, with such activity of animosity, demands that the opportunity of exposing him should not be lost; and it is for the cause that I speak. The Senator from South Carolina has read many books of chivalry, and believes himself a chivalrous knight, with sentiments of honor and courage.

Of course he has chosen a mistress to whom he has made his vows, and who, though ugly to others, is always lovely to him; though polluted in the sight of the world, is chaste in his sight—I mean the harlot, Slavery. For her, his tongue is always profuse in words. Let her be impeached in character, or any proposition made to shut her out from the extension of her wantonness, and no extravagance of manner or hardihood of assertion is then too great for this Senator. The frenzy of Don Quixote, in behalf of his wench, Dulcinea del Toboso, is all surpassed. The asserted rights of slavery, which shock equality of all kinds, are cloaked by a fantastic claim of equality. If the slave States cannot enjoy what, in mockery of the great fathers of the Republic, he misnames equality under the Constitution—in other words, the full power in the national territories to compel fellow-men to unpaid toil, to separate husband and wife, and to sell little children at the auction block—then, sir, the chivalric Senator will conduct the State of South Carolina out of the Union! Heroic knight! Exalted Senator! A second Moses come for a second Exodus!

But not content with this poor menace, which we have been twice told was "measured," the Senator in the unrestrained chivalry of his nature, has undertaken to apply opprobrious words to those who differ from him on this floor. He calls them "sectional and fanatical"; and opposition to the usurpation in Kansas he denounces as "an uncalculating fanaticism." To be sure these charges lack all grace of originality, and all sentiments of truth; but the adventurous Senator does not hesitate. He is the uncompromising, unblushing representative on this floor of a flagrant sectionalism, which now domineers over the Republic. . . .

As the Senator from South Carolina is the Don Quixote, the Senator from Illinois (Mr. Douglas) is the squire of slavery, its very Sancho Panza, ready to do all its humiliating offices. This Senator, in his labored address, vindicating his labored report— piling one mass of elaborate error upon another mass—constrained himself, as you will remember, to unfamiliar decencies of speech. Of that address I have nothing to say at this moment, though before I sit down I shall show something of its fallacies. But I go back now to an earlier occasion, when, true to his native impulses, he threw into this discussion, "for a charm of powerful trouble," personalities most discreditable to this body. I will not stop to repel the imputations which he cast upon myself; but I mention them to remind you of the "sweltered venom sleeping got," which, with other poisoned ingredients, he cast into the cauldron of this debate.

. . . Standing on this floor, the Senator issued his rescript, requiring submission to the usurped power of Kansas; and this was accompanied by a manner—all his own—such as befits the tyrannical threat. Very well. Let the Senator try. I tell him now that he cannot enforce any such submission. The Senator, with the slave power at his back, is strong; but he is not strong enough for this purpose. . . . He may convulse this country with a civil feud. Like the ancient madman, he may set fire to this temple of constitutional liberty, grander than the Ephesian dome; but he cannot enforce obedience to that tyrannical usurpation.

ABRAHAM LINCOLN

"I believe this government cannot endure permanently, half slave and half free."

SPRINGFIELD, Ill., June 16, 1858 —Abraham Lincoln today challenged the Federal Government and the very decisions of Federal courts with the thesis, advanced in the slavery issue, that eventually there must be no slavery within the United States, or this institution itself will bring down the whole structure of the Republic.

He spoke in accepting the Republican nomination for the Senate. In this contest his opponent is Stephen A. Douglas, the Democrat whose smallness of stature (compared with Mr. Lincoln's unusual height) makes a startling contrast with his nationally known oratorical gifts.

The two candidates will campaign for the election, not by popular vote, but in the accepted present custom of attempting to impress the members of the State Legislature, by whose vote one or the other will be chosen.

The theme of Mr. Lincoln's acceptance speech was the Biblical quotation, "A house divided against itself cannot stand."

However, his speech is more notable for the detailed and yet graphic exposition given to the whole issue of slavery and its political ramifications, with the qualification that he speaks the viewpoint of the Abolitionists.

What effect this will have upon Mr. Lincoln's political future is as yet hard to predict, but he has laid down a new summary of the Northern argument that makes a notable paper in political annals.

MR. PRESIDENT and Gentlemen of the Convention: If we could first know where we are, and whither we are tending, we could better judge what to do, and how to do it. We are now far into the fifth year since a policy was initiated with the avowed object, and confident promise, of putting an end to slavery agitation. Under the operation of that policy, that agitation not only has not ceased, but has constantly augmented. In my opinion, it will not cease until a crisis shall have been reached and passed. "A house divided against itself cannot stand." I believe this government cannot endure permanently, half slave and half free. I do not expect the Union to be dissolved; I do not expect the house to fall; but I do expect that it will cease to be divided. It will become all one thing, or all the other.

Either the opponents of slavery will arrest the further spread of it, and place it where the public mind shall rest in the belief that it is in the course of ultimate extinction; or its advocates will push it forward till it shall become alike lawful in all the States, old as well as new, North as well as South. . . .

The new year of 1854 found slavery excluded from more than half the states by state constitutions, and from most of the national territory by Congressional prohibition. Four days later commenced the struggle which ended in repealing that Congressional prohibition. This opened all the national territory to slavery, and was the first point gained. But, so far, Congress only had acted, and an indorsement, by the people, real or apparent, was indispensable, to save the point already gained and give chance for more. This necessity had not been overlooked, but had been provided for, as well as might be, in the notable argument of "squatter sovereignty," otherwise called "sacred right of self-government"; which latter phrase though expressive of the only rightful basis of any government, was so perverted in this attempted use of it as to amount to just this: That, if any one man choose to enslave another, no third man shall be allowed to object. That argument was incorporated with the Nebraska bill itself. . . . Then opened the roar of loose declamation in favor of "squatter sovereignty," and "sacred right of self-government." "But," said opposition members, "let us amend the bill so as to expressly declare that the people of the territory may exclude slavery." "Not we," said the friends of the measure; and down they voted the amendment.

While the Nebraska bill was passing through Congress, a law-case, involving the question of a Negro's freedom, by reason of his owner having voluntarily taken him first into a free State, and then into a territory covered by the Congressional prohibition, and held him as a slave for a long time in each, was passing through the United States Circuit Court for the District of Missouri; and both Nebraska bill and lawsuit were brought to a decision in the same month of May, 1854. The Negro's name was Dred Scott, which name now designates the decision finally made in the case. Before the then next Presidential election, the law-case came to, and was argued in, the Supreme Court of the United States; but the decision of it was deferred until after the election. Still, before the election, Senator Trumbull, on the floor of the Senate, requested the leading advocate of the Nebraska bill to state his opinion whether the people of a territory can constitutionally exclude slavery from their limits; and the latter answers: "That is a question for the Supreme Court."

The election came, Mr. Buchanan was elected, and the indorsement, such as it was, secured. That was the second point gained. The indorsement, however, fell short of a clear popular majority by nearly four hundred thousand votes, and so, perhaps, was not overwhelmingly reliable and satisfactory. The outgoing President, in his last annual message, as impressively as possible, echoed back upon the people the weight and authority of the endorsement. The Supreme Court met again, did not announce their decision, but ordered a reargument. The Presidential inauguration came, and still no decision of the court; but the incoming President, in his inaugural address, fervently exhorted the people to abide by the forthcoming decision, whatever it might be. Then, in a few days, came the decision. The reputed author of the Nebraska bill finds an early occasion to make a speech at this capital, endorsing the Dred Scott decision, and vehemently denouncing all opposition to it. The new President, too, seizes the early occasion of the Silliman letter to indorse and strongly construe that decision, and to express his astonishment that any different view had ever been entertained.

At length a squabble springs up between the President and the author of the Nebraska bill, on the mere question of fact, whether the Lecompton constitution was, or was not, in any just sense, made by the people of Kansas; and in that quarrel the latter declares that all he wants is a fair vote for the people, and that he cares not whether slavery be voted down or voted up. I do not understand his declaration, that he cares not whether slavery be voted down or voted up, to be intended by him other than as an apt definition of the policy he would impress upon the public mind —the principle for which he declares he has suffered so much, and is ready to suffer to the end. And well may he cling to that principle. If he has any parental feeling, well may he cling to it. That principle is the only shred left of his original Nebraska doctrine. Under the Dred Scott decision squatter sovereignty squattered out of existence—tumbled down like temporary scaffolding—like the mould at the foundry, served through one blast, and fell back into loose sand—helped to carry an election, and then was kicked to the winds. His late joint struggle with the Republicans against the Lecompton constitution involves nothing of the original Nebraska doctrine. That struggle was made on a point—the right of a people to make their own constitution—upon which he and the Republicans have never differed.

The several points of the Dred Scott decision, in connection with Senator Douglas's "care-not" policy, constitute the piece of machinery in its present state of advancement. This was the third point gained. The working points of that machinery are: (1) That no Negro slave, imported as such from Africa, and no descendant of such slave, can ever be a citizen of the United States. This point is made in order to deprive the Negro, in every possible event, of the benefit of that provision of the United States constitution, which declares that "the citizens of each State shall be entitled to all privileges and immunities of citizens in the several States." (2) That, "subject to the constitution of the United States," neither Congress nor a territorial legislature can exclude slavery from any United States territory. This point is made in order that individual men may fill up the territories with slaves, without danger of losing them as property, and thus to enhance the chances of permanency to the institution through all the future. (3) That whether the holding a Negro in actual slavery in a free State makes him free, as against the holder, the United States courts will not decide, but will leave to be decided by the courts of any slave State the Negro may be forced into by the master. This point is made, not to be pressed immediately; but, if acquiesced in for a while, and apparently endorsed by the people at an election, then to sustain the logical conclusion that what Dred Scott's master might lawfully do with Dred Scott, in the State of Illinois, every other master may lawfully do with any other one or one thousand slaves, in Illinois, or in any other free State.

Auxiliary to all this, and working hand in hand with it, the Nebraska doctrine, or what is left of it, is to educate and mould public opinion, at least Northern public opinion, not to care whether slavery is voted down or voted up. This shows exactly where we now are, and partially, also, whither we are tending. . . .

Such a decision is all that slavery now lacks of being alike lawful in all the States. Welcome or unwelcome, such decision is probably coming, and will soon be upon us, unless the power of the present political dynasty shall be met and overthrown. We shall lie down pleasantly dreaming that the people of Missouri are on the verge of making their State free, and we shall awake to the reality, instead, that the Supreme Court has made Illinois a slave State. To meet and overthrow that dynasty is the work before all those who would prevent that consummation. That is what we have to do.

There are those who denounce us openly to their own friends, and yet whisper to us softly that Senator Douglas is the aptest instrument there is with which to effect that object. They wish us to infer all, from the fact that he now has a little quarrel with the present head of the dynasty; and that he has regularly voted with us on a single point, upon which he and we have never differed. They remind us that he is a great man, and that the largest of us are very small ones. Let this be granted. "But a living dog is better than a dead lion." Judge Douglas, if not a dead lion, for this work, is at least a caged and toothless one. How can he oppose the advances of slavery? He doesn't care anything about it. His avowed mission is impressing the "public heart" to care nothing about it. . . .

Now, as ever, I wish not to misrepresent Judge Douglas's position, question his motives, or do aught that can be personally offensive to him. Whenever, if ever, he and we can come together on principle, so that our cause may have assistance from his great ability, I hope to have interposed no adventitious obstacle. But, clearly, he is not now with us—he does not pretend to be, he does not promise ever to be.

Our cause then, must be intrusted to, and conducted by its own undoubted friends—those whose hands are free, whose hearts are in the work—who do care for the result. . . .

The sequel:

This campaign was a "failure" in its immediate results. The Illinois legislature, swayed partially by Senator Douglas's oratory but more largely by the logic of events and their legal interpretations, elected Douglas to the Senate.

All of which was perhaps a happy circumstance for Mr. Lincoln's political ambitions. Two years later it was Lincoln who was nominated and elected President—a result that might have been otherwise had he been pitched into the maelstrom of Washington debate between 1858 and 1860.

From this acceptance speech, with its notable contribution toward increasing Lincoln's stature, he went on to the notable series of debates with Senator Douglas, whose "Reply to Lincoln" is a classic of northern Democratic doctrine. And in the meantime, the East was seething with the same issue, debated by speakers who in some cases had never heard Lincoln speak, if they were even familiar with his name.

STEPHEN A. DOUGLAS

"Leave the people free to do as they please."

FREEPORT, Ill., 1858—Senator Stephen A. Douglas, in open and joint debate here with Abraham Lincoln, contesting for his Senate seat, today told his opponent that expansion of the United States by the admission of new States must not be hampered by conditions laid down as to slavery within the borders of each.

If the population of a new state favors slavery, he said, that is the business of that state; if slavery is opposed, the state may be counted upon to see that no police powers protecting this institution are maintained.

In this manner, the Democratic Senator—spokesman for this "free state" but openly allied with his party confreres from the South—challenged the thesis of Mr. Lincoln, repeated time after time in debates with Senator Douglas on the basis of his acceptance speech given at Springfield some months ago.

LADIES AND Gentlemen: I am glad that at last I have brought Mr. Lincoln to the conclusion that he had better define his position on certain political questions to which I called his attention at Ottawa. . . . I did not present idle questions for him to answer merely for my gratification. I laid the foundation for those interrogatories by showing that they constituted the platform of the party whose nominee he is for the Senate. . . . In a few moments I will proceed to review the answers which he has given to these interrogatories; but in order to relieve his anxiety, I will first respond to these which he has presented to me. Mark you, he has not presented interrogatories which have ever received the sanction of the party with which I am acting, and hence he has no other foundation for them than his own curiosity.

First, he desires to know if the people of Kansas shall form a constitution by means entirely proper and unobjectionable, and ask admission into the Union as a State, before they have the requisite population for a member of Congress, whether I will vote for that admission. Well, now, I regret exceedingly that he did not answer that interrogatory himself before he put it to me, in order that we might understand, and not be left to infer on which side he is. Mr. Trumbull, during the last session of Congress, voted from the beginning to the end against the admission of Oregon, although a free State, because she had not the requisite population for a member of Congress. Mr. Trumbull would not consent, under any circumstances, to let a State, free or slave, come into the Union until it had the requisite population. As Mr. Trumbull is in the field fighting for Mr. Lincoln, I would like to have Mr. Lincoln answer his own question, and tell me whether he is fighting Trumbull on that issue or not. But I will answer his question. In reference to Kansas, it is my opinion that as she has population enough to constitute a slave State, she has people enough for a free State. I will not make Kansas an exceptional case to the other States of the Union. I hold it to be a sound rule of universal application to require a territory to contain the requisite population for a member of Congress before it is admitted as a State into the Union. I made that proposition in the Senate in 1856, and I renewed it during the last session in a bill providing that no territory of the United States should form a constitution and apply for admission, until it had the requisite population. On another occasion, I proposed, that neither Kansas nor any other territory should be admitted until it had the requisite population. Congress did not adopt any of my propositions containing this general rule, but did make an exception of Kansas. I will stand by that exception. Either Kansas must come in as a free State, with whatever population she may have, or the rule must be applied to all the other territories alike.

The next question propounded to me by Mr. Lincoln is: Can the people of the territory in any lawful way, against the wishes of any citizen of the United States, exclude slavery from their limits prior to the formation of a State constitution? I answer emphatically, as Mr. Lincoln has heard me answer a hundred times from every stump in Illinois, that in my opinion the people of a territory can, by lawful means, exclude slavery from their limits prior to the formation of a State constitution. Mr. Lincoln knew that I had answered that question over and over again. He heard me argue the Nebraska Bill on that principle all over the State in 1854, in 1855, and in 1856, and he has no excuse for pretending to be in doubt as to my position on that question. It matters not what way the Supreme Court may hereafter decide as to the abstract question whether slavery may or may not go into a territory under the Constitution; the people have the lawful means to introduce it or exclude it as they please, for the reason that slavery cannot exist a day or an hour anywhere, unless it is supported by local police regulations. Those police regulations can only be established by the local legislature; and if the people are opposed to slavery, they will elect representatives to that body who will, by unfriendly legislation, effectually prevent the introduction of it into their midst. If, on the contrary, they are for it, their legislation will favor its extension. Hence, no matter what the decision of the Supreme Court may be on that abstract question, still the right of the people to make a slave territory or a free territory is perfect and complete under the Nebraska Bill. I hope Mr. Lincoln deems my answer satisfactory to that point.

The third question which Mr. Lincoln presented is: "If the Supreme Court of the United States shall decide that a State of this Union cannot exclude slavery from its own limits, will I submit to it?" I am amazed that Lincoln should ask such a question. "A schoolboy knows better." Yes, a schoolboy does know better. Mr. Lincoln's object is to cast an imputation upon the Supreme Court. He knows that there never was but one man in America, claiming any degree of intelligence or decency, who ever for a moment pretended such a thing. It is true that the Washington "Union," in an article published on the seventeenth of last December, did put forth that doctrine, and I denounced the article on the floor of the Senate in a speech which Mr. Lincoln now pretends was against the President. The Union had claimed that slavery had a right to go into the free States, and that any provisions in the constitution or laws of the free States to the contrary was null and void. I denounced it in the Senate, as I said before, and I was the first man who did. Lincoln's friends, Trumbull and Seward and Hale and Wilson, and the whole black Republican side of the Senate, were silent. They left it to me to denounce it. And what was the reply made to me on that occasion? Mr. Toombs of

Georgia, got up and undertook to lecture me on the ground that I ought not to have deemed the article worthy of notice and ought not to have replied to it; that there was not one man, woman, or child south of the Potomac, in any slave State, who did not repudiate any such pretension. Mr. Lincoln knows that that reply was made on the spot, and yet now he asks this question. He might as well ask me: "Suppose Mr. Lincoln should steal a horse, would you sanction it?" and it would be as genteel in me to ask him, in the event he stole a horse, what ought to be done with him. He casts an imputation upon the Supreme Court of the United States by supposing that they would violate the Constitution of the United States. I tell him that such a thing is not possible. It would be an act of moral treason that no man on the bench could ever descend to. Mr. Lincoln himself would never in his partisan feelings so far forget what was right as to be guilty of such an act.

The fourth question of Mr. Lincoln is: "Are you in favor of acquiring additional territory, in disregard as to how such acquisition may affect the Union on the slavery question?" This question is very ingeniously and cunningly put.

The Black Republican creed lays it down expressly, that under no circumstances shall we acquire any more territory unless slavery is first prohibited in the country. I ask Mr. Lincoln whether he is in favor of that proposition. Are you (addressing Mr. Lincoln) opposed to the acquisition of any more territory, under any circumstances, unless slavery is prohibited in it? That he does not like to answer. When I ask him whether he stands up to that article in the platform of his party he turns, Yankee fashion, and, without answering it, asks me whether I am in favor of acquiring territory without regard to how it may affect the Union on the slavery question. I answer that whenever it becomes necessary, in our growth and progress, to acquire more territory, that I am in favor of it, without reference to the question of slavery; and when we have acquired it, I will leave the people free to do as they please, either to make it slave or free territory, as they prefer. It is idle to tell me or you that we have territory enough. Our fathers supposed that we had enough when our territory extended to the Mississippi River, but a few years' growth and expansion satisfied them that we needed more, and the Louisiana Territory, from the west branch of the Mississippi to the British possessions, was acquired. Then we acquired Oregon, then California and New Mexico. We have enough now for the present, but this is a young and a growing nation. It swarms as often as a hive of bees; and as new swarms are turned out each year, there must be hives in which they can gather and make their honey. In less than fifteen years, if the same progress that has distinguished this country for the last fifteen years continues, every foot of vacant land between this and the Pacific Ocean owned by the United States will be occupied. Will you not continue to increase at the end of fifteen years as well as now? I tell you, increase and multiply and expand is the law of this nation's existence. You cannot limit this great Republic by mere boundary lines, saying: "thus far shalt thou go, and no further." Any one of you gentlemen might as well say to a son twelve years old that he is big enough, and must not grow any larger, and in order to prevent his growth, put a hoop around him to keep him to his present size. What would be the result? Either the hoop must burst and be rent asunder, or the child must die. So it would be with this great nation. With our natural increase, growing with a rapidity unknown in any other part of the globe, with the tide of emigration that is fleeing from despotism in the Old World to seek refuge in our own, there is a constant torrent pouring into this country that requires more land, more territory upon which to settle; and just as fast as our interests and our destiny require additional territory in the North, in the South, or on the islands of the ocean, I am for it, and when we acquire it, will leave the people, according to the Nebraska Bill, free to do as they please on the subject of slavery and every other question.

I trust now that Mr. Lincoln will deem himself answered on his four points.

The sequel:

When Senator Douglas won this election—in fact, he never lost one in his life—he probably diminished his own chances of eventually winning the Presidency. His alliance with the slave faction became the wrong political tactic, and never was he permitted even the chance to run for the Presidency.

As the inevitability of the Civil

War became apparent in 1860, coincident with Lincoln's election, there were times when the uncompromising stand taken by Senator Douglas subjected him to abuse and actual threats of harm.

Yet when the war did break out he proved a loyal and eloquent friend of the Union in the months during 1861 that elapsed before his death.

WILLIAM H. SEWARD

"The irrepressible conflict."

ROCHESTER, N. Y., Oct. 25, 1858 —Almost on the eve of this year's momentous election, when slavery has become virtually the sole issue— and particularly the question of how Kansas and other prospective states are to be admitted into the Union— Senator William Henry Seward challenged here today the very integrity of the Democratic party and its espousal of slavery in those present or future states where it is legal.

The Senator is not a candidate for reelection, as his term has two more years to run. His prestige is so great, beginning with his governorship of this state in 1838 and continuing through a Senate career that began in 1849, that he might well have remained out of this contest.

Nevertheless, he has taken such a forceful stand that he may be counted in the forefront of the fight just as vigorously as, for instance, Mr. Abraham Lincoln, who in Illinois is staking his political future on a campaign for a Senate seat.

More remarkable, in Senator Seward's case, is the fact that a delicate balance of political strength in New York finds the Democrats, who will put a candidate into the field against him two years hence, almost equally as strong as his own party, even though New York is permanently and irrevocably aligned with the "free states."

Against that background, his speech is not only dramatic but courageous.

THE HISTORY of the Democratic party commits it to the policy of slavery. It has been the Democratic party, and no other agency, which has carried that policy up to its present alarming culmination. Without stopping to ascertain, critically, the origin of the present Democratic party, we may concede its claim to date from the era of good feeling which occurred under the administration of President Monroe. At that time, in this State, and about that time in many others of the free States, the Democratic party deliberately disfranchised the free colored or African citizen, and it has pertinaciously continued this disfranchisement ever since. This was an effective aid to slavery; for, while the slaveholder votes for his slaves against freedom, the freed slave in the free States is prohibited from voting against slavery.

In 1824, the democracy resisted the election of John Quincy Adams—himself before that time an acceptable Democrat—and in 1828 it expelled him from the Presidency and put a slaveholder in his place, although the office had been filled by slaveholders thirty-two out of forty years.

In 1836, Martin Van Buren—the first non-slaveholding citizen of a free State to whose election the Democratic party ever consented—signalized his inauguration into the Presidency by a gratuitous announcement that under no circumstances would he ever approve a bill for the abolition of slavery in the District of Columbia. From 1838 to 1844 the subject of abolishing slavery in the District of Columbia and in the national dockyards and arsenals, was brought before Congress by repeated popular appeals. The Democratic party thereupon promptly denied the right of petition, and effectually suppressed the freedom of speech in Congress, so far as the institution of slavery was concerned.

From 1840 to 1843 good and wise men counselled that Texas should remain outside the Union until she should consent to relinquish her self-instituted slavery; but the Democratic party precipitated her admission into the Union, not only without that condition, but even with a covenant that the State might be divided and reorganized so as to constitute four slave States instead of one.

In 1846, when the United States became involved in a war with Mexico, and it was apparent that the struggle would end in the dismemberment of that republic, which was a non-slaveholding power, the Democratic party rejected a declaration that slavery should not be established within the territory to be acquired. When, in 1850, governments were to be instituted in the territories of California and New Mexico, the fruits of that war, the Democratic party refused to admit New Mexico as a free State, and only consented to admit California as a free State on the condition, as it has since explained the transaction, of leaving all of New Mexico and Utah open to slavery, to which was also added the concession of perpetual slavery in the District of Columbia and the passage of an unconstitutional, cruel and humiliating law, for the recapture of fugitive slaves, with a further stipulation that the subject of slavery should never again be agitated in either chamber of Congress. When, in 1854, the slaveholders were contentedly reposing on these great advantages, then so recently won, the Democratic party unnecessarily, officiously, and with super-serviceable liberality, awakened them from their slumber, to offer and force on their acceptance the abrogation of the law which declared that neither slavery nor involuntary servitude should ever exist within that part of the ancient territory of Louisiana which lay outside of the State of Missouri, and north of the parallel of 36° 30′ of north latitude—a law which, with the exception of one other, was the only statute of freedom then remaining in the Federal code.

In 1856, when the people of Kansas had organized a new State within the region thus abandoned to slavery, and applied to be admitted as a free State into the Union, the Democratic party contemptuously rejected their petition, and drove them with menaces and intimidations from the halls of Congress, and armed the President with military power to enforce their submission to a slave code, established over them by fraud and usurpation. At every subsequent stage of a long contest which has since raged in Kansas, the Democratic party has lent its sympathies, its aid, and all the powers of the government which it controlled, to enforce slavery upon that unwilling and injured people. And now, even at this day, while it mocks us with the assurance that Kansas is free, the Democratic party keeps the State excluded from her just and proper place in the Union, under the hope that she may be dragooned into the acceptance of slavery.

The Democratic party, finally, has procured from a supreme judiciary, fixed in its interest, a decree that slavery exists by force of the constitution in every territory of the United States, paramount to all legislative authority, either within the territory or residing in Congress.

Such is the Democratic party. It has no policy, state or federal, for finance, or trade, or manufacture, or commerce, or education, or internal improvements, or for the protection or even the security of civil or religious liberty. It is positive and uncompromising in the interest of slavery—negative, compromising, and vacillating, in regard to everything else. It boasts its love of equality, and wastes its strength, and even its life, in fortifying the only aristocracy known in the land. It professes fraternity, and, so often as slavery requires, allies itself with proscription. It magnifies itself for conquests in foreign lands, but it sends the national eagle forth always with chains, and not the olive branch, in his fangs.

This dark record shows you, fellow-citizens, what I was unwilling to announce at an earlier stage of this argument, that of the whole nefarious schedule of slaveholding designs which I have submitted to you, the Democratic party has left only one yet to be consummated—the abrogation of the law which forbids the African slave-trade.

The sequel:

Senator Seward continued for the next two years to battle for the abolition of slavery, but he cast his ambitions a little too high.

In the Republican Convention of 1860, he was an outstanding candidate for the Presidential nomination, and probably would have won it but for the emergence into national prominence of the new figure of Abraham Lincoln.

Lincoln was nominated. Seward lost.

When Lincoln became President, he named Seward as Secretary of State, and Seward's conduct of that office became his highest distinction. The friendship between Lincoln and Seward, developed during the Civil War, was intimate and exceptionally close.

JOHN BROWN

"I feel no consciousness of guilt."

CHARLES TOWN, Va., Nov. 2, 1859—What says a man when he has assayed to play the role of liberator outside the law, has finally directed his handful of followers in combat with uniformed troops of the government, and has lost; when he knows that beyond all appeal he will dangle from a gallows?

John Brown said it here today, in open court, after receiving that sentence which no power on earth could avert. How did he say it? He said it calmly and with great lucidity, as though each syllable were a brick carefully laid in a pillar of argument that was to be his memorial.

In five minutes, the leader of outlaws who seized the arsenal at Harper's Ferry nearby, and who surrendered only after a detachment of Marines under Colonel Robert E. Lee had killed 10 of their number, may have gone far toward changing his reputation in the future from that of erratic firebrand and outlaw to that of martyr.

History must judge. Today, however, it was a grizzled, bearded man of 59 years—the father of a whole squad of sons—who spoke his piece in the calm, plain language of the prairies from whence he came.

"I never did intend murder," he told the court. "I feel no consciousness of guilt."

So spoke the man who has obtained a small national reputation as "Old Brown of Oswatom," the Abolitionist and active member of the underground for spiriting slaves to freedom.

The facts of this trial were fairly simple; more complicated was its background. On the night of last October 16, Brown and 21 followers crossed the Potomac River from Charles Town, near where he rented a farm earlier this year, and captured without much resistance the Federal arsenal at Harper's Ferry. Once inside it, he remained quietly while the local militia blocked the roads. That night Colonel Lee came out with a company of marines and the following morning stormed the arsenal.

The attacking force killed 10 of Brown's men, so stubbornly did they resist, and wounded their leader. Five of the attacking force were killed. The casualties made the trial for insurrection inevitable. Today Brown was found guilty and sentenced to be hanged by the neck until dead. Then he spoke his piece.

But there is more to the affair than that—long activities as an embattled Abolitionist ranging from Kansas to Pennsylvania, and a deliberate ambush in Kansas back in 1855 by Brown, four of his sons and two friends, who killed in cold blood five pro-slavery men living on the banks of the Pottawatamie River. For this deed he escaped punishment.

After that he actively enlisted men to seize some unknown area and establish a sanctuary for escaped slaves and such Negro freedmen as might care to join them.

In all this, be it remarked, John Brown was more a symbol than an individual, a bravado acting openly in a field where more and more of his kind are acting covertly. But he got cornered.

These words he spoke today:

I HAVE, may it please the Court, a few words to say.

In the first place, I deny everything but what I have all along admitted: of a design on my part to free slaves. I intended certainly to have made a clean thing of that matter, as I did last winter, when I went into Missouri and there took slaves without the snapping of a gun on either side, moving them through the country, and finally leaving them in Canada. I designed to have done the same thing again on a larger scale. That was all I intended. I never did intend murder, or treason, or the destruction of property, or to excite or incite slaves to rebellion, or to make insurrection.

I have another objection, and that is that it is unjust that I should suffer such a penalty. Had I interfered in the manner which I admit, and which I admit has been fairly proved—for I admire the truthfulness and candor of the greater portion of the witnesses who have testified in this case—had I so interfered in behalf of the rich, the powerful, the intelligent, the so-called great, or in behalf of any of their friends, either father, mother, brother, sister, wife or children, or any of that class, and suffered and sacrificed what I have in this interference, it would have been all right. Every man in this Court would have deemed it an act worthy of reward rather than punishment.

This Court acknowledges, too, as I suppose, the validity of the law of God. I see a book kissed, which I suppose to be the Bible, or at least the New Testament, which teaches me that all things whatsoever I would that men should do to me, I should do even so to them. It teaches me, further, to remember them that are in bonds as bound with them. I endeavored to act up to the instruction. I say I am yet too young to understand that God is any respecter of persons. I believe that to have interfered as I have done, as I have always freely admitted I have done, in behalf of His despised poor, I did not wrong, but right. Now, if it is deemed necessary that I should forfeit my life for the furtherance of the ends of justice, and mingle my blood further with the blood of my children and with the blood of millions in this slave country whose rights are disregarded by wicked, cruel, and unjust enactments, I say, let it be done.

Let me say one word further. I feel entirely satisfied with the treatment I have received on my trial. Considering all the circumstances, it has been more generous than I expected. But I feel no consciousness of guilt. I have stated from the first what was my intention, and what was not. I never had any design against the liberty of any person, nor any disposition to commit treason or incite slaves to rebel or make any general insurrection. I never encouraged any man to do so, but always discouraged any idea of that kind.

Let me say, also, in regard to the statements made by some of those who were connected with me, I hear it has been stated by some of them that I have induced them to join me. But the contrary is true. I do not say this to injure them, but as regretting their weakness. Not one but joined me of his own accord, and the greater part at his own expense. A number of them I never saw, and never had a word of conversation with, till the day they came to me, and that was for the purpose I have stated.

Now, I have done.

The sequel:

John Brown was hanged at Charles Town, Va., (now West Virginia) on December 2, 1859.

He immediately became a legend in which interest grew with the years.

The gentle Colonel Lee, meticulous and firm as a military commander and probably chosen for this assignment by the War Department because of the correct manner in which he would handle it, served for two more years in the uniform he wore to Harper's Ferry.

Then, facing his own choice in the hard divisions over the many issues that divided the North and the South, he turned his own back on the government he served and went on to become the gallant leader of the foredoomed cause of the Confederacy.

General Robert E. Lee was never

an orator or a public speaker.

Perhaps what he felt was fairly summed up by a distinguished fellow Southerner, with gifts that might have carried him to the Presidency of the United States—Jefferson Davis. Instead, Davis, like Lee, went to the South, there to become the only president of a nation which never was.

RALPH WALDO EMERSON

"No man existed who could look down on Burns."

BOSTON, Mass., Jan. 25, 1859—Ralph Waldo Emerson, the philosopher and essayist, tonight paid a tribute to Robert Burns on the centenary anniversary of the late Scottish poet's birth, which constituted a eulogy any man might desire to be said about him. Dr. Emerson has lectured much and written much, but in his expression of humane love for other human beings he finds his highest expression.

MR. PRESIDENT and Gentlemen: I do not know by what untoward accident it has chanced—and I forbear to inquire—that, in this accomplished circle, it should fall to me, the worst Scotsman of all, to receive your commands, and at the latest hour, too, to respond to the sentiment just offered, and which, indeed, makes the occasion. But I am told there is no appeal, and I must trust to the inspiration of the theme to make a fitness which does not otherwise exist.

Yet, sir, I heartily feel the singular claims of the occasion. At the first announcement, from I know not whence, that the twenty-fifth of January was the hundredth anniversary of the birth of Robert Burns, a sudden consent warned the great English race, in all its kingdoms, colonies and states, all over the world, to keep the festival. We are here to hold our parliament with love and poesy, as men were wont to do in the Middle Ages. Those famous parliaments might or might not have had more stateliness, and better singers than we—though that is yet to be known—but they could not have better reason.

I can only explain this singular unanimity in a race which rarely acts together—but rather after their watchword, each for himself—by the fact that Robert Burns, the poet of the middle class, represents in the mind of men today that great uprising of the middle class against the armed and privileged minorities—that uprising which worked politically in the American and French Revolutions, and which, not in governments so much as in education and in social order, has changed the face of the world. In order for this destiny, his birth, breeding and fortune were low. His organic sentiment was absolute independence, and resting, as it should, on a life of labor. No man existed who could look down on him. They that looked into his eyes saw that they might look down on the sky as easily. His muse and teaching was common sense, joyful, aggressive, irresistible. Not Latimer, nor Luther, struck more telling blows against false theology than did this brave singer. The "Confession of Augsburg," the "Declaration of Independence," the French "Rights of Man," and the "Marseillaise," are not more weighty documents in the history of freedom than the songs of Burns. His satire has lost none of its edge. His musical arrows yet sing through the air. He is so substantially a reformer, and I find his grand, plain sense in close chain with the greatest masters—Rabelais, Shakespeare in comedy, Cervante and Butler. He is an exceptional genius. The people who care nothing for literature and poetry care for Burns. It was indifferent—they thought who saw him—whether he wrote verse or not; he could have done anything else as well.

Yet how true a poet is he! And the poet, too, of poor men, of hodden-gray, and the Guernsey-coat, and the blouse. He has given voice to all the experiences of common life; he has endeared the farmhouse and cottages, patches and poverty, beans and barley; ale the poor man's wine; hardship, the fear of debt, the dear society of weans and wife, of brothers and sisters, proud of each other, knowing so few, and finding amends for want and obscurity in books and thought. What a love of nature! and—shall I say?—of middle-class nature. Not great, like Goethe, in the stars, or like Byron, on the ocean, or Moore, in the luxurious East, but in the homely landscape which the poor see around them—bleak leagues of pasture and stubble, ice, and sleet, and rain, and snow-choked brooks; birds, hares, field-mice, thistles, and heather, which he daily knew. How many "Bonny Doons," and "John Anderson my Joes," and "Auld Lang Synes," all around the earth, have his verses been applied to! And his love songs still woo and melt the youths and maids; the farm work, the country holiday, the fishing cobble, are still his debtors today.

And, as he was thus the poet of the poor, anxious, cheerful, working humanity, so had he the language of low life. He grew up in a rural district, speaking a patois unintelligible to all but natives, and he has made that Lowland Scotch a Doric dialect of fame. It is the only example in history of a language made classic by the genius of a single man. But more than this. He had that secret of genius to draw from the bottom of society the strength of its speech, and astonish the ears of the polite with these artless words, better than art, and filtered of all offense through his beauty. It seemed odious to Luther that the devil should have all the best tunes; he would bring them into the churches; and Burns knew how to take from fairs and gypsies, blacksmiths and drovers, the speech of the market and street, and clothe it with melody.

But I am detaining you too long. The memory of Burns—I am afraid heaven and earth have taken too good care of it to leave us anything to say. The west winds are murmuring it. Open the windows behind you, and hearken for the incoming tide, what the waves say of it. The doves, perching always on the eaves of the Stone Chapel opposite, may know something about it. Every home in broad Scotland keeps his fame bright. The memory of Burns—every man's and boy's, and girl's head carries snatches of his songs, and can say them by heart, and, what is strangest of all, never learned them from a book, but from mouth to mouth. The wind whispers them, the birds whistle them, the corn, barley, and bulrushes hoarsely rustle them; nay, the music boxes at Geneva are framed and toothed to play them; the hand organs of the Savoyards in all cities repeat them, and the chimes of bells ring them in the spires. They are the property and the solace of mankind.

JEFFERSON DAVIS

"If you will have it thus, we will invoke the God of our fathers."

WASHINGTON, D. C., Jan. 21, 1861—Jefferson Davis, already a veteran of war and politics at the age of 52, and obviously wracked by the pains of illness, stood at his desk in the Senate today to deliver a calm speech that in other countries might have seen him dragged immediately to a dungeon.

It is the strange temper of these times, however, that it was possible for a courtly Southerner to announce calmly that his State had seceded from the Union, by his own advice and with his consent, and that accordingly he no longer would appear as its spokesman there.

"I do think that she has a justifiable cause," he said, "and I approve of her act."

After the heated debates over Secession that have occurred in the past decade, Senator Davis' speech was temperate and calm in tone, but the atmosphere of its delivery was ominous in the extreme. Mississippi is the sixth state to secede, following South Carolina, Alabama, Florida, Georgia and Louisiana in that order.

Virginia is known to be teetering on the brink, and if and when Virginia secedes so will all the other Southern States. There is some faint hope still expressed here that Abraham Lincoln may bring about a miracle upon his Inaugural next March 4.

Likewise, there is a notable absence from Washington of the leading figures of what is becoming known generally as the Confederacy. There are few men here of the stature of Senator Davis from the Southern States.

The Senator himself, known as a strong-willed and fearless man, spoke today in the tradition of his background. A graduate of West Point, veteran of the Mexican War and a former Secretary of War, his courage often is accounted greater than his judgment.

Already there are rumors that if the Confederacy is formed as a separate nation, he ranks high among those who may be chosen as its President.

The salient paragraphs of his speech follow:

I RISE, Mr. President, for the purpose of announcing to the Senate that I have satisfactory evidence that the State of Mississippi, by a solemn ordinance of her people in convention assembled, has declared her separation from the United States. Under these circumstances, of course my functions are terminated here. It has seemed to me proper, however, that I should appear in the Senate to announce that fact to my associates, and I will say but very little more. The occasion does not invite me to go into argument, and my physical condition would not permit me to do so if it were otherwise; and yet it seems to become me to say something on the part of the state I here represent, on an occasion so solemn as this.

It is known to Senators who have served with me here that I have for many years advocated, as an essential attribute of state sovereignty, the right of a state to secede from the Union. Therefore, if I had not believed there was justifiable cause; if I had thought that Mississippi was acting without sufficient provocation, or without an existing necessity, I should still, under my theory of the government, because of my allegiance to the state of which I am a citizen, have been bound by her action. I, however, may be permitted to say that I do think that she has justifiable cause, and I approve of her act. I conferred with her people before that act was taken, counseled them then that, if the state of things which they apprehended should exist when the convention met, they should take the action which they have now adopted.

I hope none who hear me will confound this expression of mine with the advocacy of the right of a state to remain in the Union, and to disregard its constitutional obligations by the nullification of the law. Such is not my theory. Nullification and secession, so often confounded, are indeed antagonistic principles. . . .

. . . This is done not in hostility to others, not to injure any section of the country, not even for our own pecuniary benefit; but from the high and solemn motive of defending and protecting the rights we inherited, and which it is our sacred duty to transmit unshorn to our children.

I find in myself, perhaps, a type of the general feeling of my constituents toward yours. I am sure I feel no hostility to you, Senators from the North. I am sure there is not one of you, whatever sharp discussion there may have been between us, to whom I cannot now say, in the presence of my God, I wish you well; and such, I am sure, is the feeling of the people whom I represent toward those whom you represent. I therefore feel that I but express their desire when I say I hope, and they hope, for peaceful relations with you, though we must part. They may be mutually beneficial to us in the future, as they have been in the past, if you so will it. The reverse may bring disaster on every portion of the country; and if you will have it thus, we will invoke the God of our fathers, who delivered them from the power of the lion, to protect us from the ravages of the bear; and thus, putting our trust in God, and in our own firm hearts and strong arms, we will vindicate the right as best we may.

In the course of my service here, associated at different times with a great variety of Senators, I see now around me some with whom I have served long; there have been points of collision; but whatever of offense there has been to me, I leave here; I carry with me no hostile remembrance. Whatever offense I have given which has not been redressed, or for which satisfaction has not been demanded, I have, Senators, in this hour of our parting, to offer you my apology for any pain which, in heat of discussion, I have inflicted. I go hence unencumbered of the remembrance of any injury received, and having discharged the duty of making the only reparation in my power for any injury offered.

Mr. President and Senators, having made the announcement which the occasion seemed to me to require, it only remains for me to bid you a final adieu.

The sequel:

Jefferson Davis returned to Mississippi and to the rapid drama of events inevitably leading to the War Between the States. He was immediately appointed commander of the Mississippi militia, and within a month, at Montgomery, Alabama, was named provisional President of the Confederacy.

As winter went on into spring, and Virginia, Texas and the other Southern States seceded, his government entrenched itself. In February of 1862, Jefferson Davis was inaugurated at Richmond, Virginia, as the President of the Confederate States of America.

His administration ceased to be a happy one, long before the hopeless military outlook of the South appeared. His army generals held little regard for his military leaderships, as President Lincoln also was experiencing in the Union. But in the end, whereas General Grant accepted the surrender of General Lee after Lincoln himself had chosen Grant as the general to try to end the war with victory, General Lee had to make the great decision to surrender in the face of contrary orders from Davis, his own President.

It is a notable historical contrast that while Lee went from the surrender of Appomattox Courthouse to a continuing honored career, Jefferson Davis was imprisoned for two years. He never was tried, but lived thereafter in quiet freedom.

Oddly enough, his ill health seemed to develop physical stamina rather than to shorten his life. He lived for 22 years after his release from prison in 1867 and wrote his apologia, *The Rise and Fall of the Confederacy.*

It is probable that he never enjoyed a nobler moment in subsequent years than during the half hour he addressed the Senate in his sundown speech.

ABRAHAM LINCOLN

". . . we here highly resolve that these dead shall not have died in vain."

GETTYSBURG, Pa., Nov. 19, 1863 —Standing bareheaded on a makeshift ceremonial platform overlooking bleak hills terraced by the formal lines of massed graves that forever will mark one of war's bitterest battles, President Abraham Lincoln called on the world of the living to make tangible the ideals for which 45,000 men laid down their lives in two days of bitter struggle.

Now the battlefield is a cemetery officially dedicated as a memorial to the men who lie here.

He bespoke, as was necessary and proper, the aims of the Union, but despite the fact that civil war still rages between the North and South, Mr. Lincoln neither castigated the opposing forces nor held them up to ridicule. Instead—unlike the usual debates that mark these times—he spoke only with respect for the dead and with hope for the living—"that this nation, under God, shall have a new birth of freedom."

By the time the President and his party had boarded the special train for the return trip to Washington, speculation already was voiced as to what this meant in the President's conception of the peace that will come with a Union victory. Ever since the repulse of General Robert E. Lee's forces on July 4 of this year, there has been no doubt of that victory; only speculation as to the time that will be required for the South to realize the hopelessness of its fight.

Never has Mr. Lincoln appeared more so than today as the sad and gentle President whose heart seems to bleed with every war casualty, despite his firmness in sending army after army into the campaign to destroy the arms of the Confederacy. His emotion so cloaked his words and thoughts that, as he himself predicted, his speech at this historic occasion, may seldom be recalled in future.

In fact, there already have been comments among Republican leaders in the special party that came here with Mr. Lincoln that he quite threw away a great chance to make a speech that would spark the Union to renewed vigor in support of the war, make conscription more palatable and perhaps diminish the ostentatious display on the part of civilians who have used it to enrich themselves.

To some observers it appeared also that a little more time might have been consumed by Mr. Lincoln in giving his talk, a few more encomiums heaped upon the dead, and a shade more art employed in writing a message that might have helped to nullify broad European sympathy for the South.

The battle fought here has already made its mark as a classic in military strategy, as well as inexplicable military mistakes, if not insubordination —the latter contributing largely to the greatest and perhaps most unexpected triumph of the Union arms. Furthermore, this was a test of courage and savage stamina between armies made up of battle-tested veterans, in many cases of rankers braver than their superiors were skilled.

Perhaps the battle itself symbolized all that has occurred in the past two years and six months since the start of this fratricidal war, and underneath the simplicity of his words, the President more than anyone else felt that symbolism.

FOURSCORE AND seven years ago our fathers brought forth on this continent a new nation, conceived in liberty and dedicated to the proposition that all men are created equal. Now we are engaged in a great civil war, testing whether that nation, or any nation so conceived and so dedicated, can long endure.

We are met on a great battlefield of that war. We have come to dedicate a portion of that field as a final resting place for those who here gave their lives that that nation might live. It is altogether fitting and proper that we should do this. But, in a larger sense, we cannot dedicate—we cannot consecrate—we cannot hallow—this ground.

The brave men, living and dead, who struggled here have consecrated it far above our poor power to add or to detract. The world will little note nor long remember what we say here, but it can never forget what they did here.

It is for us, the living, rather to be dedicated here to the unfinished work which they who fought here have thus far so nobly advanced. It is rather for us to be here dedicated to the great task remaining before us—that from these honored dead we take increased devotion to that cause for which they gave the last full measure of devotion; that we here highly resolve that these dead shall not have died in vain; that this nation, under God, shall have a new birth of freedom; and that government of the people, by the people, for the people, shall not perish from the earth.

The sequel:

If President Lincoln expected his words to be forgotten soon, this constituted the greatest mistake in judgment he could have made.

Just as no oration in history is shorter, so none has proved to be more enduring.

The Civil War went on and on, and Lincoln became more worn, more taciturn. But after re-election he gathered his energies for another great speech in which may be seen a fuller development of the humane ideals broached in the little speech at Gettysburg.

This was his second, and last, Inaugural Address.

ABRAHAM LINCOLN

"With malice toward none, with charity for all, with firmness in the right . . ."

WASHINGTON, D. C., March 4, 1865—A peace without malice and reconstruction of the Union in a spirit of charity were sketched in the second Inaugural Address here by which Abraham Lincoln marked his return to the trials of his high office.

The tired President exhibited neither exuberance nor triumph in his simple message delivered in the Hall of the House of Representatives, on the Capitol Hill where the new dome ordered for this structure before the war began in 1861 still lies rusting in its crates. Instead, his attitude was more that of homely prayer, as he concluded his brief talk with words that may be already marked for the ages:

"With malice toward none, with charity for all, with firmness in the right as God gives us to see the right, let us finish the work we are in, to bind up the nation's wounds, to care for him who shall have borne the battle, and for his widows and for his orphans, to do all which may achieve and cherish a just and a lasting peace among ourselves and with all nations."

No victory hymn was this, although the President might well have sung one, both in personal political triumph and at the sight of the imminent end of the battles for which he perforce carries the responsibility. His election last November was an overwhelming triumph, despite the glamorous appeal of his rival, General McClellan, and he carried with him on his ticket Andrew Johnson, into the Vice Presidency, despite the fact that politically few men could have been a heavier deadweight. But it was the military situation that counted most—the victories that were sparked with the great triumph at Gettysburg two years ago.

Since the election, events have moved at great speed, following the pattern set when the President called General U. S. Grant to the supreme command a year ago this month. Since then Atlanta has fallen to General W. T. Sherman, and Phil Sheridan has ridden Jubal Early to earth in the Shenandoah. Thomas mopped up Hood at Nashville, while Sherman went on to take Savannah. As of now, the gallant General Robert E. Lee holds Richmond, but his lines of communication with Petersburg are thin.

In sum, the end is in sight. Hence the power and the force of the President's words at this moment, a combination of determination to press on to victory, and an almost tearful appeal to the leaders of the Confederacy to realize the hopelessness of a cause that has already consumed scores of thousands of lives and billions of the nation's wealth.

The President's words follow:

FELLOW-COUNTRYMEN: At this second appearing to take the oath of the presidential office, there is less occasion for an extended address than there was at first. Then a statement, somewhat in detail, of a course to be pursued seemed very fitting and proper. Now, at the expiration of four years, during which public declarations have been constantly called forth on every point and phase of the great contest which still absorbs the attention and engrosses the energies of the nation, little that is new could be presented.

The progress of our arms, upon which all else chiefly depends, is as well known to the public as to myself, and it is, I trust, reasonably satisfactory and encouraging to all. With high hope for the future, no prediction in regard to it is ventured.

On the occasion corresponding to this four years ago, all thoughts were anxiously directed to an impending civil war. All dreaded it, all sought to avoid it. While the inaugural address was being delivered from this place, devoted altogether to saving the Union without war, insurgent agents were in the city seeking to destroy it with war—seeking to dissolve the Union and divide the effects by negotiation. Both parties deprecated war, but one of them would make war rather than let the nation survive, and the other would accept war rather than let it perish, and the war came. One-eighth of the whole population were colored slaves, not distributed generally over the Union, but localized in the Southern part of it. These slaves constituted a peculiar and powerful interest. All knew that this interest was somehow the cause of the war. To strengthen, perpetuate, and extend this interest was the object for which the insurgents would rend the Union by war, while the government claimed no right to do more than to restrict the territorial enlargement of it.

Neither party expected for the war the magnitude or the duration which it has already attained. Neither anticipated that the cause of the conflict might cease when, or even before the conflict itself should cease. Each looked for an easier triumph, and a result less fundamental and astounding. Both read the same Bible and pray to the same God, and each invokes His aid against the other. It may seem strange that any men should dare to ask a just God's assistance in wringing their bread from the sweat of other men's faces, but let us judge not that we be not judged. The prayer of both could not be answered. That of neither has been answered fully. The Almighty has His own purposes. Woe unto the world because of offences, for it must needs be that offences come, but woe to that man by whom the offence cometh. If we shall suppose that American slavery is one of those offences which, in the providence of God, must needs come, but which having continued through His appointed time, He now wills to remove, and that He gives to both North and South this terrible war as the woe due to those by whom the offence came, shall we discern there any departure from those divine attributes which the believers in a living God always ascribe to Him? Fondly do we hope, fervently do we pray, that this mighty scourge of war may speedily pass away. Yet if God wills that it continue until all the wealth piled by the bondsman's two hundred and fifty years of unrequited toil shall be sunk, and until every drop of blood drawn with the lash shall be paid by another drawn with the sword, as was said three thousand years ago, so still it must be said, that the judgments of the Lord are true and righteous altogether.

With malice toward none, with charity for all, with firmness in the right as God gives us to see the right, let us finish the work we are in, to bind up the nation's wounds, to care for him who shall have borne the battle, and for his widow and for his orphans, to do all which may achieve and cherish a just and a lasting peace among ourselves and with all nations.

The sequel:

On April 14, 1865, while Lincoln sat in a box in a Washington theatre, an assassin's bullet, fired by John Wilkes Booth, shattered the entire structure of reconstruction after the war then ended, by obliterating the only man who could build upon the blueprints he already had outlined.

With Lincoln's removal from office, and the accession of Andrew Johnson, the avengers among the Northern block (perhaps somewhat justified by the fears and divisions aroused by Lincoln's murder) gained the upper hand. Sectional animosities flamed as high or higher for a period than they had been before the War Between the States.

A generation would be marred by them.

As for Lincoln, the manner of his passing might as well have been an act of sanctification. Great though he was, his reputation was enhanced by his martyrdom to the ever-rising plateau from which even today it is difficult to draw into perspective his virtues and his faults, his greatnesses and his weaknesses.

However, the country—growing into a new and industrialized force —could not linger long over either old quarrels or the memories of dead leaders.

It was plunging now into new problems, new challenges, and new voices of leadership, while there germinated in Europe—in the as yet little known minds of such men as Marx and Engels—a new political philosophy—which would increase and spread—who knows how long?

HENRY WARD BEECHER

"Hold each other in true fellowship."

PLYMOUTH, Mass., Nov. 18, 1869 —The Rev. Henry Ward Beecher, long noted as orator, minister and voice of the public conscience, today used his pulpit for a plea for reconstruction of public ideals in the Lincoln image, which rose far above the ordinary generalities of churchly homilies.

Now is the time, he said, for the citizens of this reunited country to realize their interdependence; for the North and the South to understand that in their very differences they have much to contribute to each other.

Were Mr. Beecher simply one among his many co-religionists his words would have their due importance, but his unique stature in the country makes them today the equal of official pronouncements. In fact, one recalls that on the very day that President Lincoln and other speakers dedicated the fields of Gettysburg as a national monument, Mr. Beecher's speech of the same day received more prominence on the front page of the New York *Times* than did the President's.

A fearless individualist, who often makes as many enemies as friends, this preacher is equally as well known in England as America, and did much in 1863, on a visit abroad, to create understanding of the Union cause. More recently his espousal of the equal suffrage movement has opened a new field of contention around him. But whatever stand he takes, he takes with all his might, as today when he hesitated not at all to denounce sectarianism in religion among other evils to be avoided.

IN THE unity of the nation and the reduction of its materials, we hope much from religion; very little from sectarian churches; much from the Spirit of God blessing the Truth of his Word to the hearts of individual men; much from individual men that are nobler than their sect; much from free men whose adhesion to forms and ceremonies is the least part of their existence; much from religion as it exists in its higher forms in individual nature and in public sentiment; very little from dogmas; very little from theology as such.

And yet, if it could be understood by them, here is a new call to the sects, not to disband, but to hold each other in true fellowship; to act in harmony if not in unison.

Let us look for a true humanity, let us look for the true fruit of religion, not in the associated body of this or that denomination, but in the majesty and power of love in the individual hearts of those who are gathered into sects. Let us look no more into books, merely. Let man be the *living epistles* in which we shall read what the Spirit of the Lord has to teach in any sect.

Until man's reciprocal interests upon the higher plane of moral ideas shall be better understood, until religion shall be a uniting and not a divisive element, we must with more eagerness than ever look to the harmonizing influence of man's reciprocal interests upon the lower plane of commercial and industrial life. So widespread is this nation, that it has within itself almost all the elements of prosperity which other nations seek within their own borders. The far North and the extreme South work for different products, but in difference they find reciprocal advantage.

The States are so many points of vitality. The nation, like a banyan tree, lets down a new root when each new State is established, and when centuries have spread this gigantic commercial tree over a vast space, it will be found that the branches most remote from the center do not draw their vitality through the long intricate passages from the parent trunk, but each outlying growth has roots of its own, and draws from the ground by organisms of its own, all the food it wants, without dissociating its top from the parent branches.

Let us then all labor for the unity of the nation by working for the education of its citizens, for the spread of virtue and true morality, for the promotion of our industry which will redeem the poor from servile and social drudgery, for the freedom of its commerce, for a more just and generous sympathy between all its races and classes, for a more benignant spirit to its religion; and finally, let us implore the God of our fathers, by his own wise providence, to save us from our wanton passions, from impertinent egotism, from pride, arrogance, cruelty, and sensual lusts, that as a nation we may show forth his praise in all the earth.

Note: The above quotations are from a rare collection of Beecher's speeches collected and edited in 1889 by John R. Howard.

III

NEW HORIZONS

SUSAN B. ANTHONY

"The only question left to be settled now is: Are women persons?"

NEW YORK, N. Y., 1873—Miss Susan B. Anthony, the stormy petrel of politics in her aggressive leadership of the movement for women's suffrage, challenged the leading legal minds of the United States, to tell women why women are not members of the conglomerate mass of "we, the people," named in the Constitution.

Militant although slight in stature, and her eyes ablaze with the crusading zeal of her cause, Miss Anthony nonetheless set forth arguments based on reasons that are slowly but surely influencing an ever-widening degree of public opinion.

At last, also, she has a platform from which to argue, because Miss Anthony stands as of now under indictment and conviction for having committed the "crime" of voting in the election last November. In fact, she was fined $100 for this breach of the laws as they now stand, and the sentence is under appeal.

There is a general feeling that the fine never will be assessed against her property because her firmest opponents realize that pursuance of the action would give her the added aura among her followers of a martyr to her cause. Just as avidly, it is apparent, Miss Anthony and her followers hope to have another day in court, in order to find another platform for their argument. And while the matter rests there, she is making the most of the opportunity.

Excerpts from her words, discussing the question, "Are women persons?" follow:

FRIENDS and fellow-citizens: I stand before you tonight under indictment for the alleged crime of having voted at the last Presidential election, without having a lawful right to vote. It shall be my work this evening to prove to you that in thus voting, I not only committed no crime, but, instead, simply exercised my citi-

123

zen's rights, guaranteed to me and all United States citizens by the National Constitution, beyond the power of any State to deny.

The preamble of the Federal Constitution says:

"We, the people of the United States, in order to form a more perfect union, establish justice, insure domestic tranquillity, provide for the common defense, promote the general welfare, and secure the blessings of liberty to ourselves and our posterity, do ordain and establish this Constitution for the United States of America."

It was we, the people; not we, the white male citizens; nor yet we, the male citizens; but we, the whole people, who formed the Union. And we formed it, not to give the blessings of liberty, but to secure them; not to the half of ourselves and the half of our posterity, but to the whole people—women as well as men. And it is a downright mockery to talk to women of their enjoyment of the blessings of liberty while they are denied the use of the only means of securing them provided by this democratic-republican government—the ballot.

For any State to make sex a qualification that must ever result in the disfranchisement of one entire half of the people is to pass a bill of attainder, or an *ex post facto* law, and is therefore a violation of the supreme law of the land. By it the blessings of liberty are forever withheld from women and their female posterity. To them this government has no just powers derived from the consent of the governed. To them this government is not a democracy. It is not a republic. It is an odious aristocracy; a hateful oligarchy of sex; the most hateful aristocracy ever established on the face of the globe; an oligarchy of wealth, where the rich govern the poor. An oligarchy of learning, where the educated govern the ignorant, or even an oligarchy of race, where the Saxon rules the African, might be endured; but this oligarchy of sex, which makes father, brothers, husband, sons, the oligarchs over the mother and sisters, the wife and daughters of every household—which ordains all men sovereigns, all women subjects, carries dissension, discord and rebellion into every home of the nation.

Webster, Worcester and Bouvier all define a citizen to be a person in the United States, entitled to vote and hold office.

The only question left to be settled now is: Are women persons? And I hardly believe any of our opponents will have the hardihood to say they are not. Being persons, then, women are citizens; and no State has a right to make any law, or to enforce any old law, that shall abridge their privileges or immunities. Hence, every discrimination against women in the constitutions and laws of the several States is today null and void, precisely as is every one against Negroes.

The sequel:

Susan B. Anthony did not live to see the successful conclusion of her crusade, but with the adoption of universal suffrage 50 years later, the victory was credited to her stout espousal of the cause in a day when the movement aroused more ridicule than other reaction.

But this was a milestone, and its spokesman achieved her niche among the immortals who pioneered the now taken-for-granted fact that in politics as elsewhere women are the equal of men.

CHAUNCEY M. DEPEW

"A perfect woman, nobly planned, to warm, to comfort, and command."

NEW YORK, N. Y., Dec. 22, 1875 —Chauncey M. Depew, the noted lawyer and raconteur, tonight shattered with humor the otherwise dignified atmosphere of the annual dinner of the New England Society, of this city, with a speech responding to the usual toast to "Woman."

Paying respectful compliments in gallant language to the subject of the toast, Mr. Depew went on to twit his auditors with the remark that Priscilla "condensed the primal elements" of the New England character, when she said to John Alden, "Prythee, why don't you speak for yourself, John?"

"That motto," Mr. Depew told the collection of notable descendants of Plymouth, "has been the spear in the rear and the star in the van of the New Englander's progress."

MR. PRESIDENT: I know of no act of my life which justifies your assertion that I am an expert on this question. . . . I am called upon to respond to the best, the most suggestive, and the most important sentiment which has been delivered this evening, at this midnight hour, when the varied and ceaseless flow of eloquence has exhausted subjects and audience, when the chairs are mainly vacant, the bottles empty, and the oldest veteran and most valiant Roman of us all scarce dares meet the doom he knows awaits him at home. Bishop Berkeley, when he wrote his beautiful verses upon our Western World, and penned the line "Time's noblest offspring is the last," described not so nearly our prophetic future as the last and best creation of the Almighty—woman—whom we both love and worship.

We have here the President of the United States and the General of our armies: around these tables is gathered a galaxy of intellect, genius, and achievement seldom presented on any occasion, but none of them would merit the applause we so enthusiastically bestow, or have won their high honors, had they not been guided or inspired by the woman they revered or loved. . . .

You know that it is a physiological fact that the boys take after their mothers, and reproduce the characteristics and intellectual qualities of the maternal, and not the paternal, side. Standing here in the presence of the most worthy representatives of Plymouth, and knowing as I do your moral and mental worth, the places you fill, and the commercial, financial, humane, and catholic impetus you give to our metropolitan life, how can I do otherwise than on bended knee reverence the New England mothers who gave you birth! Your worth, the places you fill, and the commercial, financial, humane president, in his speech tonight, spoke of himself as a descendant of John Alden. In my judgment, Priscilla uttered the sentiment which gave the Yankee the keynote of success, and condensed the primal elements of his character, when she said to John Alden, "Prythee, why don't you speak for yourself, John?"

That motto has been the spear in the rear and the star in the van of the New Englander's progress. It has made him the most audacious, self-reliant, irrepressible member of the human family; and for illustration we need look no farther than the present descent of Priscilla and John Alden.

"Give me liberty, or give me death." The immortal words of Patrick Henry before the Virginia provincial convention in 1775. The engraving is by A. Jones. (Bettmann Archive)

George Washington, painted near the end of his Presidency, in 1796, by Gilbert Stuart. (In The Brooklyn Museum Collection, Dick S. Ramsay Fund.)

Daniel Webster, congressman from Massachusetts, receiving an ovation after his Bunker Hill address, June 17, 1825. (Bettmann Archive)

"Let us look to our country and our cause, elevate ourselves to the dignity of pure and disinterested patriots," urged Henry Clay in his 1850 appeal to the Senate to compromise on the slavery issue. (Bettmann Archive)

Henry Ward Beecher drew three columns of space in *The New York Times* November 20, 1863, although few today remember a line from his speech thus recorded, while in the same issue one paragraph was given to Abraham Lincoln's Gettysburg address dedicating a memorial cemetery for the 45,000 soldiers who died on the field there in two days of the Civil War.

"Just as no oration in history is shorter, so none has proved more enduring."

GETTYSBURG ADDRESS

Four score and seven years ago our fathers brought forth on this continent, a new nation, conceived in Liberty, and dedicated to the proposition that all men are created equal.

Now we are engaged in a great civil war, testing whether that nation, or any nation so conceived and so dedicated, can long endure. We are met on a great battle field of that war. We have come to dedicate a portion of that field, as a final resting place for those who here gave their lives that that nation might live. It is altogether fitting and proper that we should do this.

But, in a larger sense, we cannot dedicate — we cannot consecrate — we cannot hallow — this ground. The brave men, living and dead, who struggled here, have consecrated it, far above our poor power to add or detract. The world will little note, nor long remember what we say here, but it can never forget what they did here. It is for us the living, rather, to be dedicated here to the unfinished work which they who fought here have thus far so nobly advanced. It is rather for us to be here dedicated to the great task remaining before us — that from these honored dead we take increased devotion to that cause for which they gave the last full measure of devotion — that we here highly resolve that these dead shall not have died in vain — that this nation, under God, shall have a new birth of freedom — and that government of the people, by the people, for the people, shall not perish from the earth.

The New-York Times.

VOL. XIII—NO. 3794.　　　　　NEW-YORK, FRIDAY, NOVEMBER 20, 1863.　　　　　PRICE THREE CENTS.

IMPORTANT FROM EAST TENNESSEE.

The Rebels Advancing upon Knoxville.

THE PLACE COMPLETELY INVESTED.

HEAVY SKIRMISHING YESTERDAY.

The Position Very Strongly Fortified.

THE REBEL FORCES UNDER LONGSTREET.

THE HEROES OF JULY.

A Solemn and Imposing Event.

Dedication of the National Cemetery at Gettysburg.

IMMENSE NUMBERS OF VISITORS.

Oration by Hon. Edward Everett—Speeches of President Lincoln, Mr. Seward and Governor Seymour.

THE PROGRAMME SUCCESSFULLY CARRIED OUT

DEPARTMENT OF THE GULF.

ARRIVAL OF THE CREOLE FROM NEW-ORLEANS

The Attack upon Gen. Washburne's Column.

Our Entire Loss Six Hundred and Seventy-seven.

THE DELAWARE ELECTION.

LATE FROM CHATTANOOGA.

THE ARMY OF THE POTOMAC.

GREAT BRITAIN AND AMERICA

Welcome to Rev. Henry Ward Beecher.

Demonstration at the Brooklyn Academy of Music.

GREAT SPEECH.

How *The New York Times* treated the speech the same day Henry Ward Beecher was making one of his at the Brooklyn Academy of Music.

Chautauqua tents sprang up throughout the land when culture was on the march across America in the seventies. (Bettmann Archive)

Ralph Waldo Emerson making an address in the School of Philosophy, Concord, Mass. The woodcut dates from 1882. (Bettmann Archive)

"The only question left to be settled now is: Are women persons?"
Susan B. Anthony declaimed. The cartoonists of the seventies thought Miss
Anthony a highly caricaturable person and did their best—or worst—to
lampoon her cause of equal suffrage for women. But Susan B. Anthony
went right on—talking—and her cause advanced. (Bettmann Archive)

Chauncey M. Depew, (1834–1928), one of the brightest after-dinner speakers of his day, with George William Curtis, at his left; Horatio Seymour, Grover Cleveland and Carl Schurz, on his right. (Bettmann Archive)

Women, too, had their day, since the men had their club nights. The artist in this picture portrays his impression of the first women's suffragette meeting at Seneca Falls. (Bettmann Archive)

The only way I can reciprocate your call at this late hour is to keep you here as long as I can. I think I see now the descendant of a Mayflower immortal who has been listening here to the glories of his ancestry, and learning that he is "the heir of all the ages," as puffed and swollen with pride of race and history, he stands solitary and alone upon his doorstep, reflects on his broken promise of an early return, and remembers that within "there is a divinity which shapes his end."

In all ages woman has been the source of all that is pure, un-selfish, and heroic in the spirit and life of man. It was for love that Anthony lost a world. It was for love that Jacob worked seven long years, and for seven more; and I have often wondered what must have been his emotions when on the morning of the eighth year he awoke and found the homely, scrawny, bony Leah instead of the lovely and beautiful presence of his beloved Rachel. A distinguished French philosopher answered the narrative of every event with the question, "Who was she?"

Helen conquered Troy, plunged all the nations of antiquity into war, and gave the earliest, as it is still the grandest, epic which has come down through all time. Poetry and fiction are based upon woman's love, and the movements of history are mainly due to the sentiments or ambitions she has inspired. Semiramis, Zenobia, Queen Elizabeth, claim a cold and distant admiration; they do not touch the heart. But when Florence Nightingale, or Grace Darling, or Ida Lewis, unselfish and unheralded, perils all to succor and to save, the profoundest and holiest emotions of our nature render them tribute and homage. Mr. President, there is no aspiration which any man here tonight entertains, no achievement he seeks to accomplish, no great and honorable ambition he desires to gratify, which is not directly related to either or both a mother and a wife. From the hearthstone around which linger the recollections of our mother, from the fireside where our wife awaits us, come all the purity, all the hope, and all the courage with which we fight the battle of life. The man who is not thus inspired, who labors not so much to secure the applause of the world as the solid and more precious approval of his home, accomplishes little of good for others or of honor for himself. I close with the hope that each of us may always have near us

> *A perfect woman, nobly planned,*
> *To warm, to comfort, and command.*
> *And yet a spirit still, and bright*
> *With something of an angel light.*

SAMUEL L. CLEMENS

"There is a sumptuous variety about the New England weather that compels the stranger's admiration—and regret."

NEW YORK, N. Y., Dec. 22, 1876 —Samuel Langhorne Clemens, the "Mark Twain" so popularly regarded throughout America and in fact the world for his writings and humorous speeches, tonight paid his respects to the New England weather. This man who has delivered thousands of lectures sparkling with wit, and himself now a resident of New England, left it not a leg to stand on. The occasion of the Twainian "respects" was the annual dinner of the New England Society.

GENTLEMEN: I reverently believe that the Maker who made us all, makes everything in New England—but the weather. I don't know who makes that, but I think it must be raw apprentices in the Weather Clerk's factory, who experiment and learn how in New England for board and clothes, and then are promoted to make weather for countries that require a good article and will take their custom elsewhere if they don't get it. There is a sumptuous variety about the New England weather that compels the stranger's admiration—and regret. The weather is always doing something there; always attending strictly to business; always getting up new designs and trying them on the people to see how they will go. But it gets through more business in spring than in any other season. In the spring I have counted one hundred and thirty-six different kinds of weather inside of four and twenty hours. . . .

Yes, one of the brightest gems in the New England weather is the dazzling uncertainty of it. There is only one thing certain about it, you are certain there is going to be plenty of weather, a perfect grand review; but you never can tell which end of the procession is going to move first. You fix up for the drought; you leave your umbrella in the house and sally out with your sprinkling-pot, and ten to one you get drowned. You make up your mind that the earthquake is due; you stand from under and take hold of something to steady yourself, and the first thing you know, you get struck by lightning. . . .

Now, as to the size of the weather in New England—lengthways, I mean. It is utterly disproportioned to the size of that little country. Half the time, when it is packed as full as it can stick, you will see that New England weather sticking out beyond the edges and projecting around hundreds and hundreds of miles over the neighboring States. She can't hold a tenth part of her weather. You can see cracks all about, where she has strained herself trying to do it.

I could speak volumes about the inhuman perversity of the New England weather, but I will give but a single specimen. I like to hear rain on a tin roof, so I covered part of my roof with tin, with an eye to that luxury. Well, sir, do you think it ever rains on the tin? No, sir; skips it every time.

Mind, in this speech I have been trying merely to do honor to the New England weather; no language could do it justice. But after all, there are at least one or two things about that weather (or, if you please, effects produced by it) which we residents would not like to part with. If we had not our bewitching autumn foliage, we should still have to credit the weather with one feature which compensates for all its bullying vagaries—the ice-storm—when a leafless tree is clothed with ice from the bottom to the top—ice that is as bright and clear as crystal; every bough and twig is strung with ice-beads, frozen dewdrops, and the whole tree sparkles, cold and white, like the Shah of Persia's diamond plume. Then the wind waves the branches, and the sun comes out and turns all those myriads of beads and drops to prisms, that glow and hum and flash with all manner of colored fires, which change and change again, with inconceivable rapidity, from blue to red, from red to green, and green to gold; the tree becomes a sparkling fountain, a very explosion of dazzling jewels; and it stands there the acme, the climax, the supremest possibility in art or nature of bewildering, intoxicating, intolerable magnificence! One cannot make the words too strong.

CHARLES W. ELIOT

"You can not build a university on a sect at all; you must build it upon the nation."

NEW YORK, N. Y., Dec. 22, 1877 —The humorous approach to grave questions that characterizes Dr. Charles W. Eliot, at 43 years of age already president of Harvard University for eight years, found sparkling outlet tonight as he punctured with ridicule a current movement for the founding by the Government of a national university.

Universities must be built upon the ideals of the nation, he said, and proceeded then briefly to tear apart the thesis that the Congress could operate such an undertaking. In fact, the transcript of his remarks shows insertion of the word "applause" at almost every period.

Dr. Eliot spoke at the annual dinner of the New England Society here, in response to the toast, "Harvard and Yale," honoring jointly the universities in New England that are respectively the first and second in the United States in age.

MR. PRESIDENT and gentlemen: I am obliged to my friend Dr. Clarke (James Freeman Clarke, D. C.) for the complimentary terms in which he has presented me to you. But I must appeal to your commiseration. Harvard and Yale! Can any undergraduate of either institution, can any recent graduate of either institution, imagine a man responding to that toast? . . .

We shall all agree that it is for the best interests of this country that it have sundry universities, of diverse tone, atmosphere,

sphere, representing different opinions and different methods of study to some extent, and in different trainings, though with the same end.

Holding this view, I have been somewhat concerned to see of late that the original differences between Harvard and Yale seem to be rapidly disappearing. For example, a good many years ago, Harvard set out on what is called the "elective" system, and now I read in the Yale catalogue a long list of studies called "optional," which strikes me as bearing a strong resemblance to our elective courses. . . .

Now, it is unquestioned, that about the year 1700 a certain number of Congregationalist clergymen, who belonged to the Established Church (for we are too apt to forget that Congregationalism was the "Established Church" of that time, and none other was allowed), thought that Harvard was getting altogether too latitudinarian, and though they were every one of them graduates of Harvard, they went off and set up another college in Connecticut, where a stricter doctrine should be taught. Harvard men have rather nursed the hope that this distinction between Harvard and Yale might be permanent. But I regret to say that I have lately observed many strong indications that it is wholly likely to disappear.

For example, to come at once to the foundations, I read in the papers the other day, and I am credibly informed it is true, that the head of Yale College voted to install a minister whose opinions upon the vital, pivotal, fundamental doctrine of eternal damnation are unsound. Then, again, I look at the annual reports of the Bureau of Education on this department at Washington, and I read there for some years that Harvard College was unsectarian; and I knew that it was right, because I made the return myself. I read also that Yale College was a Congregationalist College; and I had no doubt that that was right, because I supposed Dr. Porter had made the report. But now we read in that same report that Yale College is unsectarian. That is a great progress. The fact is, both these universities have found out that in a country which has no established church and no dominant sect you cannot build a university on a sect at all—you must build it upon the nation.

But, gentlemen, there are some other points, I think, of national education on which we shall find these two early founded universities to agree. For example, we have lately read, in the Message of the Chief Magistrate, that a national university would be a good thing. Harvard and Yale are of one mind upon that subject, but they want to have a national university defined. If it means a university of national resort, we say amen. If it means a university where the youth of this land are taught to love their country and to serve her, we say amen; and we point, both of us, to our past in proof that we are national in that sense. But if it means that the national university is to be a university administered and managed by the wise Congress of the United States, then we should agree in taking some slight exceptions.

We should not question for a moment the capacity of Congress to pick out and appoint the professors of Latin and Greek, and the ancient languages, because we find that there is an astonishing number of classical orators in Congress, and there is manifested there a singular acquaintance with the legislation of all the Latin races. But when it should come to some other humbler professorships we might perhaps entertain a doubt. For example, we have not entire faith in the trust that Congress has in the unchangeableness of the laws of arithmetic. We might think that their competency to select a professor of history might be doubted. They seem to have an impression that there is such a thing as "American" political economy, which can no more be than "American" chemistry or "American" physics. Finally, gentlemen, we should a little distrust the selection by Congress of a professor of ethics. Of course, we should feel no doubt in regard to the tenure of office of the professors being entirely suitable, it being the well-known practice of both branches of Congress to select men solely for fitness, without regard to locality, and to keep them in office as long as they are competent and faithful.

The sequel:

Had Dr. Eliot closed his career at this point, he would have been remembered as one of America's great educators, as well as the first layman and scientist to be chosen for the presidency of Harvard, instead of the customary clergyman. He had been called to this position, in fact, largely because of a paper on "The New Education," published in the *Atlantic Monthly.*

But in 1877 Dr. Eliot was just beginning. He served Harvard for 40 years—as has been remarked, he found it a collection of small colleges and left it a great university.

Living until 1926, he used his "retirement" for a series of other activities that made him a world figure and, as probably his best known intellectual legacy to the public, he edited the collection of classics, still in constant demand, known throughout the world as "Dr. Eliot's Five-Foot Shelf."

JOSEPH HODGES CHOATE

"You cannot live without lawyers, and certainly you cannot die without them."

NEW YORK, N. Y., Dec. 22, 1880 —If Joseph Hodges Choate had been born without background and had grown to manhood without education or social advantages, he probably would have been a noted wit or actor.

His background having been one of privilege, he chose the law as a profession, and today ranks, either by the test of clients or of fees, as one of the bar's leading figures.

Hence his wit takes the turn of pointing up the humorous twists about which people like to laugh in his own profession.

Mr. Choate's speeches about the law and lawyers are myriad. Tonight he tackled his favorite subject as guest at a dinner given by the Chamber of Commerce of the State of New York, in response to the toast: "The Bench and the Bar—Blessed are the peacemakers."

MR. PRESIDENT: I rise with unprecedented embarrassment in this presence and at this hour to respond to this sentiment, so flattering to the feelings of all the members of the Bench and Bar, to say nothing of that shrinking modesty inherent in the breast of every lawyer and which the longer he practices seems to grow stronger and stronger. I have a specific trouble which overwhelms me at this moment, and that is that all the preparation I had made for this occasion is a complete miscarriage.

I received this sentiment yesterday with an intimation that I was expected to respond to it. I had prepared a serious and sober essay on the relations of commerce to the law—the one great relation of client and counsel, but I have laid all that aside; I do not intend to have a single sober word tonight. There is a reason, however, why nothing more of a sober sort should be uttered at this table; there is a danger that it would increase by however small a measure, the specific gravity of the Chamber of Commerce of New York. Certainly nothing could be a greater calamity than that.

At an hour like this, sir, merchants like witnesses are to be weighed as well as counted. And when I compare your appearance at this moment with what it was when you entered this room, when I look around upon these swollen girths and these expanded countenances, when I see that each individual member of the Chamber has increased his avoirdupois by at least ten pounds since he took his seat at the table, why, the total weight of the aggregate body must be startling, indeed, and as I suppose you believe in the resurrection from this long session, as you undoubtedly hope to rise again from these chairs, to which you have been glued so long, I should be the last person to add a feather's weight to what has been so heavily heaped upon you.

Mr. Blaine, freighted with wisdom from the floor of the State house and from long study of American institutions, has deplored the low condition of the carrying trade. Now, for our part, as representing one of the institutions which does its full share of the carrying trade, I repudiate the idea. We undoubtedly are still prepared to carry all that can be heaped upon us.

Lord Bacon, who was thought the greatest lawyer of his age, has said that every man owes a duty to his profession; but I think that can be amended by saying, in reference to the law, that every man in the community owes a duty to our profession; and somewhere, at some time, somewhere between the cradle and the grave, he must acknowledge the liability and pay the debt. Why, gentlemen, you cannot live without the lawyers, and certainly you cannot die without them.

It was one of the brightest members of the profession, you remember, who had taken his passage for Europe to spend his summer vacation on the other side, and failed to go; and when called upon for an explanation, he said—why, yes; he had taken his passage, and had intended to go, but one of his rich clients died, and he was afraid if he had gone across the Atlantic, the heirs would have got all of the property.

When I look around me in this solid body of merchants, all this heaped-up and idle capital, all these great representatives of immense railroad, steamship and other interests under the face of the sun, I believe that the fortunes of the Bar are yet at their very beginning. Gentlemen, the future is all before us. We have no sympathy with communism, but like Communists we have everything to gain and nothing to lose.

CARL SCHURZ

"The Old World and the New."

NEW YORK, N. Y., Nov. 5, 1881— Carl Schurz, German-born newspaper publisher, author and former Senator from Missouri, counseled his adopted country to understand that harmonious relationships with the Old World depend on the keeping of a middle course between interference and a "too sentimental fondness," one for the other.

Mr. Schurz has created an individual background for himself, with experiences ranging from work as a Washington political correspondent to editorship or proprietorship of newspapers, in both the English and German languages, located in such diverse places as New York City, St. Louis and Denver, Colorado. Missouri long ago became his adopted state.

He spoke here at a dinner given by the Chamber of Commerce of the State of New York.

MR. CHAIRMAN: If you had been called upon to respond to the toast: "The Old World and the New," as frequently as I have, you would certainly find as much difficulty as I find in saying anything of the Old World that is new or of the New World that is not old.

American independence was declared at Philadelphia on July

4, 1776, by those who were born upon this soil, but American Independence was virtually accomplished by that very warlike event I speak of on the field of Yorktown, where the Old World lent a helping hand to the New. To be sure, there was a part of the Old World consisting of the British, and I am sorry to say, some German soldiers, who strove to keep down the aspirations of the New, but they were there in obedience to the command of a power which they were not able to resist, while that part of the Old World which fought upon the American side was here of its own free will as volunteers.

The New and the Old World must and will, in the commercial point of view, be of infinite use one to another as mutual customers, and our commercial relations will grow more fruitful to both sides from year to year, and from day to day, as we remain true to the good old maxim, "Live and let live." Nor is there the least speck of danger in the horizon threatening to disturb the friendliness of an international understanding between the Old World and the New World.

That cordial international understanding rests upon a very simple, natural and solid basis. We rejoice with the nations of the Old World in all their successes, all their prosperity, and all their happiness, and we profoundly and earnestly sympathize with them whenever a misfortune overtakes them. But one thing we shall never think of doing, and that is, interfering in their affairs.

On the other hand they will give us always their sympathy in good and evil as they have done heretofore, and we expect that they will never think of interfering with our affairs on this side of the ocean. Our limits are very distinctly drawn, and certainly no just or prudent power will ever think of upsetting them. The Old World and the New will ever live in harmonious accord as long as we do not try to jump over their fences and they do not try to jump over ours.

This being our understanding, nothing will be more natural than friendship and good will between the nations of the two sides of the Atlantic. The only danger ahead of us might be that arising from altogether too sentimental a fondness for one another which may lead us into lovers' jealousies and quarrels.

JAMES G. BLAINE

"He trod the wine-press alone."

WASHINGTON, D. C., Feb. 27, 1882—James G. Blaine, who six years ago campaigned unsuccessfully for the Presidency under the Republican party's banner—as the "Plumed Knight" of Ralph G. Ingersoll's poetic description—stood today in the House of Representatives to pay a last tribute to James A. Garfield, who won the way to the White House only to be assassinated by a madman.

This funeral oration both echoed the shocked response of the country to the assassination of a President of the United States, that followed by only 17 years that of President Abraham Lincoln, and the regard for President Garfield that had healed a formerly wide breach in the Republican party.

FOR THE second time in this generation the great departments of the government of the United States are assembled in the Hall of Representatives, to do honor to the memory of a murdered president. Lincoln fell at the close of a mighty struggle, in which the passions of men had been deeply stirred. The tragical termination of his great life added but another to the lengthened succession of horrors which had marked so many lintels with the blood of the firstborn. Garfield was slain in a day of peace, when brother had been reconciled to brother, and when anger and hate had been banished from the land.

Great in life, he was surpassingly great in death. For no cause, in the very frenzy of wantonness and wickedness, by the red hand of murder, he was thrust from the full tide of this world's interest, from its hopes, its aspirations, its victories, into the visible presence of death—and he did not quail. Not alone for one short moment in which, stunned and dazed, he could give up life, hardly aware of its relinquishment, but through days of deadly languor, through weeks of agony, that was not less agony because silently borne, with clear sight and calm courage he looked into his open grave. What blight and ruin met his anguished eyes, whose lips may tell—what brilliant, broken plans, what baffled, high ambitions, what sundering of strong, warm, manhood's friendship, what bitter rending of sweet household ties! Behind him a proud, expectant nation, a great host of sustaining friends, a cherished and happy mother, wearing the full, rich honors of her early toil and tears; the wife of his youth, whose whole life lay in his; the little boys not yet emerged from childhood's day of frolic; the fair young daughter; the sturdy sons just springing into closest companionship, claiming every day and every day rewarding a father's love and care; and in his heart the eager, rejoicing power to meet all demands. And his soul was not shaken. His countrymen were thrilled with instant, profound, and universal sympathy. Masterful in his mortal weakness, he became the center of a nation's love, enshrined in the prayers of a world. But all the love and all the sympathy could not share with him his suffering. He trod the wine-press alone. With unfaltering front he faced death. With unfailing tenderness he took leave of life. Above the demoniac hiss of the assassin's bullet he heard the voice of God. With simple resignation he bowed to the Divine decree.

As the end drew near his early craving for the sea returned. The stately mansion of power had been to him the wearisome hospital of pain, and he begged to be taken from his prison walls, from its oppressive, stifling air, from it homelessness and its hopelessness. Gently, silently, the love of a great people bore the pale sufferer to the longed-for healing of the sea, to live or to die, as God should will, within sight of the heaving billows, within sound of its manifold voices. With a wan, fevered face, tenderly lifted to the cooling breeze, he looked out wistfully upon the ocean's changing wonders; on its far sails; on its restless waves, rolling shoreward to break and die beneath the noonday sun; on the red clouds of evening, arching low to the horizon; on the serene and shining pathway of the star. Let us think that his dying eyes read a mystic meaning which only the rapt and parting soul may know. Let us believe that in the silence of the receding world he heard the great waves breaking on a further shore and felt already upon his wasted brow the breath of the eternal morning.

OLIVER WENDELL HOLMES

"There were tones in the voice that whispered then
You may hear to-day in a hundred men."

BOSTON, Mass., May 23, 1884—Beloved Oliver Wendell Holmes tonight humorously turned a testimonial dinner tendered to Judge John Lowell by the Boston Merchants Association into a tribute to a long-dead woman, "Dorothy Q.," by means of a new poem in which he lauded her as a veritable matriarch.

"Dorothy Q." was Miss Dorothy Quincy, who married Edward Jackson and thereby established a succession of generations now numbering Dr. Holmes among her great-grandsons and the guest of honor among her great-great-grandsons. As Dr. Holmes expressed it, the guest of honor and the noted speaker, himself at 75 years of age New England's best-known poet, are only two among the voices of "a hundred men" who echo the tones of Dorothy Q.'s whispered "yes" to Edward Jackson.

Dr. Holmes' tribute, including in part his explanatory remarks, follows:

MR. CHAIRMAN and Gentlemen: . . . Judge Lowell's eulogy will be on every one's lips this evening. His soundness, his fairness, his learning, his devotion to duty, his urbanity—these are the qualities which have commended him to universal esteem and honor. I will not say more of the living; I wish to speak of the dead.

In respectfully proposing the memory of his great-great-grandmother I am speaking of one whom few if any of you can remember. Yet her face is as familiar to me as that of any member of my household. She looks upon me as I sit at my writing-table; she does not smile, she does not speak; even the green parrot on her hand has never opened his beak; but there she is, calm, unchanging, in her immortal youth, as when the untutored artist fixed her features on the canvas. To think that one little word from the lips of Dorothy Quincy, your great-great-grandmother, my great-grandmother, decided the question whether you and I should be here tonight, in fact whether we should be anywhere at

all, or remain two bodiless dreams of nature! But it was Dorothy
Quincy's "Yes" or "No" to Edward Jackson which was to settle
that important matter—important to both of us, certainly—yes,
Your Honor; and I can say truly, as I look at you and remember
your career, important to this and the whole American community.

The picture I referred to is but a rude one, and yet I was not
ashamed of it when I wrote a copy of verses about it, three or four
of which this audience will listen to for the sake of Dorothy's
great-grandson. I must alter the pronouns a little, for this occasion
only:

> Look not on her with eyes of scorn—
> Dorothy Q. was a lady born;
> Ay! since the galloping Normans came
> England's annals have known her name;
> And still to the three-hilled rebel town
> Dear is that ancient name's renown,
> For many a civic wreath they won,
> The youthful sire and the gray-haired son.
>
> O damsel Dorothy! Dorothy Q.!
> Strange is the gift (we) owe to you!
> Such a gift as never a king
> Save to daughter or son might bring—
> All (our) tenure of heart and hand,
> All (our) title to house and land;
> Mother and sister and child and wife
> And joy and sorrow and death and life!
>
> What if a hundred years ago
> Those close-shut lips had answered "No!"
> When forth the tremulous question came
> That cost the maiden her Norman name,
> And under the folds that look so still
> The bodice swelled with the bosom's thrill—
> Should (we) be (we), or could it be
> One-tenth (two others) and nine-tenths (we)?

Soft is the breath of a maiden's Yes:
Not the light gossamer stirs with less;
But never a cable that holds so fast
Through all the battles of wave and blast,
And never an echo of speech or song
That lives in the babbling air so long!
There were tones in the voice that whispered then
You may hear to-day in a hundred men.

O lady and lover, now faint and far
Your images hover—and here we are,
Solid and stirring in flesh and bone—
Edwards and Dorothys—all their own—
A goodly record for time to show
Of a syllable whispered so long ago.

I give you: "The memory of Dorothy Jackson, born Dorothy Quincy, to whose choice of the right monosyllable we owe the presence of our honored guest and all that his life has achieved for the welfare of the community."

HENRY CABOT LODGE, SR.

"If a man is going to be an American at all let him be so without any qualifying adjectives."

BROOKLYN, N. Y., Dec. 21, 1888 —One of this country's most brilliant younger statesmen, Congressman Henry Cabot Lodge, of Massachusetts, tonight used the occasion of the annual dinner of the New England Society of this old New York city, to appeal for an Americanism unhyphenated by divided loyalties and uneroded by Communist beliefs.

Warning that the recent urgent problems aroused by the Civil War, and now happily settled, have been followed by others equally as challenging, Mr. Lodge defined modern Americanism as one that gives complete freedom to all races and creeds, but refuses the right of any element to dominate society. It also, he said, "sets its face rightfully against the doctrines of the Anarchist and the Communist, who seek to solve the social problems not by patient endeavor, but by brutal destruction."

The Congressman's warning against communism referred most obviously to the sharp intellectual debates that have been aroused in the past year with the appearance in English translation of Karl Marx's first volume of *The Communist Manifesto,* already twenty years old in its original German, and further comments caused by the second and third volumes, still printed only in German but widely read by scholars.

The other section of his speech, denouncing hyphenated Americans, reflects more generally the profound Republican party doctrine which the descendant of numerous old New England families has carried into an already brilliant political career, on top of his distinctions—while not yet 40 years of age—as lawyer, historian, philosopher and editor.

One year after he had finished a three-degree series of studies at Harvard, in 1877, Mr. Lodge published a distinguished biography of George Cabot, his great-grandfather. He followed this with other biographies of Alexander Hamilton in 1882, and of Daniel Webster in 1883. Only two years later he produced in 1885 a monumental nine-volume series of newly edited papers of Hamilton, and has completed a biography of George Washington which is ready for publication next year.

THE PILGRIM and the Puritan whom we honor tonight were men who did a great deal of work in the world. They had their faults and their shortcomings, but they were not slothful in business and they were most fervent in spirit. They formed prosperous commonwealths and built on government by law and not of men. They carried the light of learning undimmed through the early years of settlement. They planted a schoolhouse in every village, and fought always a good fight for ordered liberty and for human rights. Their memories shall not perish, for

> *"the actions of the just*
> *"smell sweet and blossom in the dust . . ."*

. . . The war for the Union and the issues springing from it have been settled . . . But all the time other questions have been growing up with the growth of the nation and are now coming to the front for decision. It is our duty to settle them, not only in the right way, but in a thorough American fashion.

By American I do not mean that which had a brief political

existence more than 30 years ago. That movement was based on race and sect, and was therefore thoroughly un-American, and failed, as all un-American movements have failed in this country. True Americanism is opposed utterly to any political divisions resting on race and religion. To the race or to the sect which as such attempts to take possession of the politics or the public education of the country, true Americanism says, Hands off!

The American idea is a free church in a free state, and a free and unsectarian public school in every ward and in every village, with its doors wide open to the children of all races and of every creed. It goes still further, and frowns upon the constant attempt to divide our people according to origin or extraction. Let every man honor and love the land of his birth and the race from which he springs and keep their memory green. It is a pious and honorable duty. But let us have done with British-Americans and Irish-Americans and so on, and all be Americans—nothing more and nothing less. If a man is going to be an American at all let him be so without any qualifying adjectives, and if he is going to be something else, let him drop the word American from his personal description.

As there are sentiments and beliefs like these to be cherished, so there are policies which must be purely and wholly American and to the "manner born" if we would have them right and successful. True Americanism recognizes the enormous gravity of the social and labor problems which confront us. It believes that the safety of the republic depends upon well paid labor and the highest possible average of individual well-being. It believes that the right solution of this problem should be sought without rest and without stay, and that no device public or private of legislation or of individual effort, which can tend to benefit and elevate the condition of the great wage-earning masses of the country, should be left untried.

It sets its face rightfully against the doctrines of the Anarchist and the Communist, who seek to solve the social problems not by patient endeavor, but by brutal destruction. "That way madness lies,"—and such attempts and such teachings, barbarous and un-American as they are, must and will be put down with a strong and unflinching hand, in the name of the home and the church and the school and all that makes up civilization and the possibility of human progress.

The sequel:

As durable as he was brilliant, Henry Cabot Lodge was a political figure of unbroken and never-diminished energy up to the time of his death in 1924. He became a Senator in 1893 and only death removed him from his seat.

Senator Lodge ended his literary endeavors with the biography of George Washington, except for a volume of reminiscences of his youth published in 1913. As a politician, he made great contributions to development of an American ideal, and in his latter years became the center of heated controversies.

Like so many men grown old in public office he saw his convictions never greatly changing in themselves but moving him in the public scene from the position of young liberal to old conservative.

As a senior Republican strategist and Chairman of the Senate Foreign Relations Committee, he opposed the Versailles Peace Treaty and the League of Nations, following World War I, when the fury of debate was carried by younger colleagues, notably Borah.

He opposed his own party leader, President Calvin Coolidge, in attempts by the latter to gain adherence by the United States to the World Court.

In domestic affairs, his advocacy of the "gold standard" eventually gave to the Democrats one of their greatest issues, and brought to the forefront a man whose gifts of oratory alone left an indelible impress upon the thinking of America—William Jennings Bryan.

Within a generation, another Lodge—namesake and grandson of this one—would make another national mark, first as Senator and then as Chief of the United States Delegation to the United Nations.

BOOKER T. WASHINGTON

"The country demands that every race measure itself by the American standard."

BOSTON, Mass., June, 1896—A prematurely aged man, born a slave of a Negro mother and a white father, who worked in salt mines and iron foundries before he was able to go to school, came here today as honored guest of Harvard University to receive the honorary degree of Master of Arts, conferred on distinguished educators.

The recipient was Booker T. Washington, who at 38 years of age already is noted as the founder and head of Tuskegee Institute, in Alabama, which with the support of Northerners and Southerners alike offers educational opportunities to Negroes.

Mr. Washington's acceptance speech seemed to give to its auditors as much as he was receiving in honor, for it was one of rare understanding of the long road stretching ahead in the complex work of integrating a free black race into the patterns of the white culture of the United States. It was, too, the speech of a cultured man, an understanding man. It follows:

MR. PRESIDENT and Gentlemen: It would in some measure relieve my embarrassment if I could, even in a slight degree, feel myself worthy of the great honor which you do me today. Why you have called me from the Black Belt of the South, from among my humble people, to share in the honors of this occasion, is not for me to explain; and yet it may not be inappropriate for me to suggest that it seems to me that one of the most vital questions that touch our American life, is how to bring the strong, wealthy and learned into helpful touch with the poorest, most ignorant and humble, and at the same time make the one appreciate the vitalizing, strengthening influence of the other. How shall we make the mansions on yon Beacon Street feel and see the need of the spirits in the lowliest cabin in Alabama cotton fields or Louisiana sugar bottoms? This problem Harvard University is solving, not by bringing itself down but by bringing the masses up.

If through me, a humble representative, seven millions of my people in the South might be permitted to send a message to Harvard—Harvard that offered up on earth's altar, young Shaw, and Russell, and Lowell and scores of others, that we might have a free and united country—that message would be, "Tell them that the sacrifice was not in vain. Tell them that by way of the shop, the field, the skilled hand, habits of thrift and economy, by way of industrial school and college, we are coming. We are crawling up, working up, yea, bursting up. Often through oppression, unjust discrimination, and prejudice, but through them we are coming up, and with proper habits, intelligence, and property, there is no power on earth that can permanently stay our progress."

If my life in the past has meant anything in the lifting up of my people and the bringing about of better relations between your race and mine, I assure you from this day it will mean doubly more. In the economy of God, there is but one standard by which an individual can succeed—there is but one for a race. This country demands that every race measure itself by the American standard. By it a race must rise or fall, succeed or fail, and in the last analysis mere sentiment counts but little.

During the next half century or more, my race must continue passing through the severe American crucible. We are to be tested in our patience, our forbearance, our perseverance, our power to endure wrong, to withstand temptations, to economize, to acquire and use skill; our ability to compete, to succeed in commerce, to disregard the superficial for the real, the appearance for the substance, to be great and yet small, learned and yet simple, high and yet the servant of all. This, this is the passport to all that is best in the life of our Republic, and the Negro must possess it, or be debarred.

In working out our destiny, while the main burden and center of activity must be with us, we shall need in large measure in the years that are to come as we have in the past, the help, the encouragement, the guidance that the strong can give to the weak. Thus helped, we of both races in the South soon shall throw off the shackles of racial and sectional prejudices and rise as Harvard University has risen and as we all should rise, above the clouds of ignorance, narrowness and selfishness, into that atmosphere, that pure sunshine, where it will be our highest ambition to serve man, our brother, regardless of race or previous condition.

WILLIAM JENNINGS BRYAN

"You shall not crucify mankind upon a cross of gold."

CHICAGO, Ill., 1896—A young newspaper editor from Omaha, Nebraska, with the vocal cords of a bull and the persuasion of a Cataline, today gathered up the membership of the Democratic National Convention in his charm and argument, and pushed wide open the door for his nomination for the Presidency of the United States.

His name is William Jennings Bryan. He is 36 years old, still two years shy of the minimum age set by the Constitution for the President, but no one seems to be concerned about that technicality. His recorded political experience consists of four years in the House of Representatives, from 1891 to 1895, a post he vacated in order to run unsuccessfully in 1894 for the Senate.

Relatively unknown politically, Mr. Bryan still may be counted, particularly after today, as standing on the threshold of greatness, whether one approves or disapproves of the issue on which he made his debut on the national political stage—a plea for the unrestricted coinage of silver at a ratio to gold of 16-to-1.

Few persons in his immediate audience, and relatively fewer outside, understand the economic reasoning behind this appeal, but Mr. Bryan is capable of charming a very large percentage into agreement with himself, willy-nilly. His appeal, furthermore, is to labor and to the farmer, in a day when the feeling is creeping through the country that the gold standard acts as a brake upon the enlarged earning capacity of those who toil with their hands.

"You shall not press down upon the brow of labor this crown of thorns," Mr. Bryan exclaimed at the close of his oration. "You shall not crucify mankind upon a cross of gold."

The speaker's arguments were not unlike those used increasingly in debate in the past year or two—that universal prosperity requires greater issuance of coin in circulation; that increased circulation of currency backed by precious metal requires enlargement of the specie standard to include silver valued at a fixed rate compared to gold. It was the manner in which Mr. Bryan broached the argument that made it new and dramatic, as well as compelling, to many of his auditors in this gathering.

He linked broadened prosperity directly to agriculture and to the purchasing power of labor. He struck out forcefully at the conservative contention that true prosperity requires first a stable base for invested wealth, from which prosperity may spread outward and downward to the workers.

"There are two ideas of government," he conceded. "There are those who believe that, if you will only legislate to make the well-to-do prosperous, their prosperity will leak through on those below. The Democratic idea, however, has been that if you make the masses prosperous, their prosperity will find its way up through every class which rests upon them."

In this convention, most delegates agree with that thesis, but whether its development rests on the double standard of coinage is to be determined. But at least a great challenge has been voiced.

. . . HERE IS the line of battle, and we care not upon which issue they force the fight; we are prepared to meet them on either issue or on both. If they tell us that the gold standard is the standard of civilization, we reply to them that this, the most enlightened of all the nations of the earth, has never declared for a gold standard and that both the great parties this year are declaring against it. If the gold standard is the standard of civilization, why, my friends, should we not have it? If they come to meet us on that issue we can present the history of our nation. More than that; we can tell them that they will search the pages of history in vain to find a single instance where the common people of any land have ever declared themselves in favor of the gold standard. They can find where the holders of fixed investments have declared for a gold standard, but not where the masses have.

Mr. Carlisle said in 1878 that this was a struggle between "the idle holders of idle capital" and "the struggling masses, who produce the wealth and pay the taxes of the country"; and, my friends, the question we are to decide is: Upon which side will the Democratic party fight; upon the side of "the idle holders of capital" or upon the side of "the struggling masses"? That is the question which the party must answer first, and then it must be answered by each individual hereafter. The sympathies of the Democratic party, as shown by the platform, are on the side of the struggling masses who have ever been the foundation of the Democratic party.

There are two ideas of government. There are those who believe that, if you will only legislate to make the well-to-do prosperous, their prosperity will leak through on those below. The Democratic idea, however, has been that if you make the masses prosperous, their prosperity will find its way up through every class which rests upon them.

You come to us and tell us that the great cities are in favor of the gold standard; we reply that the great cities rest upon our broad and fertile prairies. Burn down your cities and leave our farms, and your cities will spring up again as if by magic; but destroy our farms and the grass will grow in the streets of every city in the country.

My friends, we declare that this nation is able to legislate for its own people on every question, without waiting for the aid or consent of any other nation on earth; and upon that issue we expect to carry every state in the Union. I shall not slander the inhabitants of the fair state of Massachusetts nor the inhabitants of the state of New York by saying that, when they are confronted with the proposition, they will declare that this nation is not able to attend to its own business. It is the issue of 1776 over again. Our ancestors, when but three millions in number, had the courage to declare their political independence of every other nation; shall we, their descendants, when we have grown to seventy millions, declare that we are less independent than our forefathers?

No, my friends, that will never be the verdict of our people. Therefore, we care not upon what lines the battle is fought. If they say bimetallism is good, but that we cannot have it until other nations help us, we reply that, instead of having a gold standard because England has, we will restore bimetallism, and then let England have bimetallism because the United States has it. If they dare to come out in the open field and defend the gold standard as a good thing, we will fight them to the uttermost. Having behind us the producing masses of this nation and the world, supported by the commercial interests, the laboring interests and the toilers everywhere, we will answer their demand for a gold standard by saying to them: You shall not press down upon the brow of labor this crown of thorns. You shall not crucify mankind upon a cross of gold.

The sequel:

Bryan's speech virtually "stampeded" the Democratic Convention into his nomination for the Presidency. He lost. He was renominated in 1900 and again in 1908, only to lose twice again.

His greatest political distinction was to become Secretary of State under Woodrow Wilson, a position he resigned when war was declared on Germany, not because of pro-German sympathies but because of a deeply sincere pacifism that was interlocked with his equally sincere fundamentalism in religious beliefs.

In a long lifetime Bryan became known as the undisputed oratorical master of his day, whether on the hustings, in Chautauqua talks, or in great debates such as his opposition as legal counsel to Clarence Darrow in the Scopes trial in Dayton, Tennessee.

Despised by conservatives, derided by an increasing number of younger liberals as he grew into old age, he was withal a sincere man. His political "failures" were due in many instances to his noncompromising attitude. Few men have sparked as many ideas and political reforms that became accepted to the eventual credit of others.

Without his introduction or espousal, it would have taken much longer to achieve acceptance of the income tax, popular election of Senators, woman suffrage, or public exposition of the ownership of newspapers, as well as prohibition.

In that box score his positives far outweigh his negatives. If it constituted failure in public life not to win the Presidency, Bryan's indeed was a magnificent failure.

It is reported that at this convention after Bryan was nominated, a railroad president offered him a private car to use for campaigning, but Willis John Abbot advised against it, with words that gave Bryan his new title, saying, "You are the Great Commoner."

THEODORE ROOSEVELT

"I wish to preach not the doctrine of ignoble ease but the doctrine of the strenuous life."

CHICAGO, Ill., April 10, 1899— New York's ebullient Governor, Theodore Roosevelt, came to the "Windy City" from the relatively calm and conservative environs of his New York background to warn his hearers—and his political party —that today's world leaves no room for calm acceptance of the status quo.

Speaking before the Hamilton Club, whose membership represents the hard core of Republican leadership in the "capital of the prairies," the leader of the Rough Riders in their charge up San Juan Hill only a year ago, and pugnacious challenger of his own State's political bosses, figuratively shook a warning finger in the face of smugness.

"The twentieth century looms before us," he said, "big with the fate of many nations. If we stand idly by, if we seek merely swollen, slothful ease, and ignoble peace, if we shrink from the hard contests where men must win at hazard of their lives and at the risk of all they hold dear, then the bolder and stronger peoples will pass us by and will win for themselves the domination of the world."

Governor Roosevelt's words were received by some as a prophetic warning that the complaisance which has settled down since victory over Spain in the recent war cannot long continue; to others it seemed that he was needlessly calling up visions of ghosts that will never rattle their chains in this country's experience. To the latter, it was difficult to differentiate between these words from a Republican and the campaign oratory of spokesmen for the Democratic party.

But regardless of individual reaction, it is becoming more and more evident that New York's Governor is not a man who will permit himself to be disregarded. He has, additionally, viewpoints—and both support and liabilities politically—arising from an extraordinary background.

To be a Roosevelt in New York State is to live above any requirement for identification; there have always been Roosevelts there, including notably a member of the State Convention that ratified the Constitution. It is more likely, however, that nationally Theodore Roosevelt would win a greater following in the West than in the East, due to his long periods of residence on his ranch in Dakota Territory, his raising and leading, with Colonel Leonard Wood, of the "Rough Riders," and his personality which exudes an atmosphere that would be marked as western in any company.

These are some of the qualities that make Theodore Roosevelt, as yet only 41 years of age and already with high offices on his record —Police Commissioner of New York City, Assistant Secretary of the Navy and now the Governorship—a man whose background is national rather than local and a speaker whose words echo far away from their point of delivery.

He is appealing to a following over the heads of the titular Republican "bosses," Thomas C. Platt and Mark Hanna, seeking to capture from the masses some of the flaming support that these already have pledged to William Jennings Bryan.

GENTLEMEN: In speaking to you, men of the greatest city of the West, men of the State which gave to the country Lincoln and Grant, men who preeminently and distinctly embody all that is most American in the American character, I wish to preach not the doctrine of ignoble ease but the doctrine of the strenuous life; the life of toil and effort; of labor and strife; to preach that highest form of success which comes not to the man who desires mere easy peace but to the man who does not shrink from danger, from hardship, or from bitter toil, and who out of these wins the splendid ultimate triumph.

The timid man, the lazy man, the man who distrusts his country, the overcivilized man, who has lost the great fighting, masterful virtues, the ignorant man and the man of dull mind, whose soul is incapable of feeling the mighty lift that thrills "stern men with empires in their brains"—all these, of course, shrink from seeing the nation undertake its new duties; shrink from seeing us build a navy and army adequate to our needs; shrink from seeing us do our share of the world's work by bringing order out of chaos in the great, fair tropic islands from which the valor of our soldiers and sailors has driven the Spanish flag.

These are the men who fear the strenuous life, who fear the only national life which is really worth leading. They believe in that cloistered life which saps the hardy virtues in a nation, as it saps them in the individual; or else they are wedded to that base spirit of gain and greed which recognizes in commercialism the be-all and end-all of national life, instead of realizing that, though an indispensable element, it is after all but one of the many elements that go to make up true national greatness. No country can long endure if its foundations are not laid deep in the material prosperity which comes from thrift, from business energy and enterprise, from hard unsparing effort in the fields of industrial activity; but neither was any nation ever yet truly great if it relied upon material prosperity alone.

All honor must be paid to the architects of our material prosperity; to the great captains of industry who have built our factories and our railroads; to the strong men who toil for wealth with brain or hand; for great is the debt of the nation to these and their kind. But our debt is yet greater to the men whose highest type is to be found in a statesman like Lincoln, a soldier like

Grant. They showed by their lives that they recognized the law of work, the law of strife; they toiled to win a competence for themselves and those dependent upon them; but they recognized that there were yet other and even loftier duties—duties to the nation and duties to the race.

I preach to you, then, my countrymen, that our country calls not for the life of ease, but for the life of strenuous endeavor. The twentieth century looms before us big with the fate of many nations. If we stand idly by, if we seek merely swollen, slothful ease, and ignoble peace, if we shrink from the hard contests where men must win at hazard of their lives and at the risk of all they hold dear, then the bolder and stronger peoples will pass us by and will win for themselves the domination of the world. Let us therefore boldly face the life of strife, resolute to do our duty well and manfully; resolute to uphold righteousness by deed and by word; resolute to be both honest and brave, to serve high ideals, yet to use practical methods. Above all, let us shrink from no strife, moral or physical, within or without the nation, provided we are certain that the strife is justified; for it is only through strife, through hard and dangerous endeavor, that we shall ultimately win the goal of true national greatness.

The sequel:

Theodore Roosevelt's forthright speech caused his party leaders such concern that they decided to shelve him. They gave him the nomination for the Vice Presidency in 1900—securely under the shadow of William McKinley's conservatism. . . . And a few months after Inauguration in 1901, McKinley was assassinated.

The devotee of the "strenuous life" became a strenuous President indeed, harrying alike the arrogant business combinations, or "trusts," and the arrogant unions. In foreign affairs he dictated peace terms between Russia and Japan, keeping either from reaping special advantage and, to bring the prestige of the United States to its highest point yet, he sent "the Great White Fleet" of his country's warships on a goodwill mission around the world.

Embittered later by the decision of the Republican party not to nominate him in 1912 for a third term, he made his own life even more strenuous by forming the Bull Moose party and running for the Presidency as its leader. He lost, but so shattered the ultra-conservative Republican forces that Woodrow Wilson was elected to the Presidency on a program that echoed the earlier programs of both Roosevelt and Bryan.

In his other activities, Roosevelt seemed to be several men. As prolific writer, as magazine editor, as explorer of the Amazon jungles and as big game hunter . . . to sum him up, it now appears almost inconceivable that this man lived only 61 years.

ROBERT G. INGERSOLL

"Life is a narrow vale between the cold and barren peaks of two eternities."

NEW YORK, 1899—Robert Green Ingersoll, who died here this year at the age of 66, is more remembered for his controversies than for his achievements, and as an orator whose words eulogizing others were more dramatic than the individuals he described.

His life was one of conflicts and contrasts on which he throve. As an agnostic he achieved the unique position of winning serious denunciation, instead of the usual quiet disdain, from leaders of orthodox religious movements; as a politician his early career in Illinois was cut short by public reaction to his agnosticism, and yet he reached the peak of leadership where he nominated James G. Blaine as the standard bearer of the Republican party in 1876. And he achieved that leadership in the Republican party after having turned his coat from the Democratic party banner under which he worked prior to the Civil War.

But perhaps the greatest paradox of his life—the element that drew hundreds of thousands of persons annually to hear his lectures—was his unique conception of being, wherein while he denied God as an orthodox deity he saw his fellow man, whom he admired, as being constructed of almost godlike qualities.

From his many memorable speeches, while deliberately pushing aside his direct and controversial challenges of formal religious beliefs, the portrait of Mr. Ingersoll as he saw beauty around him in the world, is best illustrated by excerpts from two of his talks, one public and the other relatively private, delivered more than a score of years ago.

One is the conclusion of his nomination of Blaine, the other a passage from his oration at the funeral of his brother, Ebon Clark Ingersoll.

THE REPUBLICANS of the United States demand a man who knows that prosperity and resumption, when they come, must come together; that when they come they will come hand in hand through the golden harvest fields; hand in hand by the whirling spindles and turning wheels; hand in hand past the open furnace doors; hand in hand by the flaming forges; hand in hand by the chimneys filled with eager fire—greeted and grasped by the countless sons of toil.

This money (for the resumption of "specie payment") has to be dug out of the earth. You cannot make it by passing resolutions in a political convention.

The Republicans of the United States want a man who knows that this government should protect every citizen at home and abroad; who knows that any government that will not defend its defenders and protect its protectors is a disgrace to the map of the world. They demand a man who believes in the eternal separation and divorcement of church and school. They demand a man whose political reputation is spotless as a star; but they do not demand that their candidate shall have a certificate of moral character signed by a Confederate Congress. The man who has in full, heaped and rounded measure, all these splendid qualifications is the present grand and gallant leader of the Republican Party—James G. Blaine.

Our country, crowned with the vast and marvelous achievements of its first century, asks for a man worthy of the past and prophetic of her future; asks for a man who has the audacity of genius; asks for a man who is the grandest combination of heart, conscience and brain beneath her flag. Such a man is James G. Blaine.

For the Republican host led by this intrepid man, there can be no defeat. This is a grand year; a year filled with the recollections of the Revolution, filled with proud and tender memories of the past, with the sacred legends of liberty; a year in which the sons of freedom will drink from the fountains of enthusiasm; a year in which the people call for a man who has preserved in Congress what our soldiers won upon the field; a year in which we call for the man who has torn from the throat of treason the tongue of slander—for the man who has snatched the mask of Democracy from the hidden face of Rebellion—for the man who, like an intellectual athlete, has stood in the arena of debate and challenged all comers, and who, up to the present moment, is a total stranger to defeat.

Like an armed warrior, like a plumed knight, James G. Blaine marched down the hall of the American Congress and threw his shining lance full and fair against the brazen foreheads of the defamers of his country and the maligners of his honor. For the Republicans to desert this gallant leader now is as though an army should desert their general upon the field of battle.

James G. Blaine is now, and has been for years, the bearer of the sacred standard of the Republican Party. I call it sacred, because no human being can stand beneath its folds without becoming and without remaining free.

Gentlemen of the convention, in the name of the great Republic, the only republic that ever existed upon this earth; in the name of all her defenders and all her supporters; in the name of all her soldiers living; in the name of all her soldiers dead upon the field of battle; and in the name of those who perished in the skeleton clutch of famine at Andersonville and Libby, whose sufferings he so vividly remembers, Illinois—Illinois nominates for the next President of this country that prince of parliamentarians, that leader of leaders, James G. Blaine.

The sequel:

The "plumed knight" did not win the nomination; this went to Rutherford B. Hayes, who became the next President. But Ingersoll's nomination has lived as the expression of its speaker, not its subject.

AT HIS BROTHER'S GRAVE

THE LOVED and loving brother, husband, father, friend died where manhood's morning almost touches noon, and while the shadows still were falling toward the West.

He had not passed on life's highway the stone that marks the highest point, but, being weary for a moment, he lay down by the wayside, and, using his burden for a pillow, fell into that dreamless sleep that kisses down his eyelids still. While yet in love with life and raptured with the world he passed to silence and pathetic dust.

Yet, after all, it may be best, just in the happiest, sunniest hours of all the voyage, while eager winds are kissing every sail, to dash against the unseen rock, and in an instant hear the billows roar above a sunken ship. For, whether in mid-sea or 'mong the breakers of the farther shore, a wreck at last must mark the end of each and all. And every life, no matter if its hour is rich with love and every moment jeweled with joy will, at its close, become a tragedy as sad and deep and dark as can be woven of the warp and woof of mystery and death.

This brave and tender man in every storm of life was oak and rock but in the sunshine he was vine and flower. He was the friend of all heroic souls. He climbed the heights and left all superstitions far below, while on his forehead fell the golden dawning of the grander day.

He loved the beautiful, and was with color, form and music touched to tears. He sided with the weak, and with a willing hand gave alms; with loyal heart and with purest hands he faithfully discharged all public trusts.

He was a worshiper of liberty, a friend of the oppressed. A thousand times I have heard him quote these words: "For justice all places a temple, and all seasons summer." He believed that happiness was the only good, reason the only torch, justice the only worship, humanity the only religion, and love the only priest. He added to the sum of human joy; and were every one to whom he did some loving service to bring a blossom to his grave, he would sleep tonight beneath a wilderness of flowers.

Life is a narrow vale between the cold and barren peaks of two eternities. We strive in vain to look beyond the heights. We cry aloud, and the only answer is the echo of our wailing cry. From the voiceless lips of the unreplying dead there comes no word; but in the night of death hope sees a star, and listening love can hear the rustle of a wing.

He who sleeps here, when dying, mistaking the approach of death for the return of health, whispered with his latest breath: "I am better now." Let us believe, in spite of doubts and dogmas, and tears and fears, that these dear words are true of all the countless dead.

ROBERT M. LA FOLLETTE

"The right to cast the ballot is regarded as sacred. The right to make the ballot is equally sacred."

MILWAUKEE, Wis., 1902—Governor Robert Marion La Follette summed up the arguments for primary elections for the choice of candidates for public office in a notable address wherein he said that the choice of candidates is as much a "sacred right" of the citizen as his right to cast a ballot later for the candidates for public office.

Mr. La Follette was striking alike at the systems used in many states whereby party conventions choose candidates for public office and the practice whereby some State legislatures name members of the Senate. In all such cases where political leaders select the candidates of office holders, rather than the voters themselves, he argued, the way is paved for public-service corporations and for political bosses to choose slates of candidates who—regardless of what party wins—will work for special rather than the public interest.

He quoted a remark by the notorious Boss Tweed of New York: "You may elect whatever candidates you please to office, if you will allow me to select the candidates."

While Governor La Follette was speaking directly for reform in Wisconsin, he emphasized that the problem he cited is nation-wide, and reiterated that, "the only result sought by a primary election is to give to every man an equal voice in the selection of all candidates."

It may be remarked here that while Governor La Follette is noted as a radical in politics, particularly for his watch-dog attitude toward the power of wealth in politics, he is aligned in this question on the side of many persons of diverse political views. This issue is a favorite of William Jennings Bryan as well as of President Roosevelt and has wide support in the legal fraternity.

WE BELIEVE with the President, as recognized by him in daily speech, that these great monopolies constitute the foremost of national questions. We uphold his hands in his effort to curb these trusts by the enforcement of laws now upon the statute books. There is probably not an important trust in the United States which does not have the assistance of railroads in destroying its competitors in business. The limitation and control of these public-service corporations in the legitimate field, as common carriers, are an important element in the practical solution of the problem with which we have to deal.

In accepting renomination for the office of governor at the hands of the Republican party, I said:

"The greatest danger menacing public institutions today is the overbalancing control of city, state, and national legislatures by the wealth and power of public-service corporations."

I made this statement advisedly then. I repeat it now. Not in a spirit of hostility to any interest, but deeply impressed with its profound significance to republican institutions and its ultimate influence upon all citizens and all citizenship.

The idea is not new. It is not peculiar to Wisconsin.

The responsibility it brings cannot be shirked or pushed aside or postponed. The national government, every state government—particularly that of every rich and prosperous state—every city government—particularly that of every large city—has this problem to solve; not at some other time, but now.

The question of primary elections is one of government for the people and by the people. Under our system of government by political parties, two elements, equal in importance, are involved in the exercise of suffrage; one, the making of the ballot; the other, the casting of the ballot. The right to cast the ballot is regarded as sacred. The right to make the ballot is equally sacred. No man would be willing to delegate his power to vote the ballot at general elections. No man shall be compelled to delegate his power to make his ballot. Boss Tweed said: "You may elect whichever candidates you please to office, if you will allow me to select the candidates." The boss can always afford to say, "You may vote any ticket you please so long as I make all the tickets." The character of the men nominated and the influences to which they owe their nomination determine the character of government.

The result and the only result sought by a primary election is to give to every man an equal voice in the selection of all candidates; to lodge in the people the absolute right to say who their candidates for office shall be; to root out forever the power of the political boss to control the selection of officials through the manipulation of caucuses and conventions. A primary election should provide the same safeguards for nominating candidates as for electing them. It should fix the day, name the hour, use the same polling places, have the same election officers, provide the Australian ballot, containing the names of all the candidates to be voted upon at the election. It should be an election, possessing all the legal sanctions of an election.

It is needless to trace the evolution of the political machine, its combination with aggregate wealth and corporate power, making the interests of the citizen and the state subservient to their selfish ends. The names of the great bosses today are better known than the great statesmen. The tendency to monopolization of political control by a few men in each party, county, city, state, and community has operated, except in cases of profound interest, excitement, and tremendous effort, to disfranchise the great majority of citizens in so far as participating in the caucus and convention is concerned.

The day that Chief Justice Ryan prophesied would come is here. The issue he said would arise is pending.

"Which shall rule—wealth or man; which shall lead—money or intellect; who shall fill pubic stations—educated and patriotic freemen, or the feudal servants of corporate power?"

If the chosen representative does not represent the citizen, his voice is stifled; is denied any part in government. If majority decision as determined by the law of the land is ignored and reversed, if the expressed will of the people is scorned and scorned again— then the popular government fails, then government of the people, by the people, and for the people is at an end. Its forms may be observed—you may have the mockery of "elections," and the force of "representation," but a government based upon the will of the people has perished from the earth.

The sequel:

Partly due to Senator La Follette's efforts, the cause for primary elections as the means of nominating candidates has spread widely, although New York State, among others, retains at this writing the convention system for choosing its leading officials.

In many states, there are "preferential primaries" where slates of delegates to Presidential nominating conventions or to State political conventions are voted by citizens.

In his personal career, this fight was only one of many facets of Mr. La Follette's long political leadership that still is the subject of controversy, but that left on his memory the mark of a forceful and influential thinker.

He won his fight in Wisconsin for the direct primary. In 1906 he was elected to the Senate where he served until his death in 1925.

Mr. La Follette's wife, Belle Case La Follette, was his closest adviser throughout his long political career as well as a prominent member of the woman's suffrage movement. A son, Robert Jr., served as his assistant from 1919 to 1925, succeeded to his seat in the Senate, and served until 1947 when he was defeated in a primary election in Wisconsin.

GEORGE GRAHAM VEST

"He guards the sleep of his pauper master as if he were a prince."

WASHINGTON, D. C., 1903—Senator George Graham Vest ended this year four consecutive terms, 24 years, as a Senator from Missouri.

His career was distinguished, but his reputation with posterity will rest less on his actions as a Senator than on a brief argument he was inspired to make in a court action while still a young lawyer. In this case he represented a man suing another who had killed his dog.

The young lawyer won his case with a plea that has become nationally known, and which he has been asked to repeat a thousand times:

GENTLEMEN of the Jury: The best friend a man has in the world may turn against him and become his enemy. His son or daughter that he has reared with loving care may prove ungrateful. Those who are nearest and dearest to us, those whom we trust with our happiness and our good name may become traitors to their faith.

The money that a man has he may lose. It flies away from him, perhaps when he needs it most. A man's reputation may be sacrificed in a moment of ill-considered action. The people who are prone to fall on their knees when success is with us, may be the first to throw the stone of malice when failure settles its cloud upon our head.

The one absolutely unselfish friend that man can have in this selfish world, the one that never deserts him, the one that never proves ungrateful or treacherous, is his dog. A man's dog stands by him in prosperity and in poverty, in health and in sickness. He will sleep on the cold ground, where the wintry winds blow and the snow drives fiercely, if only he may be near his master's side. He will kiss the hand that has no food to offer; he will lick the wounds and sores that come in encounters with the roughness of the world. He guards the sleep of his pauper master as if he were a prince.

When all other friends desert, he remains. When riches take wings, and reputation falls to pieces, he is as constant in his love as the sun in its journey through the heavens.

If fortune drive his master forth an outcast in the world, friendless and homeless, the faithful dog asks no higher privilege than that of accompanying him, to guard him against danger, to fight against his enemies. And when the last scene of all comes, and death takes his master in its embrace and his body is laid away in the cold ground, no matter if all other friends pursue their way, there by the graveside will the noble dog be found, his head between his paws, his eyes sad, but open in alert watchfulness, faithful and true even in death.

JANE ADDAMS

*". . . one who has looked through the confusion of the
moment and has seen the moral issue involved."*

CHICAGO, Ill., Feb. 23, 1903—
Members of the Union League Club,
who invited Miss Jane Addams, co-
founder of Hull House, to deliver the
Washington's Birthday Address, today heard new definitions given to the
words *greatness* and *commemoration.*

Greatness she defined as the character of one "who has looked
through the confusion of the moment and has seen the moral issue
involved." As for the meaning of
commemoration, Miss Addams
tossed into the discard the normal
heaping of encomiums upon the past
and said charmingly but forcefully
that nothing honors the past except
present strivings to live up to its
teachings.

It is 14 years since Miss Addams,
now 43 years old, turned her back on
the prosperous society in which she
holds by birth an assured place, to
found, in association with Miss El-
len Gates Starr, the famous settlement house patterned after the older
English university settlements. Already it has made her a national
figure, overshadowing her otherwise distinguished labors in behalf

of woman suffrage and various peace
movements. Thus when Miss Addams
cautions her auditors to displace
what amounts to ancestor worship
with present-doing she furnishes in
herself an unparalleled example.

So today, while paying the highest
tributes to George Washington, she
made of him an example, not a dead
figure of glory: a prime example of
those who have "looked through the
confusion of the moment."

Citing George Washington's examples as soldier, statesman, citizen,
Miss Addams found in his career
challenges to present activity through
the whole sphere of modern activity
—the fight for social equality, the
elevation of ideals above material
ambitions, and the avid desire for
universal freedom that prompted the
Father of His Country to order in his
will that his former slaves be freed.

"A man who a century ago could
do that," Miss Addams commented,
"would he, do you think, be indifferent now to the great questions of
social adjustment which we feel all
around us?"

Her words, in abridged form, follow:

WE MEET together upon these birthdays of our great men, not
only to review their lives, but to revive and cherish our own patri-

otism. This matter is a difficult task. In the first place, we are prone to think that by merely reciting these great deeds we get a reflected glory, and that the future is secure to us because the past has been so fine.

In the second place, we are apt to think that we inherit the fine qualities of those great men, simply because we have had a common descent and are living in the same territory.

As for the latter, we know full well that the patriotism of common descent is the mere patriotism of the clan—the early patriotism of the tribe. We know that the possession of a like territory is merely an advance upon that, and that both of them are unworthy to be the patriotism of a great cosmopolitan nation whose patriotism must be large enough to obliterate racial distinction and to forget that there are such things as surveyor's lines. Then when we come to the study of great men it is easy to think only of their great deeds, and not to think enough of their spirit.

What is a great man who has made his mark upon history? Every time, if we think far enough, he is a man who has looked through the confusion of the moment and has seen the moral issue involved; he is a man who has refused to have his sense of justice distorted; he has listened to his conscience until conscience becomes a trumpet call to like-minded men, so that they gather about him and together, with mutual purpose and mutual aid, they make a new period in history. . . .

If we go back to George Washington, and ask what he would be doing were he bearing our burdens now, and facing our problems at this moment, we would, of course, have to study his life bit by bit; his life as a soldier, as a statesman, and as a simple Virginia planter.

First, as a soldier. What is it that we admire about the soldier? It certainly is not that he goes into battle; what we admire about the soldier is that he has the power of losing his own life for the life of a larger cause; that he holds his personal suffering of no account; that he flings down in the gage of battle his all, and says, "I will stand or fall with this cause." That, it seems to me, is the glorious thing we most admire, and if we are going to preserve that same spirit of the soldier, we will have to found a similar spirit in the civil life of the people, the same pride in civil warfare, the spirit of courage, and the spirit of self-surrender which lies back of this. . . .

Let us take, for a moment, George Washington as a statesman. What was it he did, during those days when they were framing a Constitution, when they were meeting together night after night, and trying to adjust the rights and privileges of every class in the community? What was it that sustained him during all those days, all those weeks, during all those months and years? It was the belief that they were founding a nation on the axiom that all men are created free and equal. What would George Washington say if he found that among us there were causes constantly operating against that equality? If he knew that any child which is thrust prematurely into industry has no chance in life with children who are preserved from that pain and sorrow; if he knew that every insanitary street, and every insanitary house, cripples a man so that he has no health and no vigor with which to carry on his life labor; if he knew that all about us are forces making against skill, making against the best manhood and womanhood, what would he say? He would say that if the spirit of equality means anything, it means like opportunity, and if we once lose like opportunity we lose the only chance we have toward equality throughout the nation.

Let us take George Washington as a citizen. What did he do when he retired from office, because he was afraid holding office any longer might bring a wrong to himself and harm to his beloved nation? . . . What were his thoughts during the all too short days that he lived there? He thought of many possibilities, but, looking out over his country, did he fear that there should rise up a crowd of men who held office, not for their country's good, but for their own good? . . .

He would tell us that anything which makes for better civic service, which makes for a merit system, which makes for fitness for office, is the only thing which will tell against this wrong, and that this course is the wisest patriotism. What did he write in his last correspondence? He wrote that he felt very unhappy on the subject of slavery, that there was, to his mind, a great menace in the holding of slaves. We know that he neither bought nor sold slaves himself, and that he freed his own slaves in his will. That was a century ago. A man who a century ago could do that, would he, do you think, be indifferent now to the great questions of social maladjustment which we feel all around us? . . .

A wise patriotism, which will take hold of these questions by careful legal enactment, by constant and vigorous enforcement, because of the belief that if the meanest man in the Republic is deprived of his rights, then every man in the Republic is deprived of his rights, is the only patriotism by which public-spirited men and women, with a thoroughly aroused conscience, can worthily serve this Republic. Let us say again that the lessons of great men are lost unless they re-enforce upon our minds the highest demands which we make upon ourselves; that they are lost unless they drive our sluggish wills forward in the direction of their highest ideals.

The sequel:

It would be presumptuous to attempt to appraise the wide-ranging effect of the actions and expressed views of Jane Addams.

By the time she died in 1935, she was a world force and considered as the primary developer of the modern field of settlement house work. In Chicago, she also was credited with having originated an entirely new spirit of orientation among the foreign-born.

The wide range of her interests was such that in 1931 Miss Addams was chosen to share with Nicholas Murray Butler, President of Columbia University, the award of the Nobel Peace Prize.

EMMA GOLDMAN

"Patriotism—a menace to liberty."

NEW YORK, N. Y., 1910—The contention that patriotism is a poison for the minds of free men is the keynote of a recent speech successfully delivered before audiences across the country by Miss Emma Goldman, the Russian immigrant who has become one of the leading voices of anarchism, permitted free rein under the liberties of her adopted country.

Miss Goldman, at 46, is a well-educated Russian woman who came to the United States in 1886 and, after a preliminary period of hard labor in the looms and mills of New York and New England, turned to the movement of radicals that preaches the total destruction of organized society as the means of "freeing" individuals.

She is notable as an anachronism in American development, gaining vast audiences for her spell-binding talks, primarily from amongst the more recent immigrant group, who apparently are entertained by her ideas, but who with few exceptions go from her meetings back to their jobs and their sober political beliefs.

The following was taken from Miss Goldman's own transcription as reprinted by the Mother Earth Publishing Company, New York:

WHAT IS patriotism? Is it love of one's birthplace, the place of childhood's recollections and hopes, dreams and aspirations? Is it the place where, in childlike naïveté, we would watch the floating clouds, and wonder why we, too, could not run so swiftly? In short, is it love for the spot, every inch representing dear and precious recollections of a happy, joyous and playful childhood?

If that were patriotism, few American men of today would be called upon to be patriotic, since the place of play has been turned into factory, mill, and mine, while deepening sounds of machinery have replaced the music of the birds. No longer can we hear the tales of great deeds, for the stories our mothers tell today are but those of sorrow, tears and grief.

What, then, is patriotism? "Patriotism, sir, is the last resort of scoundrels," said Dr. Johnson. Leo Tolstoy, the greatest anti-patriot of our time, defines patriotism as the principle that will justify the training of wholesale murderers.

Indeed, conceit, arrogance and egotism are the essentials of patriotism. Let me illustrate. Patriotism assumes that our globe is divided into little spots, each one surrounded by an iron gate. Those who have had the fortune of being born on some particular spot consider themselves nobler, better, grander, more intelligent than those living beings inhabiting any other spot. It is, therefore, the duty of everyone living on that chosen spot to fight, kill and die in the attempt to impose his superiority upon all the others.

The inhabitants of the other spots reason in like manner, of course, with the result that from early infancy the mind of the child is provided with blood-curdling stories about the Germans, the French, the Italians, Russians, etc.

Thinking men and women the world over are beginning to realize that patriotism is too narrow and limited a conception to meet the necessities of our time. The centralization of power has brought into being an international feeling of solidarity among the oppressed nations of the world; a solidarity which represents a greater harmony of interests between the workingman of America and his brothers abroad than between the American miner and his exploiting compatriot; a solidarity which fears not foreign invasion, because it is bringing all the workers to the point when they will say to their masters, "Go and do your own killing. We have done it long enough for you."

The proletariat of Europe has realized the great force of that solidarity and has, as a result, inaugurated a war against patriotism and its bloody spectre, militarism. Thousands of men fill the prisons of France, Germany, Russia and the Scandinavian countries because they dared to defy the ancient superstition.

America will have to follow suit. The spirit of militarism has already permeated all walks of life. Indeed, I am convinced that militarism is a greater danger here than anywhere else, because of the many bribes capitalism holds out to those whom it wishes to destroy.

The beginning has already been made in the schools. Children are trained in military tactics, the glory of military achievements extolled in the curriculum, and the youthful mind perverted to suit the government. Thus innocent boys are morally shanghaied into patriotism, and the military Moloch strides conquering through the nation.

When we have undermined the patriotic lie, we shall have cleared the path for the great structure where all shall be united into a universal brotherhood—a truly free society.

The sequel:

Emma Goldman lived out thirty embittered years after delivering this speech. In 1916 she was imprisoned briefly for publicly advocating birth control and in 1917 for the more serious crime of obstructing the draft.

In 1919 she was deported to Russia, but in 1921 left Russia because of dissatisfaction with communism, and emigrated to England, where in 1926 she married James Colton, a Welshman.

In 1924 she visited the United States for the last time on a speaking tour, permitted by the authorities on her pledge to avoid political discussion. The year 1936 found her actively participating in the Spanish civil war, but now she was old and tired. She died in Toronto, Canada, in 1940.

STEPHEN S. WISE

"Lincoln is become for us the test of human worth."

SPRINGFIELD, Ill., Feb. 12, 1914 —In the years since Abraham Lincoln's martyrdom, tributes by the thousand paid to him on countless occasions have made him seem at times almost unreal.

Today, however, at special exercises commemorating the centennial of Lincoln's birth, Rabbi Stephen S. Wise, the principal speaker chosen by the Lincoln Centennial Association, brought the Lincoln image into a true perspective because of a picture of him as less godlike and more the concept of the highest standard of manhood.

INSTEAD OF following Lincoln we too often strive to make it appear that he is following us. Instead of emulating him we too often venture to appropriate him. Instead of sitting at his feet as disciples, and humbly heeding the echoes of his lips, we attribute to him our own petty slogans.

Men and measures must not claim him for their own. He remains the standard by which to measure men. His views are not binding upon us, but his point of view will always be our inspiration. He would not be blindly followed who was open-minded and open-visioned. He did not solve all the problems of the future, but he did solve the problem of his own age. Ours is not to claim his name for our standards but his aim as our standard.

Lincoln is become for us the test of human worth, and we honor men in the measure in which they approach the absolute standard of Abraham Lincoln.

In his lifetime Lincoln was maligned and traduced, but detraction during a man's lifetime affords no test of his life's value nor offers any forecast of history's verdict. It would almost seem as if the glory of immortality were anticipated in the life of the great by detraction and denial whilst they yet lived. When a Lincoln-like man arises, let us recognize and fitly honor him. There could be no poorer way of honoring the memory of Lincoln than to assume, as we sometimes do, that the race of Lincolns has perished from the earth, and that we shall never look upon his like again.

One way to ensure the passing of the Lincolns is to assume that another Lincoln can nevermore arise. Would we find Lincoln today, we must not seek him in the guise of a rail-splitter, nor as a wielder of a backwoodman's axe, but as a mighty smiter of wrong in high places and low.

I have sometimes thought that the noblest tribute paid to the memory of Lincoln was the word of Phillips Brooks in Westminster Abbey when, pointing out that the test of the world to every nation was—show us your man—he declared that America names Lincoln. But the first word spoken after the death of Lincoln is truest and best—the word of Secretary of War Stanton, standing by the side of that scene of peace—"Now he belongs to the ages."

It was a verdict and prophecy alike, for Lincoln is not America's, he is the world's; he belongs not to our age, but to the ages; and yet, though he belongs to all time and to all peoples, he is our own, for he was an American.

WILLIAM A. (BILLY) SUNDAY

"I like to have a man have a definite experience in religion."

NEW YORK, N. Y., 1914—The era of religious revivalists—energetic preachers exhorting their au-ditors to "hit the sawdust trail" and emotionally get religion—has probably reached its peak in the mission of Billy Sunday, former baseball star who now fills baseball parks with his earthy preaching "performances."

Prior to entering the active field of religious work (he now is an ordained minister and holds the degree of Doctor of Divinity), Billy Sunday played major league baseball for eight years in Chicago, Pittsburgh and Philadel-phia. A notably fast base runner, he once was clocked at 14 seconds in circling a diamond. In 1891, he turned down a contract to play the following season for $3,500 and went to work as a junior secretary in the Y.M.C.A. at $83.33 a month.

Excerpts from an often-repeated Billy Sunday revival sermon follow:

THE TROUBLE with many men is that they have got just enough religion to make them miserable. If there is not joy in religion, you have got a leak in your religion. Some haven't religion enough to pay their debts. Would that I might have a hook and for every debt that you left unpaid I might jerk off a piece of clothing. If I did some of you fellows would have not anything on but a celluloid collar and a pair of socks.

Some of you have not got religion enough to have family prayer. Some of you haven't got religion enough to take the beer bottles out of your cellar and throw them in the alley. You haven't got religion enough to tell the proprietor of the red light, "No, you can't rent my house after the first of June"; to tell the saloon-keeper, "You can't have my house when the lease runs out"; and I want to tell you that the man who rents his property to a saloon-keeper is as low-down as the saloon-keeper. The trouble with you is that you are so taken up with business, with politics, with making money, with your lodges, and each and every one is so dependent on the other, that you are scared to death to come out and live clean-cut for God Almighty.

The matter with a lot of you people is that your religion is not complete. Why, I am almost afraid to make some folks laugh for fear that I will be arrested for breaking a costly piece of antique bric-a-brac.

To see some people you would think that the essential of orthodox Christianity is to have a face so long you could eat oatmeal out of the end of a gas pipe. Sister, that is not religion; I want to tell you that the smiling, happy, sunny-faced religion will win more people to Jesus Christ than the miserable old, grim-faced kind will in 10 years.

I pity anyone who can't laugh. There must be something wrong with their religion or their lives. The devil can't laugh.

I have seen women come down the aisle by the thousands, men who drank whiskey enough to sink a ship. I see fallen women come to the front by scores and hundreds, and I have seen them go away cleansed by the power of God.

I saw a woman that for 27 years had been proprietor of a disorderly house, and I saw her come down the aisle, close her doors, turn the girls out of her house, to live for God. I saw enough converted in one town where there were four disorderly houses to close their doors; they were empty; the girls have all fled home to their mothers.

Out in Iowa a fellow came to me and spread a napkin on the platform—a napkin as big as a tablecloth. He said, "I want a lot of shavings and sawdust."

"What for?"

"I'll tell you: I want enough to make a sofa pillow. Right here is where I knelt down and was converted, and my wife and four children, and my neighbors. I would like to have enough to make a sofa pillow to have something in the house to help me talk to God. I don't want to forget God, or that I was saved. Can you give me enough?"

I said: "Yes indeed, and if you want to make a mattress, all right, take it; and if you want enough of that tent to make a pair of breeches for all the boys, why take your scissors and cut it right out, if it will help you to keep your mind on God."

That is why I like to have people come down to the front and publicly acknowledge God. I like to have a man have a definite experience in religion—something to remember."

WOODROW WILSON

"Only a peace between equals can last."

WASHINGTON, D. C., Jan. 21, 1917—President Woodrow Wilson, in a speech before the Senate, today called upon the warring nations of Europe whose actions daily threaten to involve the United States in the conflict, to aim for a "peace without victory" patterned after a fashion upon the Monroe Doctrine as it operates in the Western Hemisphere.

Mr. Wilson specified that he spoke largely as an individual, but noted that as President of the United States he is—in this twilight of world conflict—today the only head of a major state free to speak his mind and policies openly without giving perhaps some advantage to an enemy.

His talk, in fact, seemed to some observers to constitute a flashback to the Virginia scholar noted, prior to his political career, as the president of one of the country's great universities, Princeton, and a writer who has won a touch of the promise of immortality in his historical works. Yet, he also must be today a President who sees in the threat of unrestricted warfare already broached by Germany, a public optimist and a private pessimist who reads in the daily despatches the threat of Armageddon overhanging America.

GENTLEMEN of the Senate: On the 18th of December last I addressed an identical note to the Governments of the nations now at war requesting them to state, more definitely than they had yet been stated by either group of belligerents, the terms upon which they would deem it possible to make peace. I spoke on behalf of humanity and of the rights of all neutral nations like our own, many of whose most vital interests the war puts in constant jeopardy.

The Central Powers united in a reply which stated merely that they were ready to meet their antagonists in conference to discuss terms of peace.

The Entente Powers have replied much more definitely, and have stated, in general terms, indeed, but with sufficient definiteness to imply details, the arrangements, guarantees, and acts of reparation which they deem to be the indispensable conditions of a satisfactory settlement.

We are that much nearer a definite discussion of the peace which shall end the present war.

I have sought this opportunity to address you because I thought that I owed it to you, as the council associated with me in the final determination of our international obligations, to disclose to you without reserve the thought and purpose that have been taking form in my mind in regard to the duty of our Government in those days to come when it will be necessary to lay afresh and upon a new plan the foundations of peace among the nations.

It is inconceivable that the people of the United States should play no part in that great enterprise. To take part in such a service will be the opportunity for which they have sought to prepare themselves by the very principles and purposes of their polity and the approved practices of their Government, ever since the days when they set up a new nation in the high and honorable hope that it might in all that it was and did show mankind the way to liberty. They cannot, in honor, withhold the service to which they are now about to be challenged. They do not wish to withold it. But they owe it to themselves and to the other nations of the world to state the conditions under which they will feel free to render it.

That service is nothing less than this—to add their authority and their power to the authority and force of other nations to guarantee peace and justice throughout the world.

Is the present war a struggle for a just and secure peace or only for a new balance of power? If it be only a struggle for a new balance of power, who will guarantee, who can guarantee, the stable equilibrium of the new arrangement? Only a tranquil Europe can be a stable Europe. There must be not only a balance of power, but a community of power; not organized rivalries, but an organized common peace.

Fortunately, we have received very explicit assurances on this point. The statesmen of both of the groups of nations, now arrayed against one another, have said, in terms that could not be misinterpreted, that it was no part of the purpose they had in mind to crush their antagonists. But the implications of these assurances may not be equally clear to all, may not be the same on both sides of the water. I think it will be serviceable if I attempt to set forth what we understand them to be.

They imply first of all that it must be a peace without victory. It is not pleasant to say this. I beg that I may be permitted to put my own interpretation upon it and that it may be understood that no other interpretation was in my thought. I am seeking only to face realities and to face them without soft concealments. Victory would mean peace forced upon the loser, a victor's terms imposed upon the vanquished. It would be accepted in humiliation, under duress, at an intolerable sacrifice, and would leave a sting, a resentment, a bitter memory, upon which terms of peace would rest, not permanently, but only as upon quicksand.

Only a peace between equals can last; only a peace the very principle of which is equality and a common participation in a common benefit.

I have spoken upon these great matters without reserve, and with the utmost explicitness because it has seemed to me to be necessary if the world's yearning desire for peace was anywhere to find free voice and utterance. Perhaps I am the only person in high authority among all the peoples of the world who is at liberty to speak and hold nothing back. I am speaking as an individual, and yet I am speaking also, of course, as the responsible head of a great Government, and I feel confident that I have said what the people of the United States would wish me to say.

May I not add that I hope and believe that I am, in effect, speaking for liberals and friends of humanity in every nation and of every program of liberty? I would fain believe that I am speaking for the silent mass of mankind everywhere who have as yet had no place or opportunity to speak their real hearts out concerning the death and ruin they see to have come already upon the persons and the homes they hold most dear.

And in holding out the expectation that the people and the Government of the United States will join the other civilized nations of the world in guaranteeing the permanence of peace upon such terms as I have named, I speak with the greater boldness and confidence because it is clear to every man who can think that there is in this promise no breach in either our traditions or our policy as a nation, but a fulfillment rather of all that we have professed or striven for.

I am proposing, as it were, that the nations should with one accord adopt the doctrine of President Monroe as the doctrine of the world: That no nation should seek to extend its policy over any other nation or people, but that every people should be left free to determine its own policy, its own way of development, unhindered, unthreatened, unafraid, the little along with the great and powerful.

I am proposing that all nations henceforth avoid entangling alliances which would draw them into competition of power, catch them in a net of intrigue and selfish rivalry, and disturb their own affairs with influences intruded from without. There is no entangling alliance in a concert of power. When all unite to act in the same sense and with the same purpose, all act in the common interest and are free to live their own lives under a common protection.

I am proposing government by the consent of the governed; that freedom of the seas which in international conference after conference representatives of the United States have urged with the eloquence of those who are the convinced disciples of liberty; and that moderation of armaments which makes of armies and navies a power for order merely, not an instrument of aggression or of selfish violence.

These are American principles, American policies. We can stand for no others. And they are also the principles and policies of forward-looking men and women everywhere, of every modern nation, of every enlightened community. They are the principles of mankind, and must prevail.

The sequel:

The sequel was blighted hope, of course.

Within three months, unrestricted submarine warfare put into practice by Germany and other rebuffs of the peaceful offers of good offices by the United States had changed this country from a "neutral" into a combatant.

But the thoughts put forth by Wilson still live, running as a refrain through much of the subsequent expression of democratic hopes.

WOODROW WILSON

". . . we will not choose the path of submission and
suffer the most sacred rights of our nation and our
people to be ignored and violated."

WASHINGTON, D. C., April 2, 1917—Appearing before a Joint Session of the Congress, listening in hushed expectancy to hear the words leading up to a conclusion which came as a surprise to no one, Woodrow Wilson today exercised the ultimate responsibility of the Presidency by plunging the United States into the war that has laid waste much of Europe and pushed the Allied friendly powers to the point of desperation.

As with so many dramatic steps in the 150-year history of the United States, Mr. Wilson's declaration involved an acceptance of great events that already had dictated their own conclusion, rather than a broaching of new ventures. In his audience were men who remembered the Civil War and the Spanish-American War.

As a historian and student, a distinguished Virginian by birth, former President of the University of Princeton and Governor of New Jersey, he was as keenly aware as any other of the meaning of this step, the irrevocable commitment of the United States to its fate in a world where dominance beckons it.

But he attempted in every paragraph of this long message to lay down for the permanent record the reluctant nature of the step: that it is purely defensive and not predatory; that this is a peaceful country goaded to extremity; that no hate for the peoples of the enemy governments enters into the great decision.

Sketching briefly what everyone already knew—the start of unrestricted submarine warfare by the Central Powers and the violation of our neutrality in flagrant manner—President Wilson said that our involvement beside our new Allies would be complete until victory is assured.

"We are at the beginning of an age," he declared, "in which it will be insisted that the same standards of conduct and of responsibility for wrong done shall be observed among nations and their governments that are observed among the individual citizens of the civilized states."

WHEN I addressed the Congress on the twenty-sixth of February last I thought that it would suffice to assert our neutral rights with arms, our right to use the seas against unlawful interference, our right to keep our people safe against unlawful violence. But armed neutrality, it now appears, is impracticable . . . it is practically certain to draw us into the war without either the rights or the effectiveness of belligerents. There is one choice we cannot make, we are incapable of making; we will not choose the path of submission and suffer the most sacred rights of our nation and our people to be ignored or violated. The wrongs against which we now array ourselves are no common wrongs; they cut to the very roots of human life.

With a profound sense of the solemn and even tragical character of the step I am taking and of the grave responsibilities which it involves, but in unhesitating obedience to what I deem my constitutional duty, I advise that the Congress declare the recent course of the Imperial German Government to be in fact nothing less than war against the Government and people of the United States; that it formally accept the status of belligerent which has thus been thrust upon it; and that it take immediate steps not only to put the country in a more thorough state of defense, but also to exert all its power and employ all its resources to bring the Government of the German Empire to terms and end the war.

What this will involve is clear. It will involve the utmost practicable cooperation in counsel and action with the governments now at war with Germany, and, as incident to that, the extension to those governments of the most liberal financial credits, in order that our resources may so far as possible be added to theirs. It will involve the organization and mobilization of all the material resources of the country to supply the materials of war and serve the incidental needs of the nation in the most abundant and yet the most economical and efficient way possible.

It will involve the immediate full equipment of the navy in all respects but particularly in supplying it with the best means of dealing with the enemy's submarines. It will involve the immediate addition to the armed forces of the United States already provided for by law in case of war of at least five hundred thousand men, who should, in my opinion, be chosen upon the principle of universal liability to service, and also the authorization of subsequent additional increments of equal force so soon as they may be needed and can be handled in training. It will involve also, of course, the granting of adequate credits to the Government, sustained, I hope, so far as they can equitably be sustained by the present generation, by well-conceived taxation. . . .

While we do these things, these deeply momentous things, let us be very clear, and make very clear to all the world, what our motives and our objects are. My own thought has not been driven from its habitual and normal course by the unhappy events of the last two months. . . .

We have no quarrel with the German people. We have no feeling toward them but one of sympathy and friendship. It was not upon their impulse that their government acted in entering this war. It was not with their previous knowledge or approval. It was a war determined upon as wars used to be determined upon in the old, unhappy days when peoples were nowhere consulted by their rulers and wars were provoked and waged in the interest of dynasties or of little groups of ambitious men who were accustomed to use their fellow-men as pawns and tools. . . .

A steadfast concert for peace can never be maintained except by a partnership of democratic nations. No autocratic government could be trusted to keep faith within it or observe its covenants. It must be a league of honor, a partnership of opinion. Intrigue would eat its vitals away; the plottings of inner circles who could plan what they would and render account to no one would be a corruption seated at its very heart. Only free peoples can hold their purpose and their honor steady to a common end and prefer the interests of mankind to any narrow interest of their own.

The sequel:

While these words laid down the humane and intellectual background of the reasoning that guided the United States into its first great involvement in foreign wars, the question thereafter remained: What comes afterward, and how will victory be exploited, in line with these high principles?

In reply to that question, the President again went before a Joint Session of the Congress nine months later to state a program.

WOODROW WILSON

"The program of the world's peace, therefore, is our program."

WASHINGTON, D. C., Jan. 8, 1918—President Woodrow Wilson today laid before the Congress a peace program, predicated on ultimate victory in this present war, containing fourteen points whose keystone is the proposal that peace see the formation of an association of nations guaranteeing the political and territorial freedom of every country.

This message, delivered in person before an assemblage as respectful as that which heard the Declaration of War last April, but now more confident as the result of the mustering of America's great resources, comes in the middle of a period mingling new threats for prolongation of the war with reasons for confidence in victory.

On the debit side, Russia is negotiating with the Germans for peace, with the prospect of thus freeing great armies for movement into the western theatre where the conclusion of the war ultimately must occur. On the credit side, American troops are now beginning to move in force to Europe, the country is truly united in this war effort, and a combination of vast new supplies and raised morale has stiffened the will and the vigor of Great Britain and France.

"There is no confusion of counsel among the adversaries of the Central Powers," President Wilson could state with candor, "no uncertainty of principle, no vagueness of detail."

Our war aims, as he delineated them, are simple: complete and unrestrained freeing of conquered peoples, granting of freedom to heretofore conquered races such as the Poles, and machinery to safeguard this peace. The last point is No. 14 and by far the greatest of all of the "points."

"A general association of nations must be formed under special covenants for the purpose of affording mutual guarantees of political independence and territorial integrity to great and small states alike."

While this statement will be linked for the future to the "Fourteen Points," observers recalled its origin, in expressed thought, long before the United States became a belligerent. It was on May 27, 1916, at a White House meeting of the now forgotten League to Enforce Peace that the President spoke the same thoughts as he declaimed the organization's proposals, written under the chairmanship of former President William Howard Taft—"an universal association of the nations to maintain the inviolate security of the highway of the seas for the common and unhindered use of all the nations of the world, and to prevent any war begun either contrary to treaty covenants or without warning and full submission of the causes to the opinion of the world—a virtual guarantee of territorial integrity and political independence."

sentiments with specific war aims, the more important part of the President's message, in the view of many observers, was the spirit of force and power for ideals that the elderly and scholarly war leader wove into his statement.

While today's speech coupled these

. . . IT WILL be our wish and purpose that the processes of peace, when they are begun, shall be absolutely open, and that they shall involve and permit henceforth no secret understandings of any kind. The day of conquest and aggrandizement is gone by; so is also the day of secret covenants entered into in the interest of particular Governments and likely at some unlooked-for moment to upset the peace of the world. It is this happy fact, now clear to the view of every public man whose thoughts do not still linger in an age that is dead and gone, which makes it possible for every nation whose purposes are consistent with justice and the peace of the world to avow now or at any other time the objects it has in view.

We entered this war because violations of right had occurred which touched us to the quick and made the life of our own people impossible unless they were corrected and the world secured once for all against their recurrence. What we demand in this war, therefore, is nothing peculiar to ourselves. It is that the world be made fit and safe to live in; and particularly that it be made safe for every peace-loving nation which, like our own, wishes to live its own life, determine its own institutions, be assured of justice and fair dealings by the other peoples of the world, as against force and selfish aggression. All of the peoples of the world are in effect partners in this interest and for our own part we see very clearly that unless justice be done to others it will not be done to us. . . .

In regard to these essential rectifications of wrong and assertions of rights, we feel ourselves to be intimate partners of all the Governments and peoples associated together against the imperialists. We cannot be separated in interest or divided in purpose. We stand together until the end.

For such arrangements and covenants we are willing to fight and to continue to fight until they are achieved; but only because we wish the right to prevail and desire a just and stable peace, such as can be secured only by removing the chief provocations to war, which this program does remove. We have no jealousy of German greatness, and there is nothing in this program that impairs it. We grudge her no achievement or distinction of learning or of pacific enterprise such as have made her record very bright and very enviable. We do not wish to injure her or to block in any way her legitimate influence or power. We do not wish to fight her either with arms or with hostile arrangements of trade, if she is willing to associate herself with us and the other peace-loving nations of the world in covenants of justice and law and fair dealing. We wish her only to accept a place of equality among the peoples of the world—the new world in which we now live—instead of a place of mastery.

Neither do we presume to suggest to her any alteration or modification of her institutions. But it is necessary, we must frankly say, and necessary as a preliminary to any intelligent dealings with her on our part, that we should know whom her spokesmen speak for when they speak to us, whether for the Reichstag majority or for the military party and the men whose creed is imperial domination.

We have spoken now, surely, in terms too concrete to admit of any further doubt or question. An evident principle runs through the whole program I have outlined. It is the principle of justice to all peoples and nationalities, and their right to live on equal terms of liberty and safety with one another, whether they be strong or weak. Unless this principle be made its foundation, no part of the structure of international justice can stand.

The people of the United States could act upon no other principle, and to the vindication of this principle they are willing to devote their lives, their honor and everything that they possess. The moral climax of this, the culminating and final war for human liberty, has come, and they are ready to put their own strength, their own integrity and devotion to the test.

The sequel:

Victory came that year, in November, at a price which could not be reckoned at the time. There was irony in the fact that two generations later, the Russian nation, whose plight primarily prompted the utterance of this program in January of 1917, would be the pawn of, and supporting force behind, another form of conquest ironically called a "cold war."

But in all wars there come to nations certain high points of inspiration—or at least to their leaders—when the aims of victory seem to give their framers some kinship with the gods.

Wilson felt himself strong enough and clever enough to carry his points to the battles of the conference table, despite openly expressed doubts that came into public debate the instant the shooting stopped in Europe. And this he did.

EUGENE V. DEBS

"I am prepared to receive your sentence."

CHICAGO, Ill., Sept., 1918—Eugene V. Debs, founder of the Socialist party and nationally known labor leader, became the first man who had run as a candidate for the Presidency at the head of a recognized party to be sent to prison for openly violating the laws of our government.

He was found guilty of violating the Espionage Act, through his leadership of the Socialist party's obstruction of the draft as well as the whole war effort in 1917–18.

Debs actually was no stranger to prison; in 1895 he served six months as a result of leadership of a strike in Illinois which was put down by troops sent into that State by President Cleveland. His life has been a stormy one, marked by such highlights as labor organizing work, establishment of the radical International Workmen of the World, and finally of the more conservative Socialist party.

In a speech before receiving sentence on this critical charge of which he has been found guilty, the veteran agitator said flatly: "I am opposed to the form of our present Government; and I am opposed to the social system in which we live."

For this he was sentenced to serve 10 years in prison.

. . . IF THE law under which I have been convicted is a good law, then there is no reason why sentence should not be pronounced upon me. I listened to all that was said in this court in support and justification of this law, but my mind remains unchanged. I look upon it as a despotic enactment in flagrant conflict with democratic principles and with the spirit of free institutions.

Your Honor, I have stated in this court that I am opposed to the form of our present Government; that I am opposed to the social system in which we live; that I believed in the change of both—but by perfectly peaceable and orderly means.

I believe, Your Honor, in common with all Socialists, that this nation ought to own and control its industries. I believe, as all Socialists do, that all things that are jointly needed and used ought to be jointly owned—that industry, the basis of life, instead of being the private property of the few and operated for their en-richment, ought to be the common property of all, democratically administered in the interest of all.

I have been accused, Your Honor, of being an enemy of the soldier. I hope I am laying no flattering unction to my soul when I say that I don't believe the soldier has a more sympathetic friend than I am. If I had my way there would be no soldiers. But I realize the sacrifice they are making, Your Honor. I can think of them. I can feel for them. I can sympathize with them. That is one of the reasons why I have been doing what little has been in my power to bring about a condition of affairs in this country worthy of the sacrifices they have made and that they are now making in its behalf.

Your Honor, I wish to make acknowledgment of my thanks to the counsel for the defense. They have not only defended me with exceptional legal ability, but with a personal attachment and devotion of which I am deeply sensible, and which I can never forget.

Your Honor, I ask no mercy. I plead for no immunity. I realize that finally the right must prevail. I never more clearly compre-hended than now the great struggle between the powers of greed on the one hand and upon the other the rising hosts of freedom.

I can see the dawn of a better day of humanity. The people are awakening. In due course of time they will come to their own.

When the mariner, sailing over tropic seas, looks for relief from his weary watch, he turns his eyes toward the Southern Cross, burning luridly above the tempest-tossed ocean. As the midnight approaches, the Southern Cross begins to bend, and the whirling worlds change their places, and with starry finger-points the Almighty marks the passage of time upon the dial of the universe, and though no bell may beat the glad tidings, the lookout knows that the midnight is passing—that relief and rest are close at hand.

Let the people take heart and hope everywhere, for the cross is bending, the midnight is passing, and joy cometh with the morning.

Your Honor, I thank you, and I thank all of this court for their courtesy, for their kindness, which I shall remember always.

I am prepared to receive your sentence.

The sequel:

Eugene Debs was sent to prison to serve his sentence, and he remained in prison until pardoned by President Harding in a period when pardons were granted generally to most persons who for non-violent pacifist activities had been convicted. While still in prison, Debs stood in the 1920 elections as candidate for President, and polled more than 900,-000 votes.

However, his rights of citizenship were not restored and his career and health both were broken. Soon leadership of the Socialist party passed to Norman Thomas, who over the years reshaped it into a more conservative pattern, and whose support of World War II is recorded in other pages of this volume. Debs died in 1926.

WOODROW WILSON

". . . to make permanent arrangements that justice shall be rendered and peace maintained."

VERSAILLES, France, Jan. 25, 1919—Standing before the delegates of a score of countries, in the Hall of Mirrors in the most beautiful palace left to history by the Bourbons of France, a President who had lost the support of his own country today outlined a dream of future world security based upon an idealism for which it is doubtful whether the world is ready.

The President is Woodrow Wilson, wartime leader of a victorious United States that in the past two years has become a major world power. As the "architect of allied victory" he is in world affairs the peer or superior of the European giants with whom he walks—Prime Minister David Lloyd George and Premiers Clemenceau and Orlando. Yet at home he saw two months ago his own country, voting in an interim election, swamp his own party by the election of majorities from the opposition party—the Republican—to both the Senate and the House.

But if this is his swan song, it is magnificent, because he projected today the final argument in a world forum for the League of Nations, an idea first embodied in a program written before the United States entered the war and later incorporated in what are now known around the world as the Fourteen Points. As he painted it, the League of Nations will rise above national governments, and be the guardian of liberty for the people of the world.

"We must concert our best judgment," said the drawling, sparse-figured man in Prince Albert coat, slightly stooped and peering through thick-lensed eyeglasses, "to make the League of Nations a vital thing— not merely a formal thing, not an oc-casional thing, not a thing sometimes called into life to meet an exigency, but always functioning in watchful attendance upon the interests of the nations, and that its continuity should be a vital continuity."

The delegations listened in respectful silence to Mr. Wilson, but with some mental reservations as to his latter arguments. How strong, many were asking by evening, is the support represented by the President of the United States? Or is his own enthusiasm carrying him out of the depths of realism?

There are other questions, too, principally as to how to fit together this idealistic statement with the concerted arrangements by Clemenceau and Lloyd George who, while paying public lip-service to the League, are using it as an obvious cloak to cover widely differing attitudes over reparations from Germany? And what is the attitude of the Russian Bear, now thrashing about in a titanic struggle between opposing factions, with the Bolsheviks daily gaining greater force in government?

WE HAVE assembled here for the purpose of doing very much more than making the present settlements that are necessary. We are assembled under very peculiar conditions of world opinion. I may say, without straining the point, that we are not representatives of governments, but representatives of peoples. It will not suffice to satisfy governmental circles anywhere. It is necessary that we should satisfy the opinion of mankind. . . .

It is a solemn obligation on our part, therefore, to make permanent arrangements that justice shall be rendered and peace maintained. This is the central object of our meeting. Settlements may be temporary, but the action of the nations in the interest of peace and justice must be permanent. We can set up permanent processes. We may not be able to set up permanent decisions. Therefore, it seems to me that we must take, so far as we can, a picture of the world into our minds.

Is it not a startling circumstance, for one thing, that the great discoveries of science, that the quiet studies of men in laboratories, that the thoughtful developments which have taken place in quiet lecture-rooms, have now been turned to the destruction of civilization? The powers of destruction have not so much multiplied as gained facility. The enemy whom we have just overcome had at his seats of learning some of the principle centers of scientific study and discovery, and he used them in order to make destruction sudden and complete; and only the watchful, continuous co-operation of men can see to it that science, as well as armed men, is kept within the harness of civilization.

In a sense, the United States is less interested in this subject than the other nations here assembled. With her great territory and her extensive sea borders, it is less likely that the United States should suffer from the attack of enemies than that many of the other nations here should suffer; and the ardor of the United States—for it is a very deep and genuine ardor—for the society of nations is not an ardor springing out of fear or apprehension, but an ardor springing out of the ideals which have come to consciousness in this war. In coming into this war the United States never for a moment thought that she was intervening in the politics of Europe, or the politics of Asia, or the politics of any part of the world. Her thought was that all the world had now become conscious that there was a single cause which turned upon the issues of this war. That was the cause of justice and of liberty for men of every kind and place. Therefore, the United States would feel that her part in this war had been played in vain if there ensued upon it a body of European settlements. She would feel that she could not take part in guaranteeing those European settlements unless that guaranty involved the continuous superintendence of the peace of the world by the associated nations of the world.

Therefore, it seems to me that we must concert our best judgment in order to make this League of Nations a vital thing—not merely a formal thing, not an occasional thing, not a thing sometimes called into life to meet an exigency, but always functioning in watchful attendance upon the interests of the nations, and that its continuity should be a vital continuity. . . .

. . . Gentlemen, the select classes of mankind are no longer the governors of mankind. The fortunes of mankind are now in the hands of the plain people of the whole world. Satisfy them, and you have not only justified their confidence, but established peace. Fail to satisfy them, and no arrangement that you can make will either set up or steady the peace of the world.

You can imagine, gentlemen, I dare say, the sentiments and the purpose with which representatives of the United States support this great project for a League of Nations. We regard it as the keystone of the whole program which expressed our purposes and ideals in this war and which the associated nations accepted as the basis of the settlement. If we return to the United States without having made every effort in our power to realize this program, we should return to meet the merited scorn of our fellow-citizens. For they are a body that constitutes a great democracy. They expect their leaders to speak their thoughts and no private purpose of their own. They expect their representatives to be their servants. We have no choice but to obey their mandate. But it is with the greatest enthusiasm and pleasure that we accept that mandate; and because this is the keystone of the whole fabric, we have pledged our every purpose to it, as we have to every item of the fabric. We would not dare abate a single item of the program which constitutes our instruction. We would not dare compromise upon any matter as the champion of this thing—this peace of the world, this attitude of justice, this principle that we are the masters of no people, but are here to see that every people in the world shall choose its own masters and govern its own destinies, not as we wish but as it wishes. We are here to see, in short, that the very foundations of this war are swept away.

Those foundations were the private choice of small coteries of civil rulers and military staffs. Those foundations were the agression of great powers upon small. Those foundations were the holding together of empires of unwilling subjects by the duress of arms. Those foundations were the power of small bodies of men to work their will and use mankind as pawns in a game. And nothing less than the emancipation of the world from these things will accomplish peace. . . .

The sequel:

In retrospect, it is evident that the ideals of the League of Nations might have fared better had their utterance been less of a personal venture by President Wilson.

His determination carried him past the point of the all-important element of willingness to negotiate that is the essence of success in putting over ideas molded in the great design.

On his return to Washington, when he laid the projected peace treaty incorporating the league idea before the new powers in Congress, Wilson so antagonized these Republicans, including the now mature Henry Cabot Lodge with his demand for ratification of the treaty without the "crossing of a t or the dotting of an i," that he pronounced the death sentence for his own idea.

In the fall of 1919, Wilson set forth on a tour of the country to rescue his child and, by the very force of public opinion, to overcome the opposition of the Senate Republican majority to it. But his mission was foredoomed, and so was his public career.

On September 25, 1919, while speaking at Pueblo, Colorado, Wilson collapsed.

Home demobilization was not yet accomplished, and the unscrambling of a war-torn world was hardly started. But Wilson there and then passed from the effective stage of political leadership.

Within two months, other persons would be battling his ideas, using as the principal lever of argument the contention that the United States, if it subscribed to the League, would sacrifice its own independence to the whims of an international combine.

In this debate, no voice carried more weight than that of William E. Borah.

WILLIAM EDGAR BORAH

*"Peace upon any other basis than national
independence . . . is fit only for slaves."*
(On the League of Nations.)

WASHINGTON, D. C., Nov. 19, 1919—The death sentence of the League of Nations—however much debate may be protracted—was written here today by one towering, lion-maned orator from the wide spaces of Idaho, who tore to shreds with the whip of national pride the gossamer fabric woven by Woodrow Wilson into the pattern of the League.

It is too soon to know whether Borah did the right or the wrong thing, but of his sincerity there can be no doubt. As an orator, he seemed to have been mustering all the force of experience, since he took his seat in the Senate in 1907, for this day.

As he spoke, he knew that for a generation more, at least, he would be reviled in some quarters as well as venerated in others, for the stand he bespoke. But he obviously did not care any more for the expected criticism than for the prospective adulation. To many, he recalled the personality displayed in other argu-

ments and in other causes by William Jennings Bryan, arch political opponent of Borah but still best known today for his resignation as Woodrow Wilson's Secretary of State in protest against entry by the United States into the steps precedent to formal participation in the late World War.

To pluck any single quotation from Borah's speech would be only to give a fragment out of context. The text is given at some length because it sums up all the replies of his colleagues to the many speeches heretofore given by the spokesman for the master plan.

Excerpts from the speech, delivered in an historical moment before packed galleries that included alike Mrs. Woodrow Wilson, on a rare absence from her stricken husband's side, and Mrs. Nicholas Longworth, wife of the Speaker of the House and daughter of the late President Theodore Roosevelt who died earlier this year, embittered by Wilson's policies, follow:

IF THE league includes the affairs of the world, does it not include the affairs of all the world? Is there any limitation on the jurisdiction of the council or of the assembly upon the question of peace or war? Does it not have now, under the reservations, the same as it had before, the power to deal with all matters of peace or war throughout the entire world? How shall you keep from meddling in the affairs of Europe or keep Europe from meddling in the affairs of America?

Mr. President, there is another and even more commanding reason why I shall record my vote against this treaty. It imperils what I conceive to be the underlying, the very first principles of this Republic. It is in conflict with the right of our people to govern themselves free from all restraint, legal or moral, of foreign powers. It challenges every tenet of my political faith. If this faith were one of my contriving, if I stood here to assert principles of government of my own evolving, I might well be charged with intolerable presumption, for we all recognize the ability of those who urge a different course. But I offer in justification of my course nothing of my own—save the deep and abiding reverence I have for those whose policies I humbly but most ardently support. I claim no merit save fidelity to American principles and devotion to American ideals as they were wrought out from time to time by those who built the Republic and as they have extended and maintained throughout these years. In opposing the treaty I do nothing more than decline to renounce and tear out of my life the sacred traditions which throughout fifty years have been translated into my whole intellectual and moral being. I will not, I cannot, give up my belief that America must, not alone for the happiness of her own people, but for the moral guidance and greater contentment of the world, be permitted to live her own life. Next to the tie which binds a man to his God is the tie which binds a man to his country, and all schemes, all plans, however ambitious and fascinating they seem in their proposal, but which would embarrass or entangle and impede or shackle her sovereign will, which would compromise her freedom of action, I unhesitatingly put behind me.

Sir, we are told that this treaty means peace. Even so, I would not pay the price. Would you purchase peace at the cost of any part of our independence? We could have had peace in 1776—the price was high, but we could have had it. James Otis, Sam Adams, Hancock, and Warren were surrounded by those who urged peace and British rule. All through the long and trying struggle, particularly when the clouds of adversity lowered upon the cause there was a cry of peace—let us have peace. We could have had peace in 1860; Lincoln was counseled by men of great influence and accredited wisdom to let our brothers—and thank heaven, they are brothers—depart in peace. But the tender, loving Lincoln, bending under the fearful weight of impending civil war, an apostle of peace, refused to pay the price, and a reunited country will praise his name forevermore—bless it because he refused peace at the price of national honor and national integrity. Peace upon any other basis than national independence, peace purchased at the cost of any part of our national integrity, is fit only for slaves, and even when purchased at such a price it is a delusion, for it cannot last.

But your treaty does not mean peace—far, very far, from it. If we are to judge the future by the past it means war. Is there any guaranty of peace other than the guaranty which comes of the control of the war-making power by the people? Yet what great rule of democracy does the treaty leave unassailed? The people in whose keeping alone you can safely lodge the power of peace or war nowhere, at no time and in no place, have any voice in this scheme for world peace. Autocracy which has bathed the world in blood for centuries reigns supreme. Democracy is ever excluded. This, you say, means peace.

Can you hope for peace when love of country is disregarded in your scheme, when the spirit of nationality is rejected, scoffed at? Yet what law of that moving and mysterious force does your treaty not deny? With a ruthlessness unparalleled your treaty in a dozen instances runs counter to the divine law of nationality. Peoples who speak the same language, kneel at the same ancestral tombs, moved by the same traditions, animated by a common hope, are torn asunder, broken in pieces, divided, and parceled out to antagonistic nations. And this you call justice. This, you cry, means peace. Peoples who have dreamed of independence, struggled and been patient, sacrificed and been hopeful, peoples who were told that through this Peace Conference they should realize the aspirations of centuries, have again had their hopes dashed to earth. One of the most striking and commanding figures in this war, soldier and statesman, turned away from the peace table at Versailles declaring to the world, "The promise of the new life, the victory of the great humane ideals, for which the peoples have shed their blood and given their treasure without stint, the fulfillment of their aspirations toward a new international order and a fairer and better world are not written into the treaty." No; your treaty means injustice. It means slavery. It means war. And to all this you ask this Republic to become a party. You ask it to abandon the creed under which it has grown to power and accept the creed of autocracy, the creed of repression and force.

Mr. President, I turn from this scheme based upon force to another scheme, planned one hundred and forty-three years ago in old Independence Hall, in the city of Philadelphia, based upon liberty. I like it better. I have become so accustomed to believe in it that it is difficult for me to reject it out of hand. I have difficulty in subscribing to the new creed of oppression, the creed of dominant and subject peoples. I feel a reluctance to give up the belief that all men are created equal—the eternal principle in government that all governments derive their just powers from the consent of the governed. I cannot get my consent to exchange the doctrine of George Washington for the doctrine of Frederick the Great translated into mendacious phrases of peace. I go back to that serene and masterful soul who pointed the way to power and glory for the new and then weak Republic, and whose teachings and admonitions even in our majesty and dominance we dare not disregard.

I know well the answer to my contention. It has been piped about of late from a thousand sources—venal sources, disloyal sources, sinister sources—that Washington's wisdom was of his day only and that his teachings are out of fashion—things long since sent to the scrap heap of history—that while he was great in character and noble in soul he was untrained in the arts of statecraft and unlearned in the science of government. The puny demagogue, the barren editor, the sterile professor now vie with each other in apologizing for the temporary and commonplace expedients which the Father of our Country felt constrained to adopt in building a republic!

What is the test of statesmanship? Is it the formation of theories, the utterance of abstract and incontrovertible truths, or is it the capacity and the power to give to a people that concrete thing called liberty, that vital and indispensable thing in human happiness called free institutions and to establish over all and above all the blessed and eternal reign of order and law? If this be the test, where shall we find another whose name is entitled to be written beside the name of Washington? His judgment and poise in the hour of turmoil and peril, his courage and vision in times of adversity, his firm grasp of fundamental principles, his almost inspired power to penetrate the future and read there the result, the effect of policies, have never been excelled, if equaled, by any of the world's commonwealth builders. Peter the Great, William the Silent, and Cromwell the Protector, these and these alone perhaps are to be associated with his name as the builders of States and the founders of governments. But in exaltation of moral purpose, in the unselfish character of his work, in the durability of his policies, in the permanency of the institutions which he more than any one else called into effect, his service to mankind stands out separate and apart in a class by itself. The works of these other great builders, where are they now? But the work of Washington is still the most potent influence for the advancements of civilization and the freedom of the race.

Reflect for a moment over his achievements. He led the Revolutionary Army to victory. He was the very first to suggest a union instead of a confederacy. He presided over and counseled with great wisdom the convention which framed the Constitution. He guided the Government through its first perilous years. He gave dignity and stability and honor to that which was looked upon by the world as a passing experiment, and finally, my friends, as his own peculiar and particular contribution to the happiness of his countrymen and to the cause of the Republic, he gave us his great foreign policy under which we have lived and prospered and strengthened for nearly a century and a half. This policy is the most sublime confirmation of his genius as a statesman. It was then, and now is, an indispensable part of our whole scheme of government. It is today a vital, indispensable element in our entire plan, purpose, and mission as a nation. To abandon it is nothing less than a betrayal of the American people. I say betrayal deliberately, in view of the suffering and the sacrifice which will follow in the wake of such a course.

But under the stress and strain of these extraordinary days, when strong men are being swept down by the onrushing forces of disorder and change, when the most sacred things of life, the most cherished hopes of a Christian world seem to yield to the mad forces of discontent—just such days as Washington passed through when the mobs of Paris, wild with new liberty and drunk with power, challenged the established institutions of all the world, but his steadfast soul was unshaken—under these conditions come again we are about to abandon this policy so essential to our happiness and tranquillity as a people and our stability as a Government. No leader with his commanding influence and his unquailing courage stands forth to stem the current. But what no leader can or will do, experience, bitter experience, and the people of this country in whose keeping, after all, thank God, is the Republic, will ultimately do. If we abandon his leadership and teachings, we will go back. We will return to this policy. Americanism shall not, cannot die. We may go back in sackcloth and ashes, but we will return to the faith of the fathers. America will live her own life. The independence of this Republic will have its defenders. Thousands have suffered and died for it, and their sons and daughters are not of the breed who will be betrayed into the hands of foreigners. The noble face of the Father of his Country, so familiar to every boy and girl, looking out from the walls of the capitol in stern reproach, will call those who come here for public service to a reckoning. The people of our beloved country will finally speak, and we will return to the policy which we now abandon. America, disenthralled and free, in spite of all these things, will continue her mission in the cause of peace, of freedom, and of civilization.

The sequel:

If there was a winner or loser in this contest, the victory was Borah's.

For 21 more years he held a dominant position in the Senate, achieving the seniority in 1925 by which he could become, under Republican organization, chairman of the Foreign Relations Committee of the Senate.

In this commanding position he likewise defeated attempts by his own party leadership—exerted by

Presidents Calvin Coolidge and Herbert Hoover—to obtain adherence by the United States to the World Court.

On the other hand, he sparked the idea for the so-called Washington Conference on naval disarmament, held in 1921–22, and the five year "naval holiday" adopted by the Hoover Administration in 1931.

When Franklin D. Roosevelt won the Presidency, and with it the Democratic party again captured control of the Congress, Borah had to relinquish in 1933 his powerful committee chairmanship, but even in the shadows as a minority spokesman he rose to roar and growl his opposition on such occasions as promised either to enlarge the control of the Federal Government over the States or to involve the United States in foreign intrigues.

He died in 1940, after 33 years in the Senate. By that time, the League of Nations lay in another grave, dug by its erstwhile supporters. In their widowhood Mrs. Wilson and Mrs. Borah ("Little Borah" as she called herself) were the closest of friends, and inseparable companions.

CLARENCE S. DARROW

"I am pleading that we overcome cruelty with kindness and hatred with love."

CHICAGO, Ill., 1924—Clarence S. Darrow, at 65 years of age the most famous living advocate for the defense in criminal cases, who can boast that he has never seen a client executed, delivered here an appeal for mercy in concluding the most sensational murder trial of the century.

Mr. Darrow strove (and successfully) to save from the gallows the youths Loeb and Leopold, both sons of relatively prominent Chicago families, who confessedly carried out the crime of mutilating and murdering a boy named Bobby Franks.

The trial lasted for months, not on the basis of guilt or innocence because it was preceded by a full confession in court, but on the sole question whether the youths should be hanged or imprisoned.

In his closing argument and plea to the court, Mr. Darrow seemed to push aside all the mountains of testimony that had been taken. He virtually admitted that he loathed both the case and his clients.

What made his plea notable—

even to those who in the press have been expressing open doubt as to his sincerity and speculating on the size of the fee paid to him—was its general mustering of arguments against the imposition of the death penalty for any crime.

The highlights of his argument follow:

THERE ARE causes for this terrible crime. There are causes, as I have said, for everything that happens in the world. War is a part of it; education is a part of it; birth is a part of it; money is a part of it—all these conspired to compass the destruction of these two poor boys.

Has the court any right to consider anything but these two boys? The State says that your Honor has a right to consider the welfare of the community, as you have. If the welfare of the community would be benefited by taking these lives, well and good. I think it would work evil that no one could measure. Has your Honor a right to consider the families of these two defendants? I have been sorry, and I am sorry for the bereavement of Mr. and Mrs. Frank, for those broken ties that cannot be healed. All I can hope and wish is that some good may come from it all. But as compared with the families of Leopold and Loeb, the Franks are to be envied—and every one knows it.

I do not know how much salvage there is in these two boys. I hate to say it in their presence, but what is there to look forward to? I do not know but what your Honor would be merciful if you tied a rope around their necks and let them die; merciful to them, but not merciful to civilization, and not merciful to those who would be left behind. To spend the balance of their days in prison is mighty little to look forward to, if anything. Is it anything? They may have the hope that as the years roll around they might be released. I do not know. I do not know. I will be honest with this court as I have tried to be from the beginning. I know that these boys are not fit to be at large. I believe they will not be until they pass through the next stage of life, at forty-five or fifty. Whether they will then, I cannot tell. I am sure of this; that I will not be here to help them. So far as I am concerned, it is over. . . .

But there are others to consider. Here are these two families, who have led honest lives, who will bear the name that they bear, and future generations must carry it on.

Here is Leopold's father—and this boy was the pride of his life. He watched him, he cared for him, he worked for him; the boy was brilliant and accomplished, he educated him, and he thought that fame and position awaited him, as it should have awaited. It is a hard thing for a father to see his life's hopes crumble into dust.

Should he be considered? Should his brothers be considered? Will it do society any good or make your life safer, or any human being's life safer, if it should be handed down from generation to generation, that this boy, their kin, died upon the scaffold?

And Loeb's the same. Here are the faithful uncle and brother, who have watched here day by day, while Dickie's father and his mother are too ill to stand this terrific strain, and shall be waiting for a message which means more to them than it can mean to you or me. Shall these be taken into account in this general bereavement?

Have they any rights? Is there any reason, your Honor, why their proud names and all the future generations that bear them shall have this bar sinister written across them? How many boys and girls, how many unborn children will feel it? It is bad enough as it is, God knows. It is bad enough, however it is. But it's not yet death on the scaffold. It's not that. And I ask your Honor, in addition to all that I have said, to save two honorable families from a disgrace that never ends, and which could be of no avail to help any human being that lives.

Now, I must say a word more and then I will leave this with you where I should have left it long ago. None of us are unmindful of the public; courts are not, and juries are not. We placed our fate in the hands of a trained court, thinking that he would be more mindful and considerate than a jury. I cannot say how people feel. I have stood here for three months as one might stand at the ocean trying to sweep back the tide. I hope the seas are subsiding and the wind is falling, and I believe they are, but I wish to make no false pretense to this court. The easy thing and the popular thing to do is to hang my clients. I know it. Men and women who do not think will applaud. The cruel and thoughtless will approve. It will be easy today; but in Chicago, and reaching out over the length and breadth of the land, more and more fathers and mothers, the humane, the kind and the hopeful, who are gaining an understanding and asking questions not only about these poor boys, but about their own—these will join in no acclaim at the death of my clients. These would ask that the shedding of blood be stopped, and that the normal feelings of man resume their sway. And as the days and the months and the years go on, they will ask it more and more. But, your Honor, what they shall ask may not count. I know the easy way. I know your Honor stands between the future and the past. I know the future is with me, and what I stand for here; not merely for the lives of these two unfortunate lads, but for all boys and all girls; for all of the young, and as far as possible, for all of the old. I am pleading for life, understanding, charity, kindness, and the infinite mercy that considers all. I am pleading that we overcome cruelty with kindness and hatred with love. I know the future is on my side. Your Honor stands between the past and the future. You may hang these boys; you may hang them by the neck until they are dead. But in doing it you will turn your face toward the past. In doing it you are making it harder for every other boy who in ignorance and darkness must grope his way through the mazes which only childhood knows. In doing it you will make it harder for unborn children. You may save them and make it easier for every child that sometime may stand where these boys stand. You will make it easier for every human being with an aspiration and a vision and a hope and a fate. I am pleading for the future; I am pleading for a time when hatred and cruelty will not control the hearts of men. . . .

WILL ROGERS

"I am here tonight representing poverty."

NEW YORK, N. Y., Dec. 4, 1924— Will Rogers, the cowboy sage who has become America's leading comedian through the simple technique of reading the newspapers and thereafter commenting upon events of the day from the stage of the Ziegfeld Follies, tonight made one of his rare "speeches" at a formal dinner. The occasion was a memorial to Alexander Hamilton, arranged by Nicholas Murray Butler, university president.

While Mr. Rogers wove his theme largely around the wealth of the Columbia alumni among whom he sat— the poor boy from Claremore, Oklahoma—some of his auditors were aware of the fact that he long ago joined the ranks of millionaires himself.

PRESIDENT BUTLER paid me a compliment a while ago in mentioning my name in his introductory remarks, and he put me ahead of the Columbia graduates. I am glad he did that, because I got the worst of it last week. The Prince of Wales last week, in speaking of the sights of America, mentioned the Woolworth Building, the subway, the slaughterhouse, Will Rogers and the Ford factory. He could at least put me ahead of the hogs.

Everything must be in contrast at an affair like this. You know to show anything off properly you must have the contrast. Now, I am here tonight representing poverty. We have enough wealth right here at this table, right here at the speaker's table alone—their conscience should hurt them, which I doubt if it does—so that we could liquidate our national debt. Every rich man reaches a time in his career when he comes to a turning point and starts to give it away. I have heard that of several of our guests here tonight, and that is one of the reasons I am here. I would like to be here at the psychological moment.

We are here, not only to keep cool with Coolidge, but to do honor to Alexander Hamilton. Now, he was the first Secretary of the Treasury. The reason he was appointed that was because he and Washington were the only men in America at that time who knew how to put their names on a check. Signing a check has remained the principal qualification of a U. S. Secretary of the Treasury.

I am glad President Butler referred to it in this way. The principal reason, of course, was that the man he fought against wanted to be President. He was a Princeton man—or I believe it was Harvard—anyway it was one of those primary schools. In fighting a duel, he forgot that in America our men over here could shoot. So unfortunately one of them was killed, which had never happened in the old country. So they did away with dueling. It was all right to protect your honor, but not to go as far as you like.

If you are speaking of finance here tonight, I do not believe that you could look further than President Butler. Butler is the word—to dig up the dough. Columbia was nothing twenty years ago. Now, he has gone around and got over a hundred buildings, and has annexed Grant's Tomb. He was the first man to go around to the graduates and explain to them that by giving money to Columbia it would help on the income tax and also perpetuate their names.

We have an Alexander Hamilton Building. He landed these buildings and ran the place up to ninety millions or something like that.

There are more students in the university than there are in any other in the world. It is the foremost university. There are thirty-two hundred courses. You spend your first two years in deciding what courses to take, the next two years in finding the building that these courses are given in, and the rest of your life wishing you had taken another course. And they have this wonderful society called the Alumni Association, a bunch of men who have gone to school and after they have come out formed a society to tell the school how to run it.

RUSSELL H. CONWELL

"Money is power and you ought to be reasonably ambitious to have it."

PHILADELPHIA, Pa., 1925—The Rev. Dr. Russell H. Conwell, who died this year at the age of 82, left a legacy considered to be without parallel. It is the educational opportunity that he gave to an estimated 10,000 young men with financial help from the proceeds of a single lecture, "Acres of Diamonds." Dr. Conwell delivered this lecture to more than 6,000 audiences.

As a Baptist minister, Dr. Conwell was noted for a somewhat unorthodox interpretation of the Bible but only to the extent that he pictured it as a living guide, using its texts to teach his auditors that religion, the good life, and opportunity are present things—not matters of a future time or a distant place.

His views and his scholarship long ago won him the distinction of being named the first president of Temple University, which he opened here in 1884. In 1891 it was he who dedicated the Baptist Temple here. By 1875 he already had become a noted lecturer as well as preacher in a day when the art of lecturing was reaching its fullest flower and was a field of intense competition.

The theme of the lecture, "Acres of Diamonds," begins with a description of an Indian who spent his fortune and life hunting for diamonds in other continents, and who began his search by selling the family farm, on which the Kimberly mines later were discovered. He includes countless other examples. Then, turning to the misconception that wealth itself is evil—as preached by so many persons—he draws the line between wealth and "love of wealth" and launches, in the Philadelphia version of this lecture, into the following eloquent words.

The lecture "Acres of Diamonds" is too long for publication here in full, but may be read complete in other current works including *The Compact Treasury of Inspiration,* first published in 1955.

I SAY that you ought to get rich, and it is your duty to get rich. How many of my pious brethren say to me, "Do you, a Christian minister, spend your time going up and down the country advising young people to get rich, to get money?" "Yes, of course I do." They say, "Isn't that awful! Why don't you preach the gospel instead of preaching about man's making money?" "Because to make money honestly is to preach the gospel." That is the reason. The men who get rich may be the most honest men you can find in the community.

"Oh," but says some young man here tonight, "I have been told all my life that if a person has money he is very dishonest and dishonorable and mean and contemptible." My friend, that is the reason why you have none, because you have that idea of people. The foundation of your faith is altogether false. Let me say here clearly, and say it briefly, though subject to discussion which I have not time for here, ninety-eight out of one hundred of the rich men of America are honest. That is why they are rich. That is why they are trusted with money. That is why they carry on great enterprises and find plenty of people to work with them. It is because they are honest men.

Says another young man, "I hear sometimes of men that get millions of dollars dishonestly." Yes, of course you do, and so do I. But they are so rare a thing in fact that the newspapers talk about them all the time as a matter of news until you get the idea that all the other rich men got rich dishonestly.

My friend, you take and drive me—if you furnish the auto—out into the suburbs of Philadelphia, and introduce me to the people who own their homes around this great city, those beautiful homes with gardens and flowers, those magnificent homes so lovely in their art, and I will introduce you to the very best people in character as well as in enterprise in our city, and you know I will. A man is not really a true man until he owns his own home, and they that own their homes are made more honorable and honest and pure, and true and economical, by owning the home.

For a man to have money, even in large sums, is not an inconsistent thing. We preach against covetousness, and you know we do, in the pulpit, and oftentimes preach against it so long and use the terms about "filthy lucre" so extremely that Christians get the idea that when we stand in the pulpit we believe it is wicked for any man to have money—until the collection basket goes around, and then we almost swear at the people because they don't give more money. Oh, the inconsistency of such doctrines as that!

Money is power, and you ought to be reasonably ambitious to have it. You ought because you can do more good with it than you could do without it. Money printed your Bible, money builds your churches, money sends your missionaries, and money pays your preachers, and you would not have many of them, either, if you did not pay them. I am always willing that my church should raise my salary, because the church that pays the largest salary always raises it the easiest. You never knew an exception to it in your life. The man who gets the largest salary can do the most good with the power that is furnished to him. Of course he can, if his spirit be right to use it for what it is given to him.

I say, then, you ought to have money. If you can honestly attain unto riches in Philadelphia, it is your Christian and godly duty to do so. It is an awful mistake of those pious people to think you must be awfully poor in order to be pious.

Some men say, "Don't you sympathize with the poor people?" Of course I do, or else I would not have been lecturing these years. I won't give in but what I sympathize with the poor, but the number of poor who are to be sympathized with is very small. To sympathize with a man whom God has punished for his sins, thus to help him when God would still continue a just punishment, is to do wrong, no doubt about it, and we do that more than we help those who are deserving.

While we should sympathize with God's poor—that is, those who cannot help themselves—let us remember there is not a poor person in the United States who was not made poor by his own shortcomings, or by the shortcomings of someone else. It is all wrong to be poor, anyhow. Let us give in to that argument and pass that to one side.

A gentleman gets up back there, and says, "Don't you think there are some things in this world that are better than money?" Of course I do, but I am talking about money now. Oh yes, I know by the grave that has left me standing alone that there are some things in the world that are higher and sweeter and purer than money. Well do I know there are some things higher and grander than gold. Love is the grandest thing on God's earth, but fortunate the lover who has plenty of money. Money is power, money is force, money will do good as well as harm. In the hands of good men and women it could accomplish, and it has accomplished, good.

WILLIAM GREEN

> *". . . Trade unionism is not a discovery or a formula. It grew and evolved slowly out of the needs of human experience."*

CAMBRIDGE, Mass., 1925—William Green, newly installed president of the American Federation of Labor, speaking before the Harvard Union, pictured the trade union movement as a logical development that has matured in modern society as a responsible and essential element of economic development.

The new spokesman for labor, whose own experience dates back to the recent and yet seemingly remote era of struggle between die-hard labor opponents on the one hand and angry and often irresponsible labor leadership on the other, in effect stated that under his direction the labor movement will be a constructive force, as interested in improving modern society as in exacting benefits from it.

The promise of this new era is highly significant, coming closely on the heels of great strikes in the coal, steel and railroad industries since the World War which, regardless of the merits of contending sides, greatly delayed recovery of the peacetime economy.

WE ALL know from a study of history the progress of the working people from the stage of barbarism to that of slavery, serfdom and later individual freedom. . . .

In the development of civilization the use of tools grew and multiplied. Later the use of steam power revolutionized the whole industrial organization and transportation. Manufacturing enterprises were formed and undertaken in all civilized countries. With these changes in civilization came a change in the mode of living. . . .

The human element played a very important part in the transition. The workers were brought together in groups upon the railroads, in the manufacturing plants and in the mines. They became the users of the tools, the operators of the engines and machines. Naturally, the question of wages and conditions of employment became a subject of vital interest to both employers and employees. Differences of opinion arose as to what the wage schedule should be and what constituted tolerable conditions of employment. Out of the differences which arose between employers and employees grew the organization of workers. In the beginning it was crude, simple and of little influence. These organizations we called unions. . . .

It is clear to all who have studied the history of this great social and economic development that trade unionism is not a discovery or a formula. It grew and evolved slowly out of the needs of human experience. In the beginning when unions were first formed their primary purpose was to defend the workers against wage reductions and unfair treatment. They were regarded almost solely as defensive measures for defensive purposes only. It seemed that the thought uppermost in the minds of the workers was the maintenance of what had been secured by them in the way of wages and working conditions. The methods employed in those days could be characterized as dominantly militant. The rule of force and might seemed to guide and influence the thoughts and actions of the workers. Concessions granted to workers by employers were usually forced through the medium of industrial warfare. There was little attention given to the thought or suggestion of conference, understanding and reasoning between employers and employees. The thought of fight to win, of force and brutality seemed to inspire both employers and employees in their industrial relationships.

From such crude and primitive beginnings trade unionism, or organized labor, has grown into the place which, with increasing influence, it occupies in our social and industrial life today. During the formative period organized labor relied almost solely upon its economic strength while today it places immeasurable value upon the convincing power of logic, facts and the righteousness of its cause. More and more organized labor is coming to believe that its best interests are promoted through concord rather than by conflict. It prefers the conference table to the strike field.

Trade unionism has kept pace with the progress which has been made in industry. It has emerged from its primitive state into a modern institution, grappling with modern problems in a modern way. It is resolutely facing the task of seeking and finding a remedy for existing industrial ills. . . .

Organized labor recognizes and appreciates the value and importance of education. It believes that the workers can advance their economic and social interests through education and knowledge. The workers believe fully that the future of the trade union movement is very largely conditioned upon the effectiveness with which we link up educational opportunities with trade union undertakings. The trade unions were truly pioneers in demanding free public schools so that there might be equal educational opportunities. Along with the adoption of the free public school institution labor is advocating a constant widening of the service rendered by the public schools. Culture should not be the heritage of any limited group. All should be enabled to make their life experiences opportunities for culture. The statement made by Lord Haldane that "class division in knowledge goes deeper than any other class division" is profoundly significant.

We believe that the only way to assure our civilization a culture instinct with life is to make the work process an agency for educating the worker. Whether that work process be making pottery, managing a steel plant, or operating a power loom, it is in the day's work that the human agent shows most clearly what manner of man he is and finds opportunity for growth. If he brings to his work an attitude of mind that is inquiring, resourceful, constructive, he increases his service many fold. When trade unions have established certain fundamental rights which assure industrial justice, and the channels through which mutual problems may be discussed and considered, there is created an opportunity for this higher kind of workmanship. If the whole industrial situation stimulates initiative and therefore workmanship, educational possibilities are quickened. Industrial development of that character will purge our civilization of the blight of commercialism and low ideals. The trade union movement is making its contribution to that end and can accomplish much more when management offers understanding cooperation.

The trade union movement has been passing through that period when physical controversies and the tactics of force were most effective; it is now in a period when its leaders must seek the conference room, and there, by exposition and demonstration, convince conferees of the justice and wisdom of Labor's position. In such service Labor is finding a special need for trained representatives and effective information.

The organizations of labor are adjusting themselves to the marked changes which have come through education and the modernization of industry. The union of the workers is not standing still. It is consolidating the gains of the past and pressing courageously along the highway of progress. The union itself is an elemental response to the human instinct for group action in dealing with group problems. Daily work in industry is now a collective undertaking. The union expresses the workmen's unsatisfied desire for self-betterment in all of the phases that desire may find expression. No substitute can hope to replace the union for it has the intrinsic right to existence which comes from service rendered to fit changing stages of development. Many wage earners have had dreams of ownership of industry but we all know that whatever the ownership, private, governmental or employee, the vital problem for us is the terms and relations we have with management. To deal with this problem, labor must always have its voluntary organizations directed and managed by itself.

The sequel:

Mr. Green proved to be the prophet of an "uneasy peace" that lasted for a while within labor's ranks and in its general dealings with mass industries.

The trade union movement forged ahead until the depression dealt it the same serious blows as were felt by the general public.

Then came demands for more aggressive leadership, and the emergence of a new form of union organization, which eleven years later saw new faces and new labor problems arising concurrently on the scene.

ALFRED E. SMITH

"I do not want any Catholic in the United States to vote for me because I am a Catholic."

OKLAHOMA CITY, Okla., Sept. 20, 1928—Governor Alfred E. Smith, of New York, now campaigning for the Presidency as nominee of the Democratic party, tonight came to grips here with a question which his background unwittingly has injected for the first time into political debate in the United States.

The basic question is whether a man's religion helps or hurts his qualifications for public office. Governor Smith is a Roman Catholic.

In the campaign, there have been many other issues. It has been an uphill fight all the way for this candidate, hurt by his lifelong political association with New York's Tammany Hall, and bitterly opposed by his own party followers in many instances because of his open opposition to prohibition. But the great controversy, unexampled before in our political contests, has been the often whispered one over the willingness of the American people to have as their President a member of the Catholic Church.

Governor Smith chose to bring this subject into the open in a speech in an area where religious controversy has fanned the whole subject into a hot flame.

I FEEL that I owe it to the Democratic party to talk out plainly. If I had listened to the counselors that advised political expediency I would probably keep quiet, but I'm not by nature a quiet man.

I never keep anything to myself. I talk it out. And I feel I owe it, not only to the party, but I sincerely believe that I owe it to the country itself to drag this un-American propaganda out into the open.

Because this country, to my way of thinking, cannot be successful if it ever divides on sectarian lines. If there are any considerable number of our people that are going to listen to appeals to their passions and to their prejudice, if bigotry and intolerance and their sister vices are going to succeed, it is dangerous for the future life of the Republic, and the best way to kill anything un-American is to drag it out into the open; because anything un-American cannot live in the sunlight.

Where does all this propaganda come from? Who is paying for its distribution? . . .

Prior to the convention the grand dragon of the Realm of Arkansas wrote to one of the delegates from Arkansas, and in the letter he advised the delegate that he not vote for me in the national convention, and he put it on the ground of upholding American ideals against institutions as established by our forefathers. Now, can you think of any man or any group of men banded together in what they call the Ku Klux Klan, who profess to be 100 per cent Americans, and forget the great principle that Jefferson stood for, the equality of man, and forget that our forefathers in their wisdom, foreseeing probably such a sight as we look at today, wrote into the fundamental law of the country that at no time was religion to be regarded as a qualification for public office.

Just think of a man breathing the spirit of hatred against millions of his fellow citizens, proclaiming and subscribing at the same time to the doctrine of Jefferson, of Lincoln, of Roosevelt and of Wilson. Why, there is no greater mockery in this world today than the burning of the Cross, the emblem of faith, the emblem of salvation, the place upon which Christ Himself made the great sacrifice for all of mankind, by these people who are spreading this propaganda, while the Christ they are supposed to adore, love and venerate, during all of His lifetime on earth, taught the holy, sacred writ of brotherly love. . . .

Let me make myself perfectly clear. I do not want any Catholic in the United States of America to vote for me on the 6th of November because I am a Catholic. If any Catholic in this country believes that the welfare, the well-being, the prosperity, the growth and the expansion of the United States is best conserved and best promoted by the election of Hoover, I want him to vote for Hoover and not for me.

But, on the other hand, I have the right to say that any citizen of this country that believes I can promote its welfare, that I am capable of steering the ship of state safely through the next four years and then votes against me because of my religion, he is not a real, pure, genuine American.

ROBERT C. BENCHLEY

"The Treasurer's Report."

NEW YORK, N. Y., 1930—Robert C. Benchley originated an individual modern theme of "public speaking," rather like creeping onto the platform, not from the side door, but out of the pages of his humorous articles and books.

A noted writer for *The New Yorker,* he wrote gems that sing as monologues even more successfully than they read as words on the printed page. Eventually, as one of the great treats of the early days of "talking pictures," Benchley became a popular screen star with his readings.

Of all his monologues, "The Treasurer's Report" is perhaps his most beloved memory. It is carried here, in full, as he delivered it, and as he annotated it for the guidance of those amateurs who sought to emulate his delivery:

(The report is delivered by an Assistant Treasurer who has been called in to pinch-hit for the regular Treasurer who is ill. He is not a very good public-speaker, this assistant, but after a few minutes of confusion is caught up by the spell of his own oratory and is hard to stop.)

I shall take but a very few minutes of your time this evening, for I realize that you would much rather be listening to this interesting entertainment than a dry financial statement . . . but I *am* reminded of a story—which you have probably all of you heard.

It seems that there were these two Irishmen walking down the street when they came to a—oh, I should have said in the first place that the parrot was hanging out in front of the store—or rather belonging to one of these two fellows—the first Irishman, that is—was—well—well—anyway, this parrot——

(After a slight cogitation, he realizes that, for all practical purposes, the story is as good as lost; so he abandons it entirely and, stepping forward, drops his facile, story-telling manner and assumes a quite spurious business-like air.)

Now, in connection with reading this report, there are one or two points which Dr. Murnie wanted brought up in connection with it, and he has asked me to bring them up in connection—to bring them up.

In the first place, there is the question of the work which we are trying to do up at our little place at Silver Lake, a work which we feel not only fills a very definite need in the community but also fills a very definite need—er—in the community. I don't think that many members of the Society realize just how big the work is we are trying to do up there.

For instance, I don't think that it is generally known that most of our boys are between the ages of fourteen. We feel that, by taking the boy at this age, we can get closer to his real nature—for a boy has a very real nature, you may be sure—and bring him into close touch not only with the school, the parent, and with each other, but also with the town in which they live, the country to whose flag they pay their allegiance, and the—ah—(*trailing off*) town in which they live.

Now to the fourth point which Dr. Murnie wanted brought up was that in connection with the installation of the new furnace last Fall. There seems to have been considerable talk going around about this not having been done quite as economically as it might—have—been—done, when, as a matter of fact, the whole thing *was* done just as economically as possible—in fact, even *more* so. I have here a report of the Furnace Committee, showing just how the whole thing was handled from start to finish.

(*Reads from report, with considerable initial difficulty with the stiff covers.*)

Bids were submitted by the following firms of furnace contractors, with a clause stating that if we did not engage a firm to do the work for us we should pay them nothing for submitting the bids. This clause alone saved us a great deal of money.

The following firms, then, submitted bids:

Merkle, Wybigant Co., the Eureka Dust Bin and Shaker Co., the Elite Furnace Shop, and Harris, Birnbauer and Harris. The bid of Merkle, Wybigant being the lowest, Harris, Birnbauer were selected to do the job.

(Here a page is evidently missing from the report, and a hurried search is carried on through all the pages, without result.)

Well, that pretty well covers up that end of the work.

Those of you who have contributed so generously last year to the floating hospital have probably wondered what became of the money. I was speaking on this subject only last week at our up-town branch and, after the meeting, a dear little old lady, dressed all in lavender, came up on the platform and, laying her hand on my arm, said, "Mr. So-and-so (calling me by name), Mr. So-and-so, what the hell did you do with all the money we gave you last year?" Well, I just laughed and pushed her off the platform, but it has occurred to the committee that perhaps some of you, like the little old lady, would be interested in knowing the disposition of the funds.

Now, Mr. Rossiter, unfortunately our treasurer—or rather Mr. Rossiter, our *treasurer, unfortunately* is confined to his home tonight with a bad head-cold and I have been asked *(he hears someone whispering to him from the wings, but decides to just ignore it)* and I have been asked if I would *(the whisper will not be denied, so he goes to the entrance and receives a brief message, returning beaming and laughing to himself)*. Well, the joke seems to be on *me*. Mr. Rossiter has *pneumonia*.

Following, then, is a summary of the Treasurer's Report:

(Reads in a very business-like manner.)

During the year 1929—and by that is meant 1928—the Choral Society received the following donations:

B.L.G.	$ 500
G.K.M.	500
Lottie and Nellie W.	500
In memory of a happy summer at Rye Beach	10
Proceeds of sale of hats and coats left in the boat-house	14.55
And the Junior League gave a performance of "Pinafore" for the benefit of the Fund which unfortunately resulted in a deficit of	300

Then from dues and charges	2,354.75
And, following the installation of the new furnace, a saving in coal amounting to which made Dr. Marnie very happy	374.75
Making a total of receipts of	$3,645.75

This is all, of course, reckoned as of June.

In the matter of expenditures the Club has not been so fortunate. There was the unsettled conditions of business, and the late Spring, to contend with, resulting in the following—er—rather discouraging figures, I am afraid.

Expenditures	$ 23,574.85
Then there was a loss, owing to several things—of	3,326.70
Carfare	4,452.25

And then Mrs. Rawlins' expense account, when she went down to see the work they are doing in Baltimore, came to $256.50, but I am sure you all agree that it was worth it to find out—er—what they are doing in Baltimore.

| And then, under the general head of odds and ends | $ 2,537.50 |
| Making a total disbursement of (*hurriedly*) | $416,546.75 |

or a net deficit of—ah—several thousand dollars.

Now, these figures bring us down to October. In October my sister was married and the house was all torn up, and in the general confusion we lost track of the figures for May and August. All those wishing the *approximate* figures for May and August, however, may obtain them from me in the vestry after dinner, where I will be with pledge cards, for those who wish to subscribe over and above your annual dues, and I hope that each and every one of you here tonight will look deeply into his heart and (*archly*) into his pocketbook, and see if he cannot find it there to help us to put this thing over with a bang (*accompanied by a wholly ineffectual gesture representing a bang*) and to help and make this just the biggest and best year the Americans have ever had. . . . I thank you.

(*Exits, bumping into proscenium.*)

OLIVER WENDELL HOLMES

"Live—I am coming."

WASHINGTON, D. C., March 7, 1931—The radio air waves of the United States flashed tonight to millions of listeners a unique program, even in an age of miracles, as the leaders of politics, the arts and science took their places before widely scattered microphones to pay tribute to a single, towering figure of his time.

The tributes were to Oliver Wendell Holmes, 90 years old today, and for more than 50 of his years a member of the Supreme Court of the United States; in his "spare time" additionally a noted wit, humanitarian and particularly interpreter of the meaning of humanity to his juniors.

At the conclusion of the program, without prior scheduling, Mr. Justice Holmes spoke extemporaneously one of the shortest and yet what must be one of the most moving little orations of all time. He said:

IN THIS symposium my part is only to sit in silence. To express one's feelings as the end draws nigh is too intimate a task.

But I may mention one thought that comes to me as a listener-in. The riders in a race do not stop short when they reach the goal. There is a little finishing canter before coming to a standstill. There is time to hear the kind voices of friends and to say to oneself: The work is done. But just as one says that, the answer comes: "The race is over, but the work never is done while the power to work remains. The canter that brings you to a standstill need not be only coming to rest. It cannot be, while you still live. For to live is to function. That is all there is to living."

And so I end with a line from a Latin poet who uttered the message more than fifteen hundred years ago, "Death plucks my ear and says: Live—I am coming."

IV

DEPRESSION, WAR AND RECONVERSION

FRANKLIN D. ROOSEVELT

"The only thing we have to fear is fear itself—nameless, unreasoning, unjustified terror which paralyzes needed efforts to convert retreat into advance."

WASHINGTON, D. C., March 4, 1933—New words of hope and courage addressed to a fear-paralyzed land, writhing in the grip of an economic depression without modern precedent, echoed from the East Portico of the Capitol here as Franklin D. Roosevelt delivered his First Inaugural Address to a crowd sitting or standing in a slashing rain.

Here was the voice of leadership in a new type of revolution—the peaceful overturning of methods of government and economic management that somehow has shrunken values, dried up commerce, caused banks to close, and cast millions of workers into unemployment.

For weeks the new President has been formulating the plans indicated in today's speech. As always during crises, he realizes that for a little while the voices of leaders—even his erstwhile political opponents—raised in the universal demand to "do something," make him the most powerful leader in the modern world. And to-day he gave that promise in broad lines that would be frightening except for the normal checks and balances preserved in our form of government.

"It is to be hoped," the new President said, "that the normal balance of the Executive and legislative authority may be wholly adequate to meet the unprecedented task before us. But it may be that an unprecedented demand and need for undelayed action may call for temporary departure from that normal balance of public procedure."

He was prepared, he added, to work under the first formula but, failing there, "and in the event that the national emergency is still critical I shall not evade the clear course of duty that will then confront me."

There was evident inspiration in these words, but to reporters on the scene there was likewise evident a thread of apprehension—the unspoken question, "What next?"

219

There was no concern that the Congress would not cooperate, for its leadership was already pledged by the time of the last election. But where would it end?

More than one person saw potential parallels between this great grant of power to the new Presi-dent and the equally overwhelming support just granted in Germany to the new Chancellor, Adolf Hitler. The deeper and unanswered question is how far angry and distraught peoples will permit or encourage strong leadership to go.

I AM certain that my fellow Americans expect that on my induction into the Presidency I will address them with a candor and a decision which the present situation of our Nation impels. This is preeminently the time to speak the truth, the whole truth, frankly and boldly. Nor need we shrink from honestly facing conditions in our country today. This great Nation will endure as it has endured, will revive and will prosper. So, first of all, let me assert my firm belief that the only thing we have to fear is fear itself—nameless, unreasoning, unjustified terror which paralyzes needed efforts to convert retreat into advance. In every dark hour of our national life a leadership of frankness and vigor has met with that understanding and support of the people themselves which is essential to victory. I am convinced that you will again give that support to leadership in these critical days.

In such a spirit on my part and on yours we face our common difficulties. They concern, thank God, only material things. Values have shrunken to fantastic levels; taxes have risen; our ability to pay has fallen; government of all kinds is faced by serious curtailment of income; the means of exchange are frozen in the currents of trade; the withered leaves of industrial enterprise lie on every side; farmers find no markets for their produce; the savings of many years in thousands of families are gone.

More important, a host of unemployed citizens face the grim problem of existence, and an equally great number toil with little return. Only a foolish optimist can deny the dark realities of the moment.

Yet our distress comes from no failure of substance. We are stricken by no plague of locusts. Compared with the perils which our forefathers conquered because they believed and were not afraid, we have still much to be thankful for. Nature still offers her bounty and human efforts have multiplied it. Plenty is at our doorstep, but a generous use of it languishes in the very sight of the supply. Primarily this is because rulers of the exchange of mankind's goods have failed through their own stubbornness and their own incompetence, have admitted their failure, and have abdicated. Practices of the unscrupulous moneychangers stand indicted in the court of public opinion, rejected by the hearts and minds of men.

True they have tried, but their efforts have been cast in the pattern of an outworn tradition. Faced by failure of credit they have proposed only the lending of more money. Stripped of the lure of profit by which to induce our people to follow their false leadership, they have resorted to exhortations, pleading tearfully for restored confidence. They know only the rules of a generation of self-seekers. They have no vision, and when there is no vision the people perish.

The moneychangers have fled from their high seats in the temple of our civilization. We may now restore that temple to the ancient truths. The measure of the restoration lies in the extent to which we apply social values more noble than mere monetary profit.

Happiness lies not in the mere possession of money; it lies in the joy of achievement, in the thrill of creative effort. The joy and moral stimulation of work no longer must be forgotten in the mad chase of evanescent profits. These dark days will be worth all they cost us if they teach us that our true destiny is not to be ministered unto but to minister to ourselves and to our fellow men.

Recognition of the falsity of material wealth as the standard of success goes hand in hand with the abandonment of the false belief that public office and high political position are to be valued only by the standards of pride of place and personal profit; and there must be an end to a conduct in banking and in business which too often has given to a sacred trust the likeness of callous and selfish wrongdoing. Small wonder that confidence languishes, for it thrives only on honesty, on honor, on the sacredness of obligations, on faithful protection, on unselfish performance; without them it cannot live.

Restoration calls, however, not for changes in ethics alone. This Nation asks for action, and action now.

Our greatest primary task is to put people to work. This is no unsolvable problem if we face it wisely and courageously. It can be accomplished in part by direct recruiting by the Government itself, treating the task as we would treat the emergency of a war, but at the same time, through this employment, accomplishing greatly needed projects to stimulate and reorganize the use of our natural resources.

Hand in hand with this we must frankly recognize the overbalance of population in our industrial centers and, by engaging on a national scale in a redistribution, endeavor to provide a better use of the land for those best fitted for the land. The task can be helped by definite efforts to raise the values of agricultural products and, with this, the power to purchase the output of our cities. It can be helped by preventing realistically the tragedy of the growing loss through foreclosure of our small homes and our farms. It can be helped by insistence that the Federal, State, and local governments act forthwith on the demand that their cost be drastically reduced. It can be helped by the unifying of relief activities which today are often scattered, uneconomical, and unequal. It can be helped by national planning for and supervision of all forms of transportation and of communications and other utilities which have a definitely public character. There are many ways in which it can be helped, but it can never be helped merely by talking about it. We must act and act quickly.

Finally, in our progress toward a resumption of work we require two safeguards against a return of the evils of the old order: there must be a strict supervision of all banking and credits and investments, so that there will be an end to speculation with other people's money; and there must be provisions for an adequate but sound currency.

These are the lines of attack. I shall presently urge upon a new Congress, in special session, detailed measures for their fulfillment, and I shall seek the immediate assistance of the several States.

Through this program of action we address ourselves to putting our own national house in order and making income balance outgo.

Our international trade relations, though vastly important, are in point of time and necessity secondary to the establishment of a sound national economy. I favor as a practical policy the putting of first things first. I shall spare no effort to restore world trade by international economic readjustment, but the emergency at home cannot wait on that accomplishment.

The basic thought that guides these specific means of national recovery is not narrowly nationalistic. It is the insistence, as a first consideration, upon the interdependence of the various elements in and parts of the United States—a recognition of the old and permanently important manifestation of the American spirit of the pioneer. It is the way to recovery. It is the immediate way. It is the strongest assurance that the recovery will endure.

In the field of world policy I would dedicate this Nation to the policy of the good neighbor—the neighbor who resolutely respects himself and, because he does so, respects the rights of others—the neighbor who respects his obligations and respects the sanctity of his agreements in and with a world of neighbors.

If I read the temper of our people correctly, we now realize as we have never realized before our interdependence on each other; that we cannot merely take but we must give as well; that if we are to go forward, we must move as a trained and loyal army willing to sacrifice for the good of a common discipline, because without such discipline no progress is made, no leadership becomes effective. We are, I know, ready and willing to submit our lives and property to such discipline, because it makes possible a leadership which aims at a larger good. This I propose to offer, pledging that the larger purposes will bind upon us all as a sacred obligation with a unity of duty hitherto evoked only in time of armed strife.

With this pledge taken, I assume unhesitatingly the leadership of this great army of our people dedicated to a disciplined attack upon our common problems.

Action in this image and to this end is feasible under the form of government which we have inherited from our ancestors. Our Constitution is so simple and practical that it is possible always to meet extraordinary needs by changes in emphasis and arrangements without loss of essential form. That is why our constitutional system has proved itself the most superbly enduring political mechanism the modern world has produced. It has met every stress of vast expansion of territory, of foreign wars, of bitter internal strife, of world relations.

It is to be hoped that the normal balance of Executive and legislative authority may be wholly adequate to meet the unprecedented task before us. But it may be that an unprecedented demand and need for undelayed action may call for temporary departure from that normal balance of public procedure.

I am prepared under my constitutional duty to recommend the measures that a stricken Nation in the midst of a stricken world may require. These measures, or such other measures as the Congress may build out of its experience and wisdom, I shall seek, within my constitutional authority, to bring to speedy adoption.

But in the event that the Congress shall fail to take one of these two courses, and in the event that the national emergency is still critical, I shall not evade the clear course of duty that will then confront me. I shall ask the Congress for the one remaining instrument to meet the crisis—broad Executive power to wage a war against the emergency, as great as the power that would be given to me if we were in fact invaded by a foreign foe.

For the trust reposed in me I will return the courage and the devotion that befit the time. I can do no less.

We face the arduous days that lie before us in the warm courage of national unity; with the clear consciousness of seeking old and precious moral values; with the clear satisfaction that comes from the stern performance of duty by old and young alike. We aim at the assurance of a rounded and permanent national life.

We do not distrust the future of essential democracy. The people of the United States have not failed. In their need they have registered a mandate that they want direct, vigorous action. They have asked for discipline and direction under leadership. They have made me the present instrument of their wishes. In the spirit of the gift I take it.

In this dedication of a Nation we humbly ask the blessing of God. May He protect each and every one of us. May He guide me in the days to come.

The sequel:

The democratic processes survived. The immediate future became known later as The Hundred Days, as one emergency activity followed another. But always the President acted within the grants of legislative authority laid down by the Congress.

Later some of the emergency activities would be ruled unconstitutional by the Supreme Court, and thus stopped. But until so ruled, they were part of the pattern of activity.

Recovery came about, both in courage and in economics, and the whole structure of life in the United States emerged from the process with so many differences that, like them all or not, we live today—and were living even before World War II—in a world that would never return to that of the 1920s.

Across the Atlantic, the German Government, first cast up by popular demand, wrote a different story, as Hitler and his Nazi party seized more and more power and led that country inexorably to its doom.

WILLIAM LYON PHELPS

"You should own no book that you are afraid to mark up."

NEW HAVEN, Conn., April 6, 1933 —William Lyon Phelps, who retired this year after 41 years of teaching students at Yale the richness and delight of literature, tonight gave to the American public a living legacy of his appreciation in a brief broadcast on the subject of owning books.

Professor Phelps noted that he lives principally in a room that contains 6,000 books; remarked that when he was asked if he had read them all, he hedged in his reply by saying, "Some of them twice."

THE HABIT of reading is one of the greatest resources of mankind; and we enjoy reading books that belong to us much more than if they are borrowed. A borrowed book is like a guest in the house; it must be treated with punctiliousness, with a certain considerate formality. You must see that it sustains no damage; it must not suffer while under your roof. You cannot leave it carelessly, you cannot mark it, you cannot turn down the pages, you cannot use it familiarly. And then, some day, although this is seldom done, you really ought to return it.

But your own books belong to you; you treat them with that affectionate intimacy that annihilates formality. Books are for use, not for show; you should own no book that you are afraid to mark up, or afraid to place on the table, wide open and face down. A good reason for marking favorite passages in books is that this practice enables you to remember more easily the significant sayings, to refer to them quickly, and then in later years, it is like visiting a forest where you once blazed a trail. You have the pleasure of going over the old ground, and recalling both the intellectual scenery and your own earlier self.

Everyone should begin collecting a private library in youth; the instinct of private property, which is fundamental in human beings, can here be cultivated with every advantage and no evils. One should have one's own bookshelves, which should not have doors, glass windows, or keys; they should be free and accessible to the hand as well as to the eye. The best of mural decorations is books; they are more varied in colour and appearance than any wall-paper, they are more attactive in design, and they have the prime advantage of being separate personalities, so that if you sit alone in the room in the firelight, you are surrounded with intimate friends. The knowledge that they are there in plain view is both stimulating and refreshing. You do not have to read them all. Most of my indoor life is spent in a room containing six thousand books; and I have a stock answer to the invariable question that comes from strangers. "Have you read all of these books?" "Some of them twice." This reply is both true and unexpected.

There are of course no friends like living, breathing, corporeal men and women; my devotion to reading has never made me a recluse. How could it? Books are of the people, by the people, for the people. Literature is the immortal part of history; it is the best and most enduring part of personality. But book-friends have this advantage over living friends; you can enjoy the most truly aristocratic society in the world whenever you want it. The great dead are beyond our physical reach, and the great living are usually almost as inaccessible; as for our personal friends and acquaintances, we cannot always see them. Perchance they are asleep, or away on a journey. But in a private library, you can at any moment converse with Socrates or Shakespeare or Carlyle or Dumas or Dickens or Shaw or Barrie or Galsworthy. And there is no doubt that in these books you see these men at their best. They wrote for *you*. They "laid themselves out," they did their ultimate best to entertain you, to make a favorable impression. You are necessary to them as an audience is to an actor; only instead of seeing them masked, you look into their inmost heart of heart.

OWEN D. YOUNG

"You must fuse at white heat the several particles of your learning."

CONWAY, Ark., Nov. 20, 1934— Owen D. Young, well known as a financier but more importantly to himself a dedicated disciple of education, came to this relatively small town, to Hendrix College, to receive a proffered degree and in return describe his conception of "culture."

Aside from his many achievements and honors in the field of domestic and international business and finance, Mr. Young's homely treatise —illustrated by an article which has been developed to high efficiency under his direction, the electric lamp— places him alongside famous professionals in the educational field.

CULTURE REPRESENTS a synthesis, a putting together of things, putting them together so completely that the combination has an individuality of its own. It may be only an amalgam; it is better if it is a chemical combination. I think of it in this way:

The vital part of the incandescent electric lamp is the tungsten wire inside the bulb. The great invention in that lamp was the discovery of a way to convert metallic tungsten into wire. It was well known that this metal would withstand the high heat required for incandescence over a long period without disintegration, but it was also known that tungsten was one of the most recalcitrant of the metals. Each particle was such a rugged individualist that it would have nothing to do with its neighbor. It seemed to have no social sense at all.

The first tungsten lamps contained so-called "pressed" filaments. The metal was subjected to tremendous pressures in small grooves the size of a wire. It was found that if pressure enough could be applied, the particles would hold together in what appeared to be a wire, sufficient to enable this fragile string to be placed into a lamp. The lamps were shipped to their destinations in cushions and finally with the greatest care inserted in the sockets.

They gave excellent light, but all of us older people can remember that if the children played tag once around the dining-room table all the lights went out. One day, courageous and daring men determined that that obstinate metal should be conquered, and it was. With high heats and extraordinarily ingenious methods, tungsten was so converted that it could be drawn into wire, and the wire became stronger than steel of equivalent size.

You must fuse at white heat the several particles of your learning into an element so ductible and so strong that nothing can destroy it without destroying you.

Let me be a little more specific. What is the use of studying Greek unless you can bring all the beauty of that language and literature into your thinking and your expression today? What is the use of studying Latin unless you can get through it a better understanding, a more complete feeling of the mighty activities in their heights and depths that made Rome both glorious and ignoble? What is the use of studying French unless through a wider outlook and more varied contacts that language brings to you a better understanding of the world in which you live and an appreciation of that grace which is the basis of good manners?

What is the use of studying history without co-relating it with the economics which for the most part has been its master? What is the use of studying economics or politics without relating them both to a knowledge of the physical sciences which shape their courses? You have only to look beyond this campus today to see that the problems both of economics and of politics arise out of the machines which the research workers of the world have made.

My point is that it is not enough for you to study economics in an insulated compartment and history and governments and the languages and science. It is not enough to gather them up as separate particles into a powder which you carry out with your diploma. They must be fused and integrated.

HERBERT HOOVER

The Bill of Rights "is the expression of the spirit of men who would be forever free."

SAN DIEGO, Calif., Sept. 17, 1935 —From this city far from the political turmoil of Washington, Herbert Hoover today reminded this country of which he so recently was President that the Bill of Rights— the first ten amendments to the Constitution—exist today as a greater force for freedom than ever before. No exigencies of emergency, he said, can nullify them.

Mr. Hoover, who has spoken in public little since his overwhelming defeat in the 1932 election for reasons far beyond the control either of himself or of his party, spoke no word of criticism of the Roosevelt Administration. He refrained from comment on the fact that throughout the last two years he has never been invited to a conference by his successor. Rather, speaking as a student and humanitarian with notable achievements to his credit prior to entry into politics, he gave new illumination to the meaning of the Constitution and the Bill of Rights embedded in it.

He pointed his talk rather at the world around the United States where "new philosophies and new theories of government have arisen . . . which militantly deny the validity of our principles."

OUR CONSTITUTION is not alone the working plan of a great Federation of States under representative government. There is embedded in it also the vital principles of the American system of liberty. That system is based upon certain inalienable freedoms and protections which not even the government may infringe and which we call the Bill of Rights. It does not require a lawyer to interpret those provisions. They are as clear as the Ten Commandments. Among others the freedom of worship, freedom of speech and of the press, the right of peaceable assembly, equality before the law, just trial for crime, freedom from unreasonable search, and security from being deprived of life, liberty, or property without due process of law, are the principles which distinguish our civilization. Herein are the invisible sentinels which guard the door of every home from invasion of coercion, of intimidation and fear. Herein is the expression of the spirit of men who would be forever free.

These rights were no sudden discovery, no over-night inspiration. They were established by centuries of struggle in which men died fighting bitterly for their recognition. Their beginnings lie in the Magna Charta at Runnymede five hundred and seventy years before the Constitution was written. Down through the centuries the Habeas Corpus, the "Petition of Rights," the "Declaration of Rights," the growth of the fundamental maxims of the Common Law, marked their expansion and security. Our forefathers migrated to America that they might attain them more fully. When they wrote the Declaration of Independence they boldly extended these rights. Before the Constitution could be ratified patriotic men who feared a return to tyranny, whose chains had been thrown off only after years of toil and bloody war, insisted that these hard-won rights should be incorporated in black and white within the Constitution—and so came the American Bill of Rights.

In the hurricane of revolutions which have swept the world since the Great War, men, struggling with the wreckage and poverty of that great catastrophe and the complications of the machine age, are in despair surrendering their freedom for false promises of economic security. Whether it be Fascist Italy, Nazi Germany, Communist Russia, or their lesser followers, the result is the same. Every day they repudiate every principle of the Bill of Rights. Freedom of worship is denied. Freedom of speech is suppressed. The press is censored and distorted with propaganda. The right of criticism is denied. Men go to jail or the gallows for honest opinions. They may not assemble for discussion. They speak of public affairs only in whispers. They are subject to search and seizure by spies and inquisitors who haunt the land. The safeguards of justice in trial or imprisonment are set aside. There is no right in one's savings or one's own home which the government need respect.

Here is a form of servitude, of slavery—a slipping back toward the Middle Ages. . . .

Even in America, where liberty blazed brightest and by its glow shed light on all the others, it is besieged from without and challenged from within. Many, in honest belief, hold that we cannot longer accommodate the growth of science, technology and mechanical power to the Bill of Rights and our form of government. With that I do not agree. Men's inventions cannot be of more value than men themselves. But it would be better that we sacrifice something of economic efficiency than to surrender these primary liberties. In them lies a spiritual right of men. Behind them is the conception which is the highest development of the Christian faith—the conception of individual freedom with brotherhood. From them is the fullest flowering of individual human personality.

Nor is respect for the Bill of Rights a fetter upon progress. It has been no dead hand that has carried the living principles of liberty over these centuries. Without violation of these principles and their safeguards we have amended the Constitution many times in the past century to meet the problems of growing civilization. We will no doubt do so many times again. Always groups of audacious men in government or out will attempt to consolidate privilege against their fellows. New inventions and new ideas require the constant remolding of our civilization. The functions of government must be readjusted from time to time to restrain the strong and protect the weak. That is the preservation of liberty itself. We ofttimes interpret some provisions of the Bill of Rights so that they override others. They indeed jostle each other in course of changing national life—but their respective domains can be defined by virtue, by reason, and by law. And the freedom of men is not possible without virtue, reason and law.

The sequel:

The voice of Herbert Hoover sounded in a very low key indeed at this time, but he never made a speech with the idea of winning a popularity poll.

As the years went by, it became more and more evident that the 31st President had many facets that had been submerged during his trying four years in the White House.

Before that time he had been an engineer of worldwide repute and success, the director of the massive famine-relief operation in Russia after World War I, and later Director General of relief work in Belgium.

For eight years his work as Secretary of Commerce was distinguished.

Aside from all this past, upon which he now turned his back, Herbert Hoover was beginning in 1935 to forge a future as "elder statesman," writer and student that would enhance his prestige progressively into an old age that remains vigorous up to the time of this writing.

JOHN L. LEWIS

"Labor, like Israel, has many sorrows."

WASHINGTON, D. C., Sept. 3, 1937—John L. Lewis, the towering labor leader who in 57 years has lifted himself from the coal-mines to the most controversial if not the outstanding individual position in the labor movement, tonight went on the radio to defend his actions in precipitating a nation-wide crisis of strikes as part of the organizing campaign for his new Congress of Industrial Organizations.

The public had a rare chance to hear the neo-classical oratory of Mr. Lewis that has swayed labor meetings for a quarter century; that, in addition, has made him a power in politics and economics as well as in the assembly halls of labor.

Mr. Lewis gave the impression that he well understood he had reached a point of crisis. Evidences of Communist support for the CIO's organizing activities at a time when the United States is just pulling out of the depression, have particularly upset the chief of the CIO, because large segments of the public in favor of breaking the monopoly heretofore held by the American Federation of Labor in all organizing fields except the railroads are still withholding support from Mr. Lewis.

THE UNITED STATES Chamber of Commerce, the National Association of Manufacturers and similar groups representing industry and financial interests are rendering a disservice to the American people in their attempts to frustrate the organization of labor and in their refusal to accept collective bargaining as one of our economic institutions.

These groups are encouraging a systematic organization under the sham pretext of local interests. They equip these vigilantes with tin hats, wooden clubs, gas masks and lethal weapons and train them in the arts of brutality and oppression.

No tin hat brigade of goosestepping vigilantes or bibble-babbling mob of blackguarding and corporation-paid scoundrels will prevent the onward march of labor, or divert its purpose to play its natural and rational part in the development of the economic, political and social life of our nation.

Unionization, as opposed to communism, presupposes the relation of employment; it is based upon the wage system and it recognizes fully and unreservedly the institution of private property and the right to investment profits. It is upon the fuller development of collective bargaining, the wider expansion of the labor movement, the increased influence of labor in our national councils, that the perpetuity of our democratic institutions must largely depend.

The organized workers of America, free in their industrial life, conscious partners of production, secure in their homes and enjoying a decent standard of living, will prove the finest bulwark against the intrusion of alien doctrines of government.

Do those who hatched this foolish cry of communism in the CIO fear the increased influence of labor in our democracy? Do they fear its influence will be cast on the side of shorter hours, a better system of distributed employment, better homes for the underprivileged, social security for the aged, a fairer distribution of our national income? Certainly the workers that are being organized want a voice in the determination of these objectives of social justice.

Certainly labor wants a fairer share of the national income. Assuredly labor wants a larger participation in increased productive efficiency. Obviously the population is entitled to participate in the fruits of the genius of our men of achievement in the field of material sciences.

Labor has suffered just as our farm population has suffered from a viciously unequal distribution of the national income. In the exploitation of both classes of workers has been the source of panic and depression, and upon the economic welfare of both rests the best assurance of a sound and permanent prosperity.

Under the banner of the Committee for Industrial Organization American labor is on the march. Its objectives today are those it had in the beginning: to strive for the unionization of our unorganized millions of workers and for the acceptance of collective bargaining as a recognized American institution.

It seeks peace with the industrial world. It seeks cooperation and mutuality of effort with the agricultural population. It would avoid strikes. It would have its rights determined under the law by the peaceful negotiations and contract relationships that are supposed to characterize American commercial life.

Until an aroused public opinion demands that employers accept that rule, labor has no recourse but to surrender its rights or struggle for their realization with its own economic power.

Labor, like Israel, has many sorrows. Its women weep for their fallen and they lament for the future of the children of the race. It ill behooves one who has supped at labor's table and who has been sheltered in labor's house to curse with equal fervor and fine impartiality both labor and its adversaries when they become locked in deadly embrace.

I repeat that labor seeks peace and guarantees its own loyalty, but the voice of labor, insistent upon its rights, should not be annoying to the ears of justice nor offensive to the conscience of the American people.

WILLIAM ALLEN WHITE

"This is a middle-class country and the middle class will have its will and way."

WASHINGTON, D. C., Sept. 20, 1937—Once in a blue moon an angry voice rises out of the mists of public debate to speak the plaints and complaints of that indefinable person—Mr. John Q. Public—torn as always between the conflicts of political parties, capital and labor, or even conservative-liberal thinking.

Here such a voice was raised by William Allen White, distinguished editor of the *Emporia* (Kansas) *Gazette*, and already revered in his lifetime as the sage of the public mind —at 69 years of age the militant spokesman for the individual with no organization behind him, the little man who is just trying to get along.

Mr. White gave one of his rare acceptances to an invitation to make a speech, in order to stand before the American Management Congress, meeting here. What he said gave little comfort to any faction among the contending forces in the American economy; but his words will be applauded by millions.

IN THIS discussion I am supposed to represent the public—the American consumer. He is a mythical character who never lived on land or sea, but for that matter, the capitalist is a myth and the worker's status is an economic hypothesis. It is trite to say that in America we are all more or less owners, all workers of high or low degrees, and certainly we are all consumers. We are all the children of John Q. Public, and our interests as members of the consuming public are after all our chief end and objective as citizens of our democracy.

Let me begin by telling you both, laborer and capitalist, that you have got us citizen consumers in a pretty sad mess. Every time we consumers think of what one of you has done we are dead sore at each of you until we begin to think of what the other has done. Let me start on capital, the employer. Not that he is more to blame than labor. But he is more responsible. He enjoys more freedom. He could have done better. You employers have wasted twenty years since the end of the World War. In those twenty years, a little intelligent self-interest, a little foresight—not much—would have solved equitably the problems that are now pressing upon us, problems that have been adjusted in haste and in the emergency of calamity. Take the eight-hour day. You knew that it was coming. Why didn't you men willingly, sensibly, grant it? But no. You had to fight it, every inch, and make the consuming public think you were greedy—when you were not. You were just dumb—dumb to give labor a sense of deep antagonism. Take the old age pension and job insurance to cover seasonal and technological unemployment. A thousand voices rose across the land, telling you of the trouble ahead. What did you do? You put cotton in your ears, and if you could hear through the cotton you began yelling "Communism!" at the academician and the liberal politician and spokesmen of the consuming public. Everyone realized 20 years ago and more that sooner or later, with the pensions of the Civil War gone which took care of the aged until the World War, we should have old age pensions as a federal problem. Yet you employers let a generation of old people, unprovided for, begin to clamor for old age pensions and begin to listen to demagogues with silly panaceas. Then, having squandered your substance, you turned your men on the street in the days of the locust, and put into the hands of the most adroit politician America has ever seen the votes of ten million men whom your slipshod social viewpoint rendered jobless. If a dozen or twenty years ago you, Mr. Capitalist, had used the social sense of the average man in the street, this problem of unemployment and old age pensions would not be handing to your arch-enemies an organized subsidized class-conscious proletariat which can be voted to your destruction. By your sloth you created the particular head devil who is mocking you. He is your baby. You begot him two decades ago in the days of your youth when you were going to handle your business in your own way and no man could come into your shop and tell you how to run it!

But labor has been no Solomon. The proper business of a labor union is to get higher wages, better hours and good shop conditions for the workmen. But when labor en masse plunks its vote for its own party, then the spirit of party loyalty begins to obscure labor's objectives—high wages, short hours, decent shop conditions. Thus class-conscious labor leaders become more interested in their party welfare than in the fundamental objectives of labor unions. So we shall have the class-conscious political worker trading his vote not for the immediate objective of wages, hours and shop conditions, but for power for his political labor boss. The political labor boss will ask the workers to swallow a whole ticket in order to dominate a whole government. He would turn a democracy into a contest between two class-conscious parties, a class-conscious proletariat and a class-conscious plutocracy. In that setup where is the Consumer; where indeed is the compromise between labor and capital under the supervision of a middle class? In short with only two class-conscious political parties what becomes of democracy? The labor union militant and undefiled—yes; the vertical union and the closed shop? Yes. But a class-conscious labor party in a democracy—no!

If labor insists upon maintaining its class lines of bitter intransigent hostility to all capital, the American middle class—old John Q. Public and his heirs and assigns—will not support labor.

This is a middle-class country and the middle class will have its will and way. For the middle class is the real owner of American industry. The middle class is also 80 per cent worker and the consumer of 80 per cent of American industrial production in the home market. The middle class thinks and feels chiefly as The Consumer. And before the middle class demands an increase in either interest for investors or higher wages for the worker, the middle class will demand fair prices and a stable industry. That means industrial peace. No peace is lasting until it is founded upon that essential equitable compromise between the contending forces— capital and labor—known as justice.

The sequel:

There has been, of course, no sequel.

Voices raised on behalf of the commonalty of us all bear little weight, since politicians, capitalists, labor—or whatever you will—know that unorganized feelings have little consequence. We divide and vote. But down through the years, there is a definite sequel that becomes known only at a time and under circumstances when, tired of being pushed around by special groups, the public forgets its immediate identification with class or mass and indicates, "a plague on both your houses."

CHARLES EVANS HUGHES

"In the great enterprise of making democracy workable we are all partners."

WASHINGTON, D. C., March 4, 1939—The chief umpire of the United States Government, in determining the fine line of division between control of the public by laws and protection of the individual in his rights under the Constitution, today reviewed the experiences of

American democracy over its first 150 years and found them good.

Charles Evans Hughes, Chief Justice of the United States, delivered this opinion in an historic appearance, by invitation, as the principal speaker before a Joint Session of the Senate and House of Representatives, celebrating their Sesquicentennial.

In this assemblage, the Chief Justice saw "the living exponents of the principle of representative government—not government by direct mass action but by representation which means leadership as well as responsiveness and accountability."

The slim, bearded figure, who spoke from the dais temporarily vacated by the Speaker of the House, holds an unique position in American history. He has been Governor of New York, Secretary of State, and, as a lawyer, his reputation ranks alongside that of the world's great; he was appointed Chief Justice after years of public service including a prior term as an Associate Justice which he resigned to become the Republican party's unsuccessful candidate for the Presidency in 1916.

At the age of 77 he is crisp, vigorous and evidently destined for many more active years.

THE MOST significant fact in connection with this anniversary is that, after 150 years, notwithstanding expansion of territory, enormous increase in population, and profound economic changes, despite direct attack and subversive influences, there is every indication that the vastly preponderant sentiment of the American people is that our form of government shall be preserved. . . .

Forms of government, however well contrived, cannot assure their own permanence. If we owe to the wisdom and restraint of the fathers a system of government which has thus far stood the test, we all recognize that it is only by wisdom and restraint in our own day that we can make that system last. If today we find ground for confidence that our institutions which have made for liberty and strength will be maintained, it will not be due to abundance of physical resources or to productive capacity, but because these are at the command of a people who still cherish the principles which underlie our system, and because of the general appreciation of what is essentially sound in our governmental structure.

With respect to the influences which shape public opinion, we live in a new world. Never have these influences operated more directly, or with such variety of facile instruments, or with such overwhelming force. We have mass production in opinion as well as in goods. The grasp of tradition and of sectional prejudgment is loosened. Postulates of the past must show cause. Our institutions will not be preserved by veneration of what is old, if that is simply expressed in the formal ritual of a shrine. The American people are eager and responsive. They listen attentively to a vast multitude of appeals and, with this receptivity, it is only upon their sound judgment that we can base our hope for a wise conservatism with continued progress and appropriate adaptation to new needs.

We shall do well on this anniversary if the thought of the people is directed to the essentials of our democracy. Here in this body we find the living exponents of the principle of representative government—not government by direct mass action but by representation which means leadership as well as responsiveness and accountability.

Here the ground swells of autocracy, destructive of parliamentary independence, have not yet upset or even disturbed the authority and responsibility of the essential legislative branch of democratic institutions. We have a National Government equipped with vast powers which have proved to be adequate to the development of a great nation, and at the same time maintaining the balance between centralized authority and local autonomy. It has been said that to preserve that balance, if we did not have States we should have to create them. In our 48 States we have the separate sources of power necessary to protect local interests and thus also to preserve the central authority, in the vast variety of our concerns, from breaking down under its own weight. . . .

We not only praise individual liberty but our constitutional system has the unique distinction of insuring it. Our guarantees of fair trials, of due process in the protection of life, liberty, and property—which stands between the citizen and arbitrary power—of religious freedom, of free speech, free press and free assembly, are the safeguards which have been erected against the abuses threatened by gusts of passion and prejudice which in misguided zeal would destroy the basic interests of democracy. We protect the fundamental right of minorities, in order to save democratic government from destroying itself by the excesses of its own power. The firmest ground for confidence in the future is that more than ever we realize that, while democracy must have its organization and controls, its vital breath is individual liberty.

I am happy to be here as the representative of the tribunal which is charged with the duty of maintaining, through the decision of controversies, these constitutional guaranties. We are a separate but not an independent arm of government. You, not we, have the purse and the sword. You, not we, determine the establishment and the jurisdiction of the lower Federal courts and the bounds of the appellate jurisdiction of the Supreme Court. The Congress first assembled on March 4, 1789, and on September 24, 1789, as its twentieth enactment, passed the Judiciary Act—to establish the judicial courts of the United States—a statute which is a monument of wisdom, one of the most satisfactory acts in the long history of notable congressional legislation. It may be said to take rank in our annals as next in importance to the Constitution itself.

In thus providing the judicial establishment, and in equipping and sustaining it, you have made possible the effective functioning of the department of government which is designed to safeguard with judicial impartiality and independence the interests of liberty. But in the great enterprise of making democracy workable we are all partners. One member of our body politic cannot say to another: "I have no need of thee." We work in successful cooperation by being true, each department to its own functions, and all to the spirit which pervades our institutions, exalting the processes of reason, seeking through the very limitations of power the promotion of the wise use of power, and finding the ultimate security of life, liberty, and the pursuit of happiness, and the promise of continued stability and a rational progress in the good sense of the American people.

The sequel:

One may ask, how is restatement of fundamental principles to be assessed in immediate or long-range impact?

The simple answer is that the words stand as reminders, and there can never be an excess of calm, reasoned reminders.

By 1939 the United States had become, among the major world powers, the oldest in unchanged form of government despite its Topsy-like growth, and certainly the most stable economically, despite the recent devastating depression.

How fortunate a country which, being given such a message in 1939, could be given the same report in 1959, after further great vicissitudes in its external and internal fortunes, and still say, "This is true."

FRANK LLOYD WRIGHT

"A new integrity of human life."

LONDON, May, 1939—Frank Lloyd Wright, one of the most celebrated (and most controversial) of American architects, aroused an ovation without precedent in this background in the last of five lectures that were anticipated as distinguished but which rose to the level of the sensational.

It was generally conceded that Mr. Wright, normally regarded as a radical if not eccentric member of the avante garde of his profession, interpreted the conception of architecture on almost a supernatural plane, while giving due regard to the normal needs of line, mass and perspective.

His talks were given in response to an invitation to deliver the annual Sir George Watson Lectures of the Sulgrave Manor Board. These have been delivered in the Royal Institute of British Architects before crowds such as usually are seen queued up at theatres in the Haymarket.

His interpretation of "An Organic Architecture," culminated in the following passages:

SO FAR as what education chooses to call culture goes we have been trying all these centuries to beat life and to defeat it, pretty nearly succeeding too. "Authority" has seldom trusted life at any time. We certainly have not trusted life in architecture, nor have we trusted it in economics, and we have not trusted it in politics or statesmanship. We have not trusted it anywhere—no—not even in religion.

The cultural lag has been greatly aided by our wily wanton, prostitute social sentimentality. Nor can any aesthetic whatsoever, no matter how mechanistic and hard it may imagine itself to be, save us

now. We have to get people, states and buildings *thought-built.*
Unless the things of life concerning culture, a natural architecture
being first among them, are now thought-built from within, I think
we are at the end of the last chapter in . . . is it a great civilization,
I wonder? Are we perhaps at the tail of something, dwindling to a
conclusion?

How many of you can feel that unless we find this upward way
from within, life is on the downward rather than on the upward
grade? For myself, I feel we *must* learn the nature of this organic
character and integrity in all that we do *now* or perish. If we do not
soon learn to call that learning "culture" we shall soon learn to call
what we now call culture, a curse.

I have seemed to belittle the nature of our time and the great
achievements of science, but I have intended to do neither because
I believe human nature still sound, and recognize that science has
done a grand job as well; but well I know that Science cannot
save us.

Science can give us only the tools in a box, mechanical miracles
that it has already given us. But of what use to us are miraculous
tools until we have mastered the humane, cultural use of them?

We do not want to live in a world where the machine has mastered the man; we want to live in a world where man has mastered
the machine.

What we call organic architecture is no mere aesthetic nor cult
nor fashion but an actual movement based upon a profound idea
of a new integrity of human life, wherein art, religion and science
are one: Form and Function seen as One, of such is Democracy.

The sequel:

When Frank Lloyd Wright was
given the high distinction of an invitation to deliver the Watson lectures, he was the "grand old man"
of the radicals creating a new func-
tional form of architecture, based on
the principles described above.

No one guessed in 1939, when he
was 70 years of age, that at this
writing in 1959 he still would be the
fiery leader of the "modern" movement, both in the lecture hall and
at the building sites of his creations.
In 1959, in his ninetieth year, just
before he died he personally super-
vised erection of the $3,000,000 Sol-
omon R. Guggenheim Museum, on
Fifth Avenue, New York—the first
building designed by himself to be
erected in New York.

WENDELL L. WILLKIE

*"Our American unity must be forged between the ideas
of the opposition and the practices and the policies of
the administration."*

NATIONAL RADIO ADDRESS, Nov. 11, 1940—A defeated candidate for the Presidency, Wendell L. Willkie, sat before a radio microphone tonight to set a new precedent in American politics. One week after losing the race for the Presidency to Franklin D. Roosevelt, he reminded his own supporters, and the public as well, that in the American system there always must be a "loyal opposition" that supports all measures for the public good but stands as the check against arbitrary assumption of power by the winning side. Such a statement he deemed necessary, he said, to calm the controversies aroused by the recent campaign.

Mr. Willkie, the relatively unknown "dark horse" who came out of political obscurity to capture the banner of his own party and to poll more votes than any other candidate except Mr. Roosevelt's total in defeating him, echoed in his speech the grave apprehensions of many persons that, while the United States is not directly involved in the European war, its path at best must lead perilously close to involvement.

Hence the great need for unity, and Mr. Willkie's clearly apparent effort to hold his party to constructive criticism, the form of "loyal opposition" that has long been formalized in the British Parliament and actually has existed in the United States on most crucial occasions.

PEOPLE of America: Twenty-two years ago today, a great conflict raging on the battlefields of Europe came to an end. The guns were silent. A new era of peace began and for that era the people of our Western World—our democratic world—held the highest hopes.

Those hopes have not been fulfilled. The democratic way of life did not become stronger—it became weaker. The spirit of constitutional government flickered like a dying lamp. And within the last year or so the light from that lamp has disappeared entirely from the continent of Europe.

We in America watched darkness fall upon Europe. And as we watched, there approached an important time for us—the national election of 1940.

In that election, and in our attitudes after that election, the rest of the world would see an example of democracy in action, an example of a great people faithful to their Constitution and to their elected representatives.

The campaign preceding this election stirred us deeply. Millions upon millions of us who had never been active in politics took part in it. The people flocked to the polling places in greater numbers than ever before in history.

Nearly 50,000,000 people exercised on November 5 the right of the franchise—the precious right which we inherited from our forefathers and which we must cherish and pass on to future generations.

Thus it came about that although constitutional government had been blotted out elsewhere, here in America men and women kept it triumphantly alive.

No matter which side you were on, on that day, remember that this great, free expression of our faith in the free system of government must have given hope to millions upon millions of others—on the heroic island of Britain—in the ruined cities of France and Belgium—yes, perhaps even to people in Germany and in Italy. It has given hope wherever man hopes to be free.

In the campaign preceding this election, serious issues were at stake. People became bitter. Many things were said which in calmer moments might have been left unsaid or might have been worded more thoughtfully.

But we Americans know that the bitterness is a distortion, not a true reflection of what is in our hearts. I can truthfully say that there is no bitterness in mine. I hope there is none in yours.

We have elected Franklin Roosevelt President. He is your President. He is my President. We all of us owe him the respect due to his high office. We give him that respect. We will support him with our best efforts for our country. And we pray that God may guide his hand during the next four years in the supreme task of administering the affairs of the people.

It is a fundamental principle of the democratic system that the majority rules. The function of the minority, however, is equally fundamental. It is about the function of that minority—22,000,000 people, nearly half of our electorate, that I wish to talk to you tonight.

A vital element in the balanced operation of democracy is a strong, alert and watchful opposition. That is our task for the next four years. We must constitute ourselves a vigorous, loyal and public-spirited opposition party.

It has been suggested that in order to present a united front to a threatening world, the minority should now surrender its convictions and join the majority. This would mean that in the United States of America there would be only one dominant party—only one economic philosophy—only one political philosophy of life. This is a totalitarian idea—it is a slave idea—it must be rejected utterly. . . .

An American President could fill his whole Cabinet with leaders of the opposition party and still our Administration would not be a two-party administration. It would be an administration of a majority President giving orders to minority representatives of his own choosing. These representatives must concur in the President's convictions. If they do not they have no alternative except to resign. . . .

Our American unity cannot be made with words or with gestures. It must be forged between the ideas of the opposition and the practices and the policies of the administration. Ours is a government of principles and not one merely of men. Any member of the minority party, though willing to die for his country, still retains the right to criticize the policies of the government. This right is imbedded in our constitutional system.

We, who stand ready to serve our country behind our Commander in Chief, nevertheless retain the right, and I will say the duty, to debate the course of our government. Ours is a two-party system. Should we ever permit one party to dominate our lives entirely, democracy would collapse and we would have dictatorship.

Therefore, to you who have so sincerely given yourselves to this cause, which you chose me to lead, I say: "Your function during the next four years is that of the loyal opposition." You believe deeply in the principles that we stood for in the recent election.

And principles are not like a football suit to be put on in order to play a game and then taken off when the game is over.

It is your constitutional duty to debate the policies of this or any other Administration and to express yourselves freely and openly to those who represent you in your state and national government.

The sequel:

Even at this writing the place of Wendell L. Willkie in American history is clouded by controversy, although his stature has grown as an individual.

A fascinating man, he burned bright and fast in a life that lasted only 52 years, from 1892 to 1944. A successful lawyer—highly successful in representing financial interests—he became an ardent political liberal within the Republican party, capturing the nomination in 1940 without the benefit of any organization whatever.

Yet he could not win over those Republican radicals who had cast their lot with Roosevelt; notably Harold L. Ickes, the former Bull Moose leader, who dubbed Willkie "the barefoot boy from Wall Street."

Soon after Willkie's defeat in the big contest, he offered his services to the Administration and traveled widely in Europe and Asia on missions for the government. He became a bitter foe of the isolationists and left, as his political legacy, two books, *One World,* published in 1943, and *An American Program,* published in 1944.

FRANKLIN D. ROOSEVELT

"With absolute faith that our common cause will greatly succeed."

WASHINGTON, D. C., Dec. 29, 1940—President Roosevelt tonight called upon the American people, in the face of ever-growing conquests by the dictator countries abroad, to make the United States "the arsenal of democracy," for the provision of all possible arms and assistance to Great Britain and the other democratic powers standing against that onslaught.

The President delivered his appeal

by radio, in one of what have become known as his "fireside chats." His talk was delivered in dramatic circumstances, with the United States in the anomalous position of not being at war, but threatened by Germany, Italy and Japan with full reprisal if this country should help in blocking their plans of conquest.

The President rejected this threat, and simultaneously discarded the implied demand by those belligerents that the United States throw its weight behind the writing of a "negotiated peace" which would pre-serve to the aggressors all of their gains, including the continent of Europe as now held by Germany and Italy and the richest part of China, held in Japan's grasp.

The President's words carried extraordinary weight, because at no time has there been greater massive national support behind his stand. It is true that some few individuals and groups feel that the United States is being far from neutral, but Congressional votes on all major questions find the Administration's security program overwhelmingly supported.

MY FRIENDS: This is not a fireside chat on war. It is a talk on national security; because the nub of the whole purpose of your President is to keep you now, and your children later, and your grandchildren much later, out of a last-ditch war for the preservation of American independence and all of the things that American independence means to you and to me and to ours. . . .

Never before since Jamestown and Plymouth Rock has our American civilization been in such danger as now.

For on Sept. 27, 1940—this year—by an agreement signed in Berlin, three powerful nations, two in Europe and one in Asia, joined themselves together in the threat that if the United States of America interfered with or blocked the expansion program of these three nations—a program aimed at world control—they would unite in ultimate action against the United States.

The Nazi masters of Germany have made it clear that they intend not only to dominate all life and thought in their own country, but also to enslave the whole of Europe, and then to use the resources of Europe to dominate the rest of the world.

It was only three weeks ago that their leader stated this: "There are two worlds that stand opposed to each other." And then in defiant reply to his opponents he said this: "Others are correct when they say: 'With this world we cannot ever reconcile ourselves.'

. . . I can beat any other power in the world." So said the leader of the Nazis.

In other words, the Axis not merely admits but the Axis proclaims that there can be no ultimate peace between their philosophy —their philosophy of government—and our philosophy of government.

In view of the nature of this undeniable threat, it can be asserted, properly and categorically, that the United States has no right or reason to encourage talk of peace until the day shall come when there is a clear intention on the part of the aggressor nations to abandon all thought of dominating or conquering the world.

At this moment the forces of the States that are leagued against all peoples who live in freedom are being held away from our shores. The Germans and the Italians are being blocked on the other side of the Atlantic by the British and by the Greeks, and by thousands of soldiers and sailors who were able to escape from subjugated countries. In Asia the Japanese are being engaged by the Chinese nation in another great defense.

In the Pacific Ocean is our fleet.

Some of our people like to believe that wars in Europe and in Asia are of no concern to us. But it is a matter of most vital concern to us that European and Asiatic war-makers should not gain control of the oceans which lead to this hemisphere. . . .

Does any one seriously believe that we need to fear attack anywhere in the Americas while a free Britain remains our most powerful naval neighbor in the Atlantic? And does any one seriously believe, on the other hand, that we could rest easy if the Axis powers were our neighbors there?

If Great Britain goes down, the Axis powers will control the Continents of Europe, Asia, Africa, Australasia, and the high seas —and they will be in a position to bring enormous military and naval resources against this hemisphere. It is no exaggeration to say that all of us in all the Americas would be living at the point of a gun—a gun loaded with explosive bullets, economic as well as military. . . .

Frankly and definitely there is danger ahead—danger against

which we must prepare. But we well know that we cannot escape danger, or the fear of danger, by crawling into bed and pulling the covers over our heads. . . .

The experience of the past two years has proven beyond doubt that no nation can appease the Nazis. No man can tame a tiger into a kitten by stroking it. There can be no appeasement with ruthlessness. There can be no reasoning with an incendiary bomb. We know now that a nation can have peace with the Nazis only at the price of total surrender.

Even the people of Italy have been forced to become accomplices of the Nazis; but at this moment they do not know how soon they will be embraced to death by their allies.

The American appeasers ignore the warning to be found in the fate of Austria, Czecho-Slovakia, Poland, Norway, Belgium, the Netherlands, Denmark and France. They tell you that the Axis powers are going to win anyway; that all of this bloodshed in the world could be saved, that the United States might just as well throw its influence into the scale of a dictated peace and get the best out of it that we can.

They call it a "negotiated peace." Nonsense! Is it a negotiated peace if a gang of outlaws surrounds your community and on threat of extermination makes you pay tribute to save your own skins? . . .

The people of Europe who are defending themselves do not ask us to do their fighting. They ask us for the implements of war, the planes, the tanks, the guns, the freighters which will enable them to fight for their liberty and for our security. Emphatically we must get these weapons to them, get them to them in sufficient volume and quickly enough so that we and our children will be saved the agony and suffering of war which others have had to endure.

Let not the defeatists tell us that it is too late. It will never be earlier. Tomorrow will be later than today.

Certain facts are self-evident.

In a military sense Great Britain and the British Empire are today the spearhead of resistance to world conquest. And they are putting up a fight which will live forever in the story of human gallantry.

There is no demand for sending an American expeditionary force outside our own borders. There is no intention by any member of your government to send such a force. You can, therefore, nail, nail any talk about sending armies to Europe as deliberate untruth.

Our national policy is not directed toward war. Its sole purpose is to keep war away from our country and away from our people.

Democracy's fight against world conquest is being greatly aided, and must be more greatly aided, by the rearmament of the United States and by sending every ounce and every ton of munitions and supplies that we can possibly spare to help the defenders who are in the front lines. And it is no more unneutral for us to do that than it is for Sweden, Russia and other nations near Germany to send steel and ore and oil and other war materials into Germany every day in the week.

We are planning our own defense with the utmost urgency, and in its vast scale we must integrate the war needs of Britain and the other free nations which are resisting aggression.

This is not a matter of sentiment or of controversial personal opinion. It is a matter of realistic, practical military policy, based on the advice of our military experts who are in close touch with existing warfare. These military and naval experts and the members of the Congress and the Administration have a single-minded purpose—the defense of the United States.

This nation is making a great effort to produce everything that is necessary in this emergency—and with all possible speed. And this great effort requires great sacrifice. . . .

But all of our present efforts are not enough. We must have more ships, more guns, more planes—more of everything. And this can be accomplished only if we discard the notion of "business as usual." This job cannot be done merely by superimposing on the existing productive facilities the added requirements of the nation for defense.

Our defense efforts must not be blocked by those who fear the future consequences of surplus plant capacity. The possible consequences of failure of our defense efforts now are much more to be feared.

And after the present needs of our defense are past, a proper handling of the country's peacetime needs will require all of the new productive capacity, if not still more.

No pessimistic policy about the future of America shall delay the immediate expansion of those industries essential to defense. We need them. . . .

I believe that the Axis powers are not going to win this war. I base that belief on the latest and best of information.

We have no excuse for defeatism. We have every good reason for hope—hope for peace, yes, and hope for the defense of our civilization and for the building of a better civilization in the future.

I have the profound conviction that the American people are now determined to put forth a mightier effort than they have ever yet made to increase our production of all the implements of defense, to meet the threat to our democratic faith.

As President of the United States, I call for that national effort. I call for it in the name of this nation which we love and honor and which we are privileged and proud to serve. I call upon our people with absolute confidence that our common cause will greatly succeed.

IRVIN S. COBB

"The pretty man with the pink clothes on."

NEW YORK, N. Y., 1941—For almost 50 of his rollicking 67 years, Irvin S. Cobb has delighted worldwide readers with a display of wit in written and spoken word. Like Mark Twain, his humor is notable for its humanity, and more apparent in his anecdotes than in his more formal speeches.

Now at the rounding out of his career, his family, his boyhood recollections and his own fantastic memory comprise the soil in which his humor flowers. The following anecdote, told perhaps a thousand times by the speaker on his feet, is here given as written in his autobiography.

IT WAS on a circus day—I was probably 10 or 12 years old—that a thing happened, which still abides in my memory, as about the first example of spontaneous humor I can think of. That year, at the last moment, two old ladies unexplainedly joined Capt. John Cobb's personally conducted caravan. One of them lived across the street from us and the other just around the corner. Mrs. Lawson, the senior of the pair, was extremely deaf. She used one of those old-fashioned flexible ear trumpets with a tip at one end and a bell-like aperture at the other. Her crony, Mrs. Rohm, had a high-pitched, far-carrying voice.

On a blue-painted seat, with the old ladies at one end, my father and mother at the other, and the customary rows of youngsters in between, we watched the unfolding pageant. The time came for the crowning feature of a circus of those times. Perhaps the reader is of sufficient age to remember what that was.

Elephants and camels and horses would be close-ranged at the foot of a springboard. Along a steep runway which slanted down this springboard, would flash in order, one behind the other, the full strength of the troupe. The acrobats would tumble over the backs of the animals to alight gracefully upon a thick padded mattress. The clowns would sprawl on the backs of the living obstacles. Always there was a clown who, dashing down the runway, would suddenly halt and fling his peaked cap across. There was another dressed as a country woman, who, as he somersaulted, lost a pair of bifurcated white garments while the audience whooped with delight.

This season, a culminating treat had been provided by the management. The lesser gymnasts had done their stunts. Now, to the head of the runway mounted the premier tumbler. He stood there, grand in his rose-colored *fleshings,* his arms folded across his swelling breast and his head almost touching the sagging canvas of the roof. The band stopped playing, the ringmaster mounted the ring-back and proclaimed that Johnnie O'Brien, foremost athlete of the world, would now perform his death-defying and unparalleled feat of turning a triple somersault over two elephants, three camels and four horses.

For many this announcement had a special interest; they knew Johnnie O'Brien as a native-born son of our town, as was Cal Wagner, an equally famous *kinker*. An expectant hush fell upon the assemblage. Mrs. Lawson turned to Mrs. Rohm and in the silence her voice rose as she asked:

"What did he say?"

Mrs. Rohm brought the blunderbuss end of Mrs. Lawson's ear trumpet to her lips, and, through its sinuous black length, in a voice so shrill that instantly every head was turned toward the pair of them, she answered:

"He says that the pretty man up there with the pink clothes on is going to jump over all those critters yonder without hurtin' himself."

On the sawdust, in his baggy white clothes, squatted one of the clowns. On the instant he leaped to his feet, ran to the head of a larger elephant, and in both hands caught that creature's long black dangling trunk which now, as everyone saw, looked so amazingly like Mrs. Lawson's ear trumpet, and raising it to his mouth, he shrieked out in a magnificent imitation of Mrs. Rohm's falsetto:

"He says that the pretty man up there, with the pink clothes . . ."

If he finished the sentence, none there heard him. From every mouth there arose a tremendous gasp of joyous appreciation and, overtopping and engulfing this, a roar of laughter which billowed the tent. Strong men dropped through the seats like ripened plums from the bough and lay upon the earth shaking with laughter. The performers rolled about in the ring. The band members laid aside their instruments and whooped.

And through it all Mrs. Lawson and Mrs. Rohm sat there wondering why the band did not play and why the pretty man in the pink clothes up at the top of the runway didn't go ahead and do his death-defying feat, but instead seemed to be having a convulsion.

CHARLES A. LINDBERGH

"Those of us who believe in an independent America must band together and organize for strength."

NEW YORK, N. Y., April 23, 1941 —Charles A. Lindbergh, who in the 1920s became the first man to fly the Atlantic Ocean alone, tonight aligned his famous name with a new and rising faction of controversy over the place of the United States in a world shaken by the great European war.

Unknown heretofore in the political arena, but holding national public regard both as a result of his courage on his historic flight and sympathy over the tragedy that saw his first son kidnaped and murdered, Mr. Lindbergh has stepped now into the center of a major storm.

It is an unpopular thing today to be an isolationist or a pacifist; Mr. Lindbergh went a step further and told the United States, contrary to popular feeling, that intervention in Europe would bring on a war that the United States cannot hope to win.

To this conclusion he added his own estimate that France and England had made a mistake in opposing Germany with arms.

By these arguments, the flying hero has taken a stand opposing the Administration, the overwhelming majority of Congress and the greater proportion of the instruments of communication—press and radio.

THERE ARE many viewpoints from which the issues of this war can be argued. Some are primarily idealistic. Some are primarily practical. One should, I believe, strive for a balance of both. But, since the subjects that can be covered in a single address are limited, tonight I shall discuss the war from a viewpoint which is primarily practical. It is not that I believe ideals are unimportant, even among the realities of war; but if a nation is to survive in a hostile world its ideals must be backed by the hard logic of military practicability. If the outcome of war depended upon ideals alone, this would be a different world than it is today.

I know I will be severely criticized by the interventionists in America when I say we should not enter a war unless we have a

"You shall not crucify mankind upon a cross of gold.
. . ." William Jennings
Bryan, in his characteristic
stance, pleading for the unrestricted coinage of silver.
The photograph was made
in 1896 by Underwood &
Underwood.

A skipper relaxes on deck—
Samuel L. Clemens, better
known as Mark Twain, tak-
ing it easy. (Bettmann
Archive)

Theodore Roosevelt, advocate of the strenuous life, a president of the United States, a wielder of the "big stick," author, and big game hunter, is shown campaigning in New Jersey in 1913. (Bettmann Archive)

Advocate of the "sawdust trail" to salvation, which meant "coming down front" at his revival meetings and "getting religion," Billy Sunday, former baseball star, was a vigorous revival speaker throughout America at the time this picture was taken in 1915. (Bettmann Archive)

"All the News That's Fit to Print."

The New York Times.

THE WEATHER

VOL. LXVI. NO. 21,619.

NEW YORK, TUESDAY, APRIL 3, 1917.—TWENTY-FOUR PAGES.

PRESIDENT CALLS FOR WAR DECLARATION, STRONGER NAVY, NEW ARMY OF 500,000 MEN, FULL CO-OPERATION WITH GERMANY'S FOES

Text of the President's Address

ARMED AMERICAN STEAMSHIP SUNK; 11 MEN MISSING

Aztec Is First Gun-Bearing Vessel Under Our Flag to Be Torpedoed.

SURPRISE ATTACK AT NIGHT

Navy Men and Their Chief Among 17 Survivors Picked Up by a Patrol.

IN A LIFEBOAT THAT SANK

MUST EXERT ALL OUR POWER

To Bring a "Government That Is Running Amuck to Terms."

WANTS LIBERAL CREDITS

And Universal Service, for "the World Must Be Made Safe for Democracy."

A TUMULTUOUS GREETING

Congress Adjourns After "State of War" Resolution Is Introduced—Acts Today.

The War Resolution Now Before Congress

This resolution was introduced in the House of Representatives last night by Representative Flood, Chairman of the Foreign Affairs Committee, immediately after the President's address:

JOINT RESOLUTION, Declaring that a State of War Exists Between the Imperial German Government and the Government and People of the United States and Making Provision to Prosecute the Same.

Whereas, The recent acts of the Imperial German Government are acts of war against the Government and people of the United States:

Resolved, By the Senate and House of Representatives of the United States of America in Congress assembled, that the state of war between the United States and the Imperial German Government which has thus been thrust upon the United States is hereby formally declared; and

That the President be, and he is hereby, authorized and directed to take immediate steps not only to put the country in a thorough state of defense but also to exert all of its power and employ all of its resources to carry on war against the Imperial German Government and to bring the conflict to a successful termination.

President Wilson on April 2, 1917 introducing into Congress his "state of war" resolution against Germany. The photograph (Wide World Photos) shows how far away in those days photographers had to stand to photograph the President. The full text appeared in *The New York Times.*

John L. Lewis defending the CIO in the thirties. (Underwood & Underwood)

Irvin S. Cobb, the humorist from Paducah, Kentucky. (Wide World Photos, November 4, 1938.)

Will Rogers, rope twirler and homespun "philosophy" spouter, in his cowboy pants. (Wide World Photos)

President Franklin Delano Roosevelt, December 8, 1941: "We are now in this war. We are all in it—all the way. Every single man, woman and child is a partner in the most tremendous undertaking of our American history. We must share together the bad news and the good news, the defeats and the victories, the changing fortunes of war." Behind him, Vice President Wallace, Speaker Rayburn. (United Press International Photo)

"In the swift rush of great events, we find ourselves groping to know the full sense and meaning of the times in which we live." President Eisenhower's first inaugural address, January 20, 1953. (Photo by United Press)

"The ordeal of the twentieth century . . . is far from over." Governor Adlai Stevenson of Illinois addressing the Democratic National Convention and accepting its nomination for the presidency. (Wide World Photos)

General MacArthur before the United States Congress, April 19, 1951. (Wide World Photos)

William Faulkner accepts the Nobel Prize for literature in Sweden. (Wide World Photos)

General Alfred M. Gruenther utters a warning as he retires from NATO. (Wide World Photos)

Eleanor Roosevelt responding to an ovation in Chicago, July, 1952. (Wide World Photos)

Henry Cabot Lodge, Jr. looking over the situation from his seat in the United Nations just before a speech in November, 1956. (Wide World Photos)

Carl Sandburg before the United States Congress on Lincoln's birthday anniversary, 1959, a rare moment when politicians listened to a poet evoke the figure of a great American. Behind the poet are Vice President Nixon and Speaker Rayburn (compare the photograph of President Roosevelt asking for a declaration of war in 1941). (Wide World Photos)

reasonable chance of winning. That, they will claim, is far too materialistic a viewpoint. . . . But I do not believe that our American ideals and our way of life will gain through an unsuccessful war. And I know that the United States is not prepared to wage war in Europe successfully at this time. We are no better prepared today than France was when the interventionists in Europe persuaded her to attack the Siegfried Line.

I have said before, and I will say again, that I believe it will be a tragedy to the entire world if the British Empire collapses. That is one of the main reasons why I opposed this war before it was declared, and why I have constantly advocated a negotiated peace. I did not feel that England and France had a reasonable chance of winning. France has now been defeated and despite the propaganda and confusion of recent months it is now obvious that England is losing the war. I believe this is realized even by the British government. But they have one last desperate plan remaining. They hope that they may be able to persuade us to send another American Expeditionary Force to Europe and to share with England militarily, as well as financially, the fiasco of this war.

I do not blame England for this hope, or for asking for our assistance. But we now know that she declared a war under circumstances which led to the defeat of every nation that sided with her from Poland to Greece. We know that in the desperation of war England promised to all these nations armed assistance that she could not send. We know that she misinformed them, as she has misinformed us, concerning her state of preparation, her military strength and the progress of the war.

In time of war, truth is always replaced by propaganda. . . .

I ask you to look at the map of Europe today and see if you can suggest any way in which we could win this war if we entered it. Suppose we had a large army in America, trained and equipped. Where would we send it to fight? The campaigns of the war show only too clearly how difficult it is to force a landing, or to maintain an army, on a hostile coast. Suppose we took our Navy from the Pacific and used it to convoy British shipping. That would not win the war for England. It would, at best, permit her to exist under the constant bombing of the German air fleet. Suppose we had an air force that we could send to Europe. Where could it operate? Some of our squadrons might be based in the British Isles, but it is physically impossible to base enough aircraft in the British Isles alone to equal in strength the aircraft that can be based on the continent of Europe.

I have asked these questions on the supposition that we had in existence an Army and an Air Force large enough and well enough equipped to send to Europe; and that we would dare to remove our Navy from the Pacific. Even on this basis, I do not see how we could invade the Continent of Europe successfully as long as all of that Continent and most of Asia is under Axis domination. But the fact is that none of these suppositions are correct. We have only a one-ocean Navy. Our Army is still untrained and inadequately equipped for foreign war. Our Air Force is deplorably lacking in modern fighting planes because most of them have already been sent to Europe. . . .

We have weakened ourselves for many months, and still worse, we have divided our own people by this dabbling in Europe's wars. While we should have been concentrating on American defense, we have been forced to argue over foreign quarrels. We must turn our eyes and our faith back to our own country before it is too late. . . .

The time has come when those of us who believe in an independent American destiny must band together and organize for strength. We have been led toward war by a minority of our people. This minority has power. It has influence. It has a loud voice. But it does not represent the American people. . . .

. . . That is why the American First Committee has been formed—to give voice to the people who have no newspaper, or news reel, or radio station at their command; to the people who must do the paying and the fighting and the dying, if this country enters the war.

. . . If you believe in an independent destiny for America, if you believe that this country should not enter the war in Europe, we ask you to join the America First Committee in its stand. . . .

DOROTHY THOMPSON

"Democracy and freedom face the bitterest of tests."

TORONTO, Can., May 2, 1941— From this Canadian vantage point the outstanding woman journalist of the United States tonight warned isolationists in Canada and the United States alike that there is no road to understanding with the Nazi German Government.

The words of Miss Dorothy Thompson, until recently a foreign correspondent specializing in reporting the resurgence of German imperialism, were not unexpected, in view of the expressions of views which she airs in her syndicated columns, but they represented a fresh approach to her audience—the International Affiliation of Sales and Advertising Clubs. And they were certain to carry some weight in the debate now being waged in the States.

EVERY NATION on this globe and every individual on this globe will presently learn what a few have always known: that there are times in history when the business of one is the business of all, when life or death is a matter of choice, and when no one alive can avoid making that choice. These times occur seldom in history, these times of inevitable decisions. But this is one of those times.

Before this epoch is over, every living human being will have chosen, every living human being will have lined up with Hitler or against him, every living human being will either have opposed this onslaught or supported it. For if he tries to make no choice that in itself will be a choice. If he takes no side, he is on Hitler's side; if he does not act that is an act—for Hitler.

The Japan *Times Advertiser,* which is a controlled organ of the Japanese Foreign Office, has set them forth. They have appeared along with the suggestion that Mr. Matsuoka come to America and induce President Roosevelt to join Japan in an attempt to mediate the war. The proposed terms affect Canada, no less than any other part of the British Empire, and affect us as intimately as though we were already an active belligerent. They reveal with complete clarity what is in the minds of the Axis powers. They reveal what they consider to be the New Order of a Thousand Years.

Let us take a look at them; let us see what is the price for peace.

The British Empire and Commonwealth will be utterly destroyed. India and South Africa are to be given independence. I leave out of account the fact that South Africa already has independence. She is to be made more independent by depriving her of the protection of the rest of the English-speaking world. She is to be made independent, as Slovakia was made independent in order to compel her dependence, her total dependence upon the Axis powers.

Thus also the freedom of India. She is to be made free between the nut-cracker of Russia and Japan. Australia is to be opened to Japanese emigration. She would be colonized by the Japanese, and being colonized, claimed as an integral part of the Japanese Empire.

All Western and all Eastern bases of the British Empire—Gibraltar, Malta, Aden, the Red Sea, Singapore, Hong Kong—are to be demilitarized in a world bristling with Axis weapons. The Dutch East Indies and French Indo-China are to be liberated from oppressive rule and put under Japanese economic control.

The seat of authority of the British Empire is to remain, for the time being, on the British Isles. But these islands will be able to exercise no authority over themselves or over any part of the world. . . .

Nazi Germany is to organize the entire continent as one corporate State, with its capital in Berlin. This means that nationality in Europe except for minor matters of local administration, is to be abolished. The whole of Western Europe is to be organized as a huge vertical trust, in which the executives, directors, and majority stockholders will be the German Nazi Party. . . .

You men and women of Canada are tied up inescapably in the destiny first of the British Empire and, should that fall, in the destiny of the United States. And the destiny of one is the destiny of the other. It is no longer a question of our will. We, who did not early enough make the choice for ourselves, have now had it made for us.

Should Britain fall, all that is left of it would be penned up together with the United States on the North American continent, completely encircled and utterly powerless to take an offensive. East and west, north and south, occupying all the strategic bases in the Atlantic and the Pacific commanding all the rest of the economic power of the globe, directing the lives of over two billion men and women of all races and colors, would be two master-races: the German and the Japanese. This is not what I say, this is what Mr. Matsuoka says.

In this world people get what they passionately desire, and woe unto them if they desire the wrong thing. If we desire isolation, we shall have it—the isolation of a prison camp in a hostile community. We shall be penned up on this Continent, while hostile nations east of us, and west of us, and north of us, and south of us, do their level best, their vicious scheming, organized, subsidized, ruthless best to destroy us from inside; to set Canadians against the people of the States; to set labor against capital and capital against labor; the masses against the intelligentsia, and the intelligentsia against the masses; the Irish against the English; the Catholics against the Protestants, the Negroes against the whites, the whites against the Negroes, and everybody against the Jews, in order that the war which we sought to avoid elsewhere may occur here in an internecine fight, the running amok and berserk of an imprisoned colony.

This is their plan. This has always been their plan, to stir nationality against nationality, race against race, class against class, creed against creed, that their mutual destruction of each other may work out for the glory of Hitler and the grandeur of Japan. They count on our freedom—our individual freedom, our individual interests, our individual pursuit of pleasure and happiness—as the means of our destruction of ourselves.

And good men, honest men, unwitting men, work together with the frustrated, the fanatic, the sick, the bitter, the cowardly, the corrupt, the greedy, the selfish, for the end that this civilization may perish from this earth. And democracy and freedom face the bitterest of all tests. It is not the test of arms, it is truly the test of whether they are worthy to survive.

HAROLD L. ICKES

"Americans fight joyously in a just cause."

NEW YORK, N. Y., May 18, 1941 —Harold L. Ickes, Secretary of the Interior and stormy petrel of the Franklin D. Roosevelt Administration, today gave a comprehensive definition to the word "American" as he spoke before 100,000 persons gathered on the Mall in Central Park to observe "I am an American" Day.

Noted for his forthright speech, and abhorrence for the circuitous phraseology which he terms "gobble-degook," Secretary Ickes always is forceful. His words today took on added significance because of the fact that they must be read in the context of these days in mid-1941 when country-wide debate is raging over the actual status of the United States in open support of the Allies.

I WANT to ask a few simple questions. And then I shall answer them.

What has happened to our vaunted idealism? Why have some of us been behaving like scared chickens? Where is the million-throated democratic voice of America?

For years it has been dinned into us that we are a weak nation; that we are an inefficient people; that we are simple-minded. For years we have been told that we are beaten, decayed, and that no part of the world belongs to us any more.

Some amongst us have fallen for this carefully pickled tripe. Some amongst us have fallen for this calculated poison. Some amongst us have begun to preach that the "wave of the future" has passed over us and left us a wet, dead fish.

What constitutes an American? Not color nor race nor religion. Not the pedigree of his family nor the place of his birth. Not the coincidence of his citizenship. Not his social status nor his bank account. Not his trade nor his profession. An American is one who loves justice and believes in the dignity of man. An American is one who will fight for his freedom and that of his neighbor. An American is one who will sacrifice prosperity, ease and security in order that he and his children may retain the rights of free men.

An American is one in whose heart is engraved the immortal second sentence of the Declaration of Independence.

Americans have always known how to fight for their rights and their way of life. Americans are not afraid to fight. They fight joyously in a just cause.

We Americans know that freedom, like peace, is indivisible. We cannot retain our liberty if three-fourths of the world is enslaved. Brutality, injustice and slavery, if practiced as dictators would have them, universally and systematically, in the long run would destroy us as surely as a fire raging in our nearby neighbor's house would burn ours if we didn't help to put out his.

If we are to retain our freedom, we must do everything within our power to aid Britain. We must also do everything to restore to the conquered peoples their freedom. This means the Germans too.

Such a program, if you stop to think, is selfishness on our part. It is the sort of enlightened selfishness that makes the wheels of history go around. It is the sort of enlightened selfishness that wins victories.

NORMAN THOMAS

"We have better work for our sons to do than to have them die."

NEW YORK, N. Y., June 29, 1941 —Norman Thomas, the graying perennial Socialist candidate for the Presidency, tonight pleaded with Americans to resist involvement in the European war, in an address broadcast nationally by radio.

Many listened to the speech, but its influence was predestined to be small. It is an anachronism of politics that Mr. Thomas has become a figure nationally respected for his integrity, his learning and his charm as a public figure, but the leader of lost causes whichever way he turns.

Ironically his public statements on nationalism and pacifism in this period of tension have tended to align him on this issue with leaders of other minority groups who in former years were among the targets of his bitterest attacks, and to separate him from spokesmen for a cultural internationalism who formerly were among his closest friends.

I INSIST that if once we let ourselves be plunged into this war, our liberties will be gone. The same oceans which are so mighty a barrier for our own defense will prove an insuperable obstacle to our conquest of distant continents by any price we can afford to pay. The probable cost of this war in the lives of our sons staggers the imagination. Its cost in money means bankruptcy, something close to a subsistence level of life during the war, and a post-war economic crisis besides which 1932 will be remembered as a year of prosperity. To make the people maintain so insensate a conflict, propaganda, censorship, and conscription, raised to the highest degree, will become necessary. Every bitterness of division among us will be increased. The last chance for the orderly development of a nobler democracy on the face of the earth will have gone. It will not come again with the signing of some sort of peace. Instead there will be a bitter and confused reaction; dictatorship, either of the government in office or some stronger, more demagogic rival, will appear the only alternative to chaos. The idealists who will have helped put us into another war for democracy or the survivors among them will live to see democracy slain in America by the war they sought.

No sincerity of their intentions can alter this fact, for it is not they who will rule the storms of war. War has its own logic, which is the logic of despotism, of the complete subordination of the individual and of groups of individuals, farmers and workers, to the needs and the will of the military state.

Even today the sincere idealists are a small minority among the war makers. Far more powerful are the banking and other business interests who hold the opinion so often voiced by Wendell Willkie that in some mysterious way another military victory by the British Empire, with our aid, in a world caught in the throes of revolution as well as war, will save the old system of private capitalism, the old gold standard, and the types of international trade. Still worse are the imperialists like Henry Luce, Dorothy Thompson in some of her moods, and the extraordinary Senator Pepper, who preach the glories of American imperialism as if that were the American destiny, and bid us grow great by joining the British in exploiting in the name of God and our own profit, the wretched poverty of the natives of Asia and Africa. Nothing alarms me more than the growth of imperialism in the last few months in America. . . .

I do not say this because I am indifferent to Europe's fate. I would go far to cooperate with the whole world to make peace more lasting and glorious. Only recently I have denounced the Administration for imposing new, shocking, and unnecessary restrictions on our already limited offer of asylum to the victims of war and fascism in Europe.

I am not affirming that we can ignore the dangers of the world in which we live, or that a Hitler victory far more complete than he has yet won will not add to those dangers. I am denouncing the hysteria which grossly exaggerates those dangers and even more dangerously minimizes the perils of our involvement in war. I am insisting that a determined America which will keep its sons out of war, can, if it will, make its own democracy work, and by the contagion of its example in a world where alleged democracy has failed, do far more for mankind than by involving itself in a war for which neither Churchill nor Roosevelt has dared to state specific aims.

America's noblest destiny is not empire. It is to demonstrate the possibility of conquering poverty and keeping freedom in a land at peace. We have better work for our sons to do than to have them die to see which of two cruel and treacherous dictators shall master the European continent or what empire shall rob the peoples of Africa, Asia and the islands of the sea.

I am against our participation in this war not only because I hate war, but because I hate Fascism and all totalitarianism, and love democracy. I speak not only for myself, but for my Party in summoning my fellow countrymen to demand that our country be kept out of war, not as an end in itself, but as a condition to the fulfillment of all our hopes and dreams for a better life for ourselves and our children, yes, and all the children of this great land. The extraordinary shifts and changes in European alliances should but confirm our resolution to stay out of Europe's war, and, ourselves at peace, to seek as occasion permits, the peace of the world.

FULTON J. SHEEN

"A revolution that will change your hearts."

WASHINGTON, D. C., March 23, 1941—A 46-year-old priest, already famous for 15 years as a writer and speaker and now an outstanding "radio personality," Mgr. Fulton J. Sheen, tonight urged a national audience to substitute thought for slogans in the present controversy over conservatism vs. radicalism in world movements.

The speaker broadcast on The Catholic Hour, under the sponsorship of the National Catholic Welfare Conference, but his audiences long since have extended far beyond the communicants of his own church.

I PLEAD with you to sweep away slogans that mean nothing and begin to be among the thinking elite who want to build a very different and happier world than the one we live in now. You have been told that the only choice possible is to be a reactionary or a liberal; that you must go either right or left.

That would be true if you lived in a two-dimensional plane and this world were all; but you have a soul as well as a body. You need therefore a three-dimensional universe, one with height where you can stretch not your necks but your hearts.

A mule can travel only in two directions: either right or left. He must be either a reactionary or a liberal. But because you have a soul there is another direction open to you, toward God for whom you were made.

Let the unthinking squabble about what a grandson ought to believe, or what a grandfather did believe, but concentrate on what a godson believes because born of the Spirit. If you are honest with yourself you will admit that you are weary of religions, politics and panaceas that flatter the way you live; you want something that will contradict the way you live and therefore be capable of redeeming you; you are sick of revolution that only changes booty and loot from one man's pocket to another's; you want a revolution that will change your hearts.

Leave it to the comedians to talk about "progress" when humanity is pressing you itself, for what they call progress is only a process—the fashion of the world passing away.

Put behind you the acceptance of nonsense because you dislike holding something with ethical consequences. Realize that you must be saved not *for* these days but *from* them; that a new order may begin whenever you can live as created in time but ordered in eternity. Do you not see that where Christ is persecuted in the world today, man is most defeated?

The sequel:

From what might have been considered the peak of a career, Mgr. Sheen progressed to the preaching and teaching field of television, and became a bishop in the Roman Catholic hierarchy.

FRANKLIN D. ROOSEVELT

"We are going to win the war and we are going to win the peace that follows."

WASHINGTON, D. C., Dec. 8, 1941—To a nation stunned by the news of Japan's sneak attack yesterday on Pearl Harbor—and while reports of that disaster still were incomplete—President Roosevelt tonight broadcast a message of confidence in the war that suddenly has burst upon the United States.

He spoke again over the radio from his study in the White House, within a few hours after sending to the Congress a message requesting affirmation of the declaration that a state of war exists with Japan—action which was taken immediately.

This would not be an easy or a short conflict, the President stated; it would be long and costly and difficult, but he expressed full confidence in victory.

THE SUDDEN criminal attacks perpetrated by the Japanese in the Pacific provide the climax of a decade of international immorality.

Powerful and resourceful gangsters have banded together to make war upon the whole human race. Their challenge has now been flung at the United States of America. The Japanese have treacherously violated the long-standing peace between us. Many American soldiers and sailors have been killed by enemy action. American ships have been sunk; American airplanes have been destroyed.

The Congress and the people of the United States have accepted that challenge.

Together with other free peoples, we are now fighting to maintain our right to live among our world neighbors in freedom and in common decency, without fear of assault.

I have prepared the full record of our past relations with Japan, and it will be submitted to the Congress. It begins with the visit of Commodore Perry to Japan eighty-eight years ago. It ends with the visit of two Japanese emissaries to the Secretary of State last Sunday, an hour after Japanese forces had loosed their bombs and machine guns against our flag, our forces and our citizens.

I can say with utmost confidence that no Americans today or a thousand years hence need feel anything but pride in our patience and in our efforts through all the years toward achieving a peace in the Pacific which would be fair and honorable to every nation, large or small. And no honest person, today or a thousand years hence, will be able to suppress a sense of indignation and horror at the treachery committed by the military dictators of Japan under the very shadow of the flag of peace borne by their special envoys in our midst.

The course that Japan has followed for the past ten years in Asia has paralleled the course of Hitler and Mussolini in Europe and in Africa. Today, it has become far more than a parallel. It is collaboration, actual collaboration, so well calculated that all the continents of the world, and all the oceans, are now considered by the Axis strategists as one gigantic battlefield.

In 1931, ten years ago, Japan invaded Manchukuo—without warning.

In 1935, Italy invaded Ethiopia—without warning.

In 1938, Hitler occupied Austria—without warning.

In 1939, Hitler invaded Czecho-Slovakia—without warning.

Later in 1939, Hitler invaded Poland—without warning.

In 1940, Hitler invaded Norway, Denmark, the Netherlands, Belgium and Luxembourg—without warning.

In 1940, Italy attacked France and later Greece—without warning.

And in this year, 1941, the Axis Powers attacked Yugoslavia and Greece and they dominated the Balkans—without warning.

In 1941 also, Hitler invaded Russia—without warning.

And now Japan has attacked Malaya and Thailand—and the United States—without warning.

It is all of one pattern.

We are now in this war. We are all in it—all the way. Every single man, woman and child is a partner in the most tremendous undertaking of our American history. We must share together the bad news and the good news, the defeats and the victories—the changing fortunes of war.

So far, the news has been all bad. We have suffered a serious set-back in Hawaii. Our forces in the Philippines, which include the brave people of that commonwealth, are taking punishment, but are defending themselves vigorously. The reports from Guam and Wake and Midway Islands are still confused, but we must be prepared for the announcement that all these outposts have been seized.

The casualty lists of these first few days will undoubtedly be large. I deeply feel the anxiety of all families of the men in our armed forces and the relatives of people in cities which have been bombed. I can only give them my solemn promise that they will get news just as quickly as possible.

This government will put its trust in the stamina of the American people and will give the facts to the public as soon as two conditions have been fulfilled; first, that the information has been definitely and officially confirmed; and, second, that the release of the information at the time it is received will not prove valuable to the enemy directly or indirectly.

Most earnestly I urge my countrymen to reject all rumors. These ugly little hints of complete disaster fly thick and fast in wartime. They have to be examined and appraised. . . .

Now a word about the recent past—and the future. A year and

a half has elapsed since the fall of France, when the whole world first realized the mechanized might which the Axis nations had been building for so many years. America has used that year and a half to great advantage. Knowing that the attack might reach us in all too short a time, we immediately began greatly to increase our industrial strength and our capacity to meet the demands of modern warfare.

Precious months were gained by sending vast quantities of our war matériel to the nations of the world still able to resist Axis aggression. Our policy rested on the fundamental truth that the defense of any country resisting Hitler or Japan was in the long run the defense of our own country. That policy has been justified. It has given us time, invaluable time, to build our American assembly lines of production.

Assembly lines are now in operation. Others are being rushed to completion. A steady stream of tanks and planes, of guns and ships, of shells and equipment—that is what these eighteen months have given us.

But it is all only a beginning of what has to be done. We must be set to face a long war against crafty and powerful bandits. The attack at Pearl Harbor can be repeated at any one of many points in both oceans and along both our coast lines and against all the rest of the hemisphere.

It will not only be a long war, it will be a hard war. That is the basis on which we now lay all our plans. That is the yardstick by which we measure what we shall need and demand: money, materials, doubled and quadrupled production—ever increasing. The production must be not only for our own Army and Navy and air forces. It must reinforce the other armies and navies and air forces fighting the Nazis and the war lords of Japan throughout the Americas and the world.

I have been working today on the subject of production. Your government has decided on two broad policies.

The first is to speed up all existing production by working on a seven-day-week basis in every war industry, including the production of essential raw materials.

The second policy, now being put into form, is to rush additions to the capacity of production by building more new plants, by adding to old plants, and by using the many smaller plants for war needs.

Over the hard road of the past months we have at times met obstacles and difficulties, divisions and disputes, indifference and callousness. That is now all past—and, I am sure, forgotten. . . .

We are going to win the war and we are going to win the peace that follows.

The sequel:

While the President delivered this "fireside chat" the United States was only at war with Japan. Technically relations were unchanged with Germany and Italy.

It was not until the morning of December 11 that Germany and Italy formally declared war on the United States, in accordance with their alliance with Japan.

But all that the President could say, or needed to say in his capacity as the country's President had been expressed in the speech digested here. The rest was anti-climax.

Not until January 6, 1942, when the President went to Capitol Hill to address the Congress in person, would he enlarge upon the theme.

FRANKLIN D. ROOSEVELT

"No compromise can end that conflict."

WASHINGTON, D. C., Jan. 6, 1942 —President Roosevelt called today for total national mobilization in the new world war thrust upon the United States—"our task is unprecedented and the time is short."

This was the all-pervading theme of his message on the state of the Union, which traditionally opens the new session of the Congress, and which today came only one month after the attack on Pearl Harbor, as a result of which the Congress already had been called into special session.

In the meantime, every possible step has been taken to place the United States on a war footing, in contrast with the defense posture of the security program which earlier was the rule.

In the meantime, also, the new and active alliance between Great Britain and the United States was dramatized by a visit to Washington by Prime Minister Winston Churchill, who both conferred with President Roosevelt and delivered an address, by invitation, to a joint session of the Congressional bodies.

MR. VICE PRESIDENT, Mr. Speaker, members of the Senate and the House of Representatives of the United States:

In fulfilling my duty to report on the state of the Union, I am proud to say to you that the spirit of the American people was never higher than it is today. The Union was never more closely knit together and this country was never more deeply determined to face the solemn tasks before it.

The response of the American people has been instantaneous, and it will be sustained until our security is assured.

Exactly one year ago today I said to this Congress: "When the dictators are ready to make war upon us they will not wait for an act of war on our part. They, not we, will choose the time and the place and the method of their attack."

We now know their choice of the time, a peaceful December morning, Dec. 7, 1941.

We know their choice of the place, an outpost, an American outpost, in the Pacific.

We know their choice of the method, the method of Hitler himself.

Japan's scheme of conquest goes back half a century. It is not merely a policy of seeking living room, it was a plan which included the subjugation of all the peoples in the Far East and in the islands of the Pacific, and the domination of that ocean by Japanese military and naval control of the western coasts of North, Central and South America. . . .

When Hitler organized his Berlin-Rome-Tokyo alliance, all these plans of conquest became a single plan. Under this, in addition to her own schemes of conquest, Japan's role was obviously to cut off our supply of weapons of war to Britain and Russia and China, weapons which increasingly were speeding the day of Hitler's doom. The act of Japan at Pearl Harbor was intended to stun us, to terrify us to such an extent that we would divert our industrial and military strength to the Pacific area or even to our own continental defense.

The plan has failed in its purpose. We have not been stunned. We have not been terrified or confused. This very reassembling of the Seventy-seventh Congress today is proof of that. For the mood of quiet grim resolution which here prevails bodes ill for those who conspired and collaborated to murder world peace. . . .

Admittedly, we have been faced with hard choices. It was bitter, for example, not to relieve the heroic and historic defenders of Wake Island. It was bitter for us not to be able to land a million men from a thousand ships in the Philippine Islands.

But this adds only to our determination to see to it that the Stars and Stripes will fly again over Wake and Guam, and that the brave people of the Philippines will be rid of Japanese imperialism and will live in freedom and security and independence.

Powerful and offensive actions must and will be taken in proper time. The consolidation of the United Nations' total war effort against our common enemy is being achieved.

That was and is the purpose of conferences which have been held during the past two weeks in Washington and Moscow and Chungking. This is the primary objective of the declaration of solidarity signed in Washington on Jan. 1, 1942, by twenty-six nations against the Axis powers.

Difficult choices may have to be made in the months to come. We do not shrink from such decisions. We and those united with us will make those decisions with courage and determination.

Plans have been laid here and in the other capitals for coordinated and cooperative action by all the United Nations, military action and economic action. Already we have established, as you know, unified command of land, sea and air forces in the Southwestern Pacific theatre of war.

There will be a continuation of conferences and consultations among military staffs, so that the plans and operations of each will fit into the general strategy designed to crush the enemy. We shall not fight isolated wars, each nation going its own way. These twenty-six nations are united not in spirit and determination alone but in the broad conduct of the war in all its phases. . . .

Our task is hard. Our task is unprecedented and the time is short. We must strain every existing armament-producing facility to the utmost. We must convert every available plant and tool to war production. That goes all the way from the greatest plants to the smallest, from the huge automobile industry to the village machine shop.

Production for war is based on men and women, the human hands and brains which collectively we call labor. Our workers stand ready to work long hours. To turn out more in a day's work. To keep the wheels turning and the fires burning twenty-four hours a day and seven days a week. They realize well that on the speed and efficiency of their work depend the lives of their sons and brothers on the fighting front. . . .

War costs money. So far we have hardly even begun to pay for it. We devoted only 15 per cent of our national income to national defense. As will appear in my budget message tomorrow, our war program for the coming fiscal year will cost $56,000,000,000, or in other words more than half of the estimated annual national income. That means taxes and bonds, and bonds and taxes. It means cutting luxuries and other nonessentials. In a word, it means an all-out war by individual effort and family effort in a united country. . . .

As the United States goes into its full stride, we must always be on guard, on guard against misconception that will arise naturally or which will be planted among us by our enemies.

We must guard against complacency. We must not underrate the enemy. He is powerful and cunning, cruel and ruthless. . . .

We must, on the other hand, guard against defeatism. That has been one of the chief weapons of Hitler's propaganda machine, used time and again with deadly results. It will not be used successfully on the American people.

We must guard against divisions among ourselves and among all the other United Nations. We must be particularly vigilant against racial discrimination in any of its ugly forms. . . .

We cannot wage this war in a defensive spirit. As our power and resources are fully mobilized we shall carry the attack against the enemy. We shall hit him, and hit him again, wherever and whenever we can reach him. . . .

Many people ask, "When will this war end?" There is only one answer to that. It will end just as soon as we make it end by our combined efforts, our combined strength, our combined determination to fight through and work through until the end, the end of militarism in Germany and Italy and Japan. Most certainly we shall not settle for less.

That is the spirit in which discussions have been conducted during the visit of the British Prime Minister to Washington. Mr. Churchill and I understand each other, our motives and our purposes. Together during the past two weeks we have faced squarely the major military and economic problems of this greatest world war.

All in our nations have been cheered by Mr. Churchill's visit. We have been deeply stirred by his great message to us. He is welcome in our midst now and in days to come. And we unite in wishing him a safe return to his home. For we are fighting on the same side with the British people who fought alone the long terrible months and withstood the enemy with fortitude and tenacity and skill.

We are fighting on the same side with the Russian people who have seen the Nazi hordes swarm up to the very gates of Moscow and who with almost superhuman will and courage have forced the invaders back into retreat.

We are fighting on the same side as the brave people of China, those millions who for four and a half long years have withstood bombs and starvation and have whipped the invaders time and again in spite of the superior Japanese equipment and arms.

Yes, we are fighting on the same side with the indomitable Dutch.

We are fighting on the same side as all the other governments in exile whom Hitler and all his armies and all his Gestapo have not been able to conquer.

But we of the United Nations are not making all this sacrifice of human effort and human lives to return to the kind of world we had after the last World War. We are fighting today for security and progress and for peace, not only for ourselves but for all men, not only for one generation but for all generations. We are fighting to cleanse the world of ancient evils, ancient ills.

Our enemies are guided by brutal cynicism, by unholy contempt for the human race. We are inspired by a faith which goes back through all the years to the first chapter of the Book of Genesis—"God created man in His own image."

We on our side are striving to be true to that divine heritage. We are fighting, as our fathers have fought, to uphold the doctrine that all men are equal in the sight of God. Those on the other side are striving to destroy this deep belief and to create a world in their own image, a world of tyranny and cruelty and serfdom.

That is the conflict that day and night now pervades our lives. No compromise can end that conflict. There never has been and never can be successful compromise between good and evil. Only total victory can reward the champions of tolerance and decency and freedom and faith.

GEORGE S. PATTON

"Flanks are something for the enemy to worry about."

ON THE AVRANCHES FRONT, France, July 31, 1944—The American Army's fightingest general, and its most controversial one—Lieutenant General George S. Patton—prepared tonight to send his newly designated Third Army into one of the war's bitterest actions, with a brief talk reminiscent of Napoleon or Sherman, to both of whom he already has been compared.

He talked to his army, now comprising the most powerful single armored unit yet put into the field, through a staff of several score officers. The scene of his talk—given by a general to a group with whom he has shared countless nights of sleepless planning—was the blacked-out interior of improvised headquarters at a secret location.

His words, from the minutes of the meeting, follow:

WE BECOME operational officially tomorrow, and doubtless from time to time there will be some complaints that we are pushing people too hard. I don't give a good goddam about such complaints. I believe in the old and sound rule that an ounce of sweat is worth a gallon of blood.

The harder we push, the more Germans we'll kill, and the more Germans we kill, the fewer of our men will be killed. Pushing means lower casualties. I want you to remember that.

There is another thing I want you to remember. Forget this goddamed business of worrying about our flanks. We must guard our flanks, but not to the extent that we don't do anything else. Some goddam fool once said that flanks must be secured, and since then sons-of-bitches all over the world have been going crazy guarding their flanks. Flanks are something for the enemy to worry about, not us.

Also, I don't want any messages saying, "I am holding my position." We're not holding anything. Let the Hun do that. We are advancing constantly and are not interested in holding anything, except onto the enemy. We're trying to hold onto him and kick the hell out of him all the time.

Our basic plan of operation is to advance and to keep on advancing regardless of whether we have to go over, under or through the enemy. We have one motto, "Audacious, audacious, always audacious." Remember that. From here on out, until we win or die in the attempt, we will always be audacious.

The sequel:

There remained yet a long period in which General Patton must instill the rule of audacity in his troops. With them after this date he experienced both great triumphs and great disappointments, but war raised his controversial figure to the highest rank.

Not long after the victory which he helped to win, he was killed—not in battle as he had once predicted he would be—but in an accident involving a truck and the car in which he was riding.

V

LOOKING FORWARD

BERNARD M. BARUCH

"We are here to make a choice between the quick and the dead."

UNITED NATIONS HEADQUARTERS, N. Y., June 14, 1946—Bernard M. Baruch, unofficial adviser to, and confidant of, each President from Woodrow Wilson to Dwight D. Eisenhower, summarized today in these dramatic words the great question of the Twentieth Century.

Speaking as United States Representative to the United Nations Atomic Energy Commission, Mr. Baruch said bluntly that discovery of atomic fission basically gives the world a choice between self-destruction in wartime or undreamed-of development through peaceful harnessing of this force.

Immediate reaction to the speech was one of optimism. However, there remained the question as to what Soviet reaction would be. At the time of this meeting only the United States had demonstrated conquest of the atom, and therefore is in the position to be generous in its offers, with no question as to its sincerity. But there are rumors that the German scientists who were captured by the Soviet armies in the last days of the war were even a year ago far advanced in their own progress toward the same goal; that their skills added to Russian scientific work may bring this other power into the picture before much time elapses.

Of great importance in today's presentation was the personality of this vigorous 76-year-old man who held posts of the highest responsibilities in World War I and II, and who wrote a report on postwar plans, in 1944, at the special request of former President Roosevelt. Many observers also recall the long years prior to World War II when Mr. Baruch, at his own expense, made searching inquiries into the defense needs of the United States, only to see his recommendations shelved as soon as they had been delivered.

With today's report, speaking as he does with the unanimous backing alike of the White House and the Congress, there is hope the result will be different.

WE ARE here to make a choice between the quick and the dead. That is our business.

Behind the black portent of the new atomic age lies a hope which, seized upon with faith, can work our salvation. If we fail, then we have damned every man to be the slave of fear. Let us not deceive ourselves: We must elect world peace or world destruction.

Science has torn from nature a secret so vast in its potentialities that our minds cower from the terror it creates. Yet terror is not enough to inhibit the use of the atomic bomb. The terror created by weapons has never stopped man from employing them. For each new weapon a defense has been produced, in time. But now we face a condition in which adequate defense does not exist.

Science, which gave us this dread power, shows that it can be made a giant help to humanity, but science does not show us how to prevent its baleful use. So we have been appointed to obviate that peril by finding a meeting of the minds and the hearts of our peoples. Only in the will of mankind lies the answer.

In this crisis we represent not only our governments but, in a larger way, we represent the peoples of the world. We must remember that the peoples do not belong to the governments, but that the governments belong to the peoples. We must answer their demands; we must answer the world's longing for peace and security.

In that desire the United States shares ardently and hopefully. The search of science for the absolute weapon has reached fruition in this country. But she stands ready to proscribe and destroy this instrument—to lift its use from death to life—if the world will join in a pact to that end.

In our success lies the promise of a new life, freed from the heart-stopping fears that now beset the world. The beginning of victory for the great ideals for which millions have bled and died lies in building a workable plan. Now we approach the fulfilment of the aspirations of mankind. At the end of the road lies the fairer, better, surer life we crave and mean to have.

Only by a lasting peace are liberties and democracies strengthened and deepened. War is their enemy. And it will not do to believe that any of us can escape war's devastation. Victor, vanquished and neutrals alike are affected physically, economically and morally.

Against the degradation of war we can erect a safeguard. That is the *guerdon* for which we reach. Within the scope of the formula we outline here, there will be found, to those who seek it, the essential elements of our purpose. Others will see only emptiness. Each of us carries his own mirror in which is reflected hope—or determined desperation—courage or cowardice.

There is famine throughout the world today. It starves men's bodies. But there is a greater famine—the hunger of men's spirit. That starvation can be cured by the conquest of fear, and the substitution of hope, from which springs faith—faith in each other; faith that we want to work together toward salvation; and determination that those who threaten the peace and safety shall be punished.

The peoples of these democracies gathered here have a particular concern with our answer, for their peoples hate war. They will have a heavy exaction to make of those who fail to provide an escape. They are not afraid of an internationalism that protects; they are unwilling to be fobbed off by mouthings about narrow sovereignty, which is today's phrase for yesterday's isolationism.

The basis of a sound foreign policy, in this new age, for all the nations here gathered, is that: anything that happens, no matter where or how, which menaces the peace of the world, or the economic stability, concerns each and all of us.

That, roughly, may be said to be the central theme of the United Nations. It is with that thought we gain consideration of the most important subject that can engage mankind—life itself.

Now, if ever, is the time to act for the common good. Public opinion supports a world movement toward security. If I read the signs aright, the peoples want a program, not composed merely of pious thoughts, but of enforceable sanctions—an international law with teeth in it.

We, of this nation, desirous of helping to bring peace to the world and realizing the heavy obligations upon us, arising from our possession of the means for producing the bomb and from the fact that it is part of our armament, are prepared to make our full contribution toward effective control of atomic energy.

But before a country is ready to relinquish any winning weapons, it must have more than words to reassure it. It must have a guarantee of safety, not only against the offenders in the atomic area, but against the illegal users of other weapons—bacteriological, biological, gas—perhaps—why not?—against war itself.

In the elimination of war lies our solution, for only then will nations cease to compete with one another in the production and use of dread "secret" weapons which are evaluated solely by their capacity to kill. This devilish program takes us back not merely to the Dark Ages, but from cosmos to chaos. If we succeed in finding a suitable way to control atomic weapons adaptable to mass destruction: when a man learns to say "A" he can, if he chooses, learn the rest of the alphabet too.

Let this be anchored in our minds:

Peace is never long preserved by weight of metal or by an armament race. Peace can be made tranquil and secure only by understanding and agreement fortified by sanctions. We must embrace international cooperation or international disintegration.

Science has taught us how to put the atom to work. But to make it work for good instead of for evil lies in the domain dealing with the principles of human duty. We are now facing a problem more of ethics than physics.

The solution will require apparent sacrifice in pride and in position, but better pain as the price of peace than death as the price of war.

The sequel:

The first high hopes aroused by international reaction to the American proposals put forward by Mr. Baruch soon withered. The wartime lessons of even the first atomic bombs' potency in usage against Hiroshima and Nagasaki had not been enough to induce true respect for the bomb, and other developments abroad were not known at the time.

These other developments were Russian progress in research, with a speed that soon obliterated the time in which the United States could guard with peaceful intent its own exclusive atomic developments.

Tension increased rather than decreased, as this research both in the United States and in Russia broadened to encompass the harnessing of the hydrogen bomb, a far more powerful weapon than the atomic bomb.

Ironically in all the arguments advanced in the intervening years, no really new thought had been introduced to supplement the stark picture laid down by the aging and thoughtful Mr. Baruch.

GEORGE C. MARSHALL

"Our policy is directed not against any country or doctrine but against hunger, poverty, desperation and chaos."

CAMBRIDGE, Mass., June 5, 1947 —Speaking from the mellowed background of Harvard University's "yard," as the latest recipient of honors awarded for more than 300 years, Secretary of State George C. Marshall today launched the most ambitious program to enhance recovery of shattered allied nations from World War II yet broached by our government.

He called in effect for a coordinated program of relief that would restore the normal flow of production and trade, and help to integrate industrial and agricultural production to "break the vicious circle" of dislocations caused both by war production programs and by occupations.

He warned, however, that such assistance requires first the submission of reasonable plans for constructive programs by each of our former allies, programs in which "political passion and prejudice should have no part."

The choice of background for this momentous announcement was an academic platform, while the speaker wore the hood and stole of an honorary Doctor of Laws which removed both the announcer and the subject about as far as possible from the electric atmosphere of political debate in Washington.

There was comment also as to the fortuitous circumstance that Secretary Marshall, already a distinguished Army officer and recently Ambassador, has kept as aloof as possible from other debates over reconstruction and relief that already have cost the American taxpayers scores of millions of dollars.

I NEED not tell you gentlemen that the world situation is very serious. That must be apparent to all intelligent people. I think one difficulty is that the problem is one of such enormous complexity that the very mass of facts presented to the public by press and radio make it exceedingly difficult for the man in the street to reach a clear appraisement of the situation. Furthermore, the people of this country are distant from the troubled areas of the earth and it is hard for them to comprehend the plight and consequent reactions of the long-suffering peoples, and the effect of those reactions on their governments in connection with our efforts to promote peace in the world.

In considering the requirements for the rehabilitation of Europe, the physical loss of life, the visible destruction of cities, factories, mines and railroads was correctly estimated but it has become obvious during recent months that this visible destruction was probably less serious than the dislocation of the entire fabric of European economy. For the past ten years conditions have been highly abnormal. The feverish preparation for war and the more feverish maintenance of the war effort engulfed all aspects of national economies. Machinery has fallen into disrepair or is entirely obsolete. Under the arbitrary and destructive Nazi rule, virtually every possible enterprise was geared into the German war machine. Long-standing commercial ties, private institutions, banks, insurance companies and shipping companies disappeared, through loss of capital, absorption through nationalization or by simple destruction. In many countries, confidence in the local currency has been severely shaken. The breakdown of the business structure of Europe during the war was complete. Recovery has been seriously retarded by the fact that two years after the close of hostilities a peace settlement with Germany and Austria has not been agreed upon. But even given a more prompt solution of these difficult problems, the rehabilitation of the economic structure of Europe quite evidently will require a much longer time and greater effort than had been foreseen.

There is a phase of this matter which is both interesting and serious. The farmer has always produced the foodstuffs to exchange with the city dweller for the other necessities of life. This division of labor is the basis of modern civilization. At the present time it is threatened with breakdown. The town and city industries are not producing adequate goods to exchange with the food-producing farmer. Raw materials and fuels are in short supply. Machinery is lacking or worn out. The farmer or the peasant cannot find the goods for sale which he desires to purchase. So the sale of his farm produce for money which he cannot use seems to him an unprofitable transaction. He, therefore, has withdrawn many fields from crop cultivation and is using them for grazing. He feeds more grain to stock and finds for himself and his family an ample supply of food, however short he may be on clothing and the other ordinary gadgets of civilization. Meanwhile people in the cities are short of food and fuel. So the governments are forced to use their foreign money and credits to procure these necessities abroad. This process exhausts funds which are urgently needed for reconstruction. Thus a very serious situation is rapidly developing which bodes no good for the world. The modern system of the division of labor upon which the exchange of products is based is in danger of breaking down.

The truth of the matter is that Europe's requirements for the next three or four years of foreign food and other essential products —principally from America—are so much greater than her present ability to pay that she must have substantial additional help, or face economic, social and political deterioration of a very grave character.

The remedy lies in breaking the vicious circle and restoring the confidence of the European people in the economic future of their own countries and of Europe as a whole. The manufacturer and the farmer throughout wide areas must be able and willing to exchange their products for currencies the continuing value of which is not open to question.

Aside from the demoralizing effect on the world at large and the possibilities of disturbances arising as a result of the desperation of the people concerned, the consequences to the economy of the United States should be apparent to all. It is logical that the United States should do whatever it is able to do to assist in the return of normal economic health in the world, without which there can be no political stability and no assured peace. Our policy is directed not against any country or doctrine but against hunger, poverty, desperation and chaos. Its purpose should be the revival of a working economy in the world so as to permit the emergence of political and social conditions in which free institutions can exist. Such assistance, I am convinced, must not be on a piece-meal basis as various crises develop. Any assistance that this Government may render in the future should provide a cure rather than a mere palliative. Any government that is willing to assist in the task of recovery will find full cooperation, I am sure, on the part of the United States Government. Any government which maneuvers to block the recovery of other countries cannot expect help from us. Furthermore, governments, political parties or groups which seek to perpetuate human misery in order to profit therefrom politically or otherwise will encounter the opposition of the United States.

It is already evident that, before the United States Government can proceed much further in its efforts to alleviate the situation and help start the European world on its way to recovery, there must be some agreement among the countries of Europe as to the requirements of the situation and the part those countries themselves will take in order to give proper effect to whatever action might be undertaken by this Government. It would be neither fitting nor efficacious for this Government to undertake to draw up unilaterally a program designed to place Europe on its feet economically. This is the business of the Europeans. The initiative, I think, must come from Europe. The role of this country should consist of friendly aid in the drafting of a European program and of later support of such a program so far as it may be practical for us to do so. The program should be a joint one, agreed to by a number, if not all European nations.

An essential part of any successful action on the part of the United States is an understanding on the part of the people of America of the character of the problem and the remedies to be applied. Political passion and prejudice should have no part. With foresight, and a willingness on the part of our people to face up to the vast responsibility which history has clearly placed upon our country, the difficulties I have outlined can and will be overcome.

The sequel:

Before the first reports of this speech had been fully distributed, newspaper headlines had given this talk its title in history. It was the "Marshall Plan."

More than a decade later the name has become so ingrained in the history of postwar foreign policy that it promises to rank along such other names as the Louisiana Purchase, the Monroe Doctrine and the Neutrality Acts as landmarks in American history.

General Marshall himself would

have been the last to claim full credit for the Plan. It was a major step in foreign policy hammered out in many conferences among many groups of government leaders, with a prominent preparatory role being played by Dean Acheson, Undersecretary of State with General Marshall and later Secretary of State in his own right.

However, just as Secretary Marshall would have borne the blame had the program failed, so his is the "program credit"—to use a theatre expression—for perhaps the greatest of the postwar relief programs, effectuated as the European Recovery Program. Its authorship already has overshadowed in world opinion the probably much more difficult and greater task he accomplished as Chief of Staff of the Army throughout World War II.

HERBERT HOOVER

"I suggest that the United Nations be reorganized without the Communist nations in it."

NEW YORK, N. Y., April 27, 1950 —Former President Herbert Hoover tonight advocated reorganization of the United Nations with membership confined to the non-Communist nations or, as an alternative, a second organization of Western powers outside the United Nations.

Mr. Hoover's recommendations were made in a nationally broadcast address delivered before the annual meeting of the American Newspaper Publishers Association. It evoked mixed reactions, but on the whole was cheered as a statesmanlike view of a question that is probably unsolvable, yet one which must be faced on a continuing basis for many years to come.

The speaker, whose stature has grown in the 17 years since he was defeated for reelection by Franklin D. Roosevelt, gave his talk as a sequel to another delivered in 1941 when, with America committed to aiding the Allies but not yet involved in actual hostilities, he proposed that victory of the Nazis be marked immediately by movements toward organization of the world's countries that would thwart the growth of communism as well as stamp out Nazism.

That was not done, he noted, and accordingly the efforts to cooperate with communism had been marred at every turn by the dictators, who had extended their ideological conquests to include China and much of the remainder of Asia.

Earlier this year, it was remarked, Russia had achieved another victory of great diplomatic importance when Great Britain withdrew recognition from the Chinese Nationalist Government and accorded this recognition to the Chinese Communist regime.

At this writing, it is noted that great military forces, armed by Russia, have been massed by Red China on its ocean borders facing Japan, Formosa and the Philippines, while North Korea has become an armed camp overshadowing the southern part of Korea being reconstructed by Western powers, principally the United States.*

I NEED not remind you that our page one international issue is Communist Russia. There are seven phases of this experience which I must recall before I come to a proposal of action.

The first phase of experience with Russia began under the Czars. Since Peter the Great they have steadily expanded their reach of Empire over the largest land mass in the world. Their method was that of a burglar going down a hall. If there was no one in the first room, he took everything including the doorknob. If he found someone in the second room who protested, he weighed the strength of the protester and might leave part of the furniture. If he found an armed man in the third room, he closed the door and waited.

Lenin and Stalin added a new apparatus for the robber. They now make the man in the second room a Party member and rob him later and by degrees. They now put the armed man in the third room asleep with a non-aggression pact or a promise of peace. Thus, he neglects his weapons. In any event they steal his secrets.

The second phase of this experience with Russia was a period of sixteen years during which four Presidents and seven Secretaries of State opposed our having any relations with this malignant government. Their attitude was that when our neighbors are living a life of spiritual and other disrepute, we do not attack them. But we can hold up standards in the world a little better if we do not invite them into our homes by so-called diplomatic recognition.

The third historical phase arrived when our left-wingers had their way in our relations with Communist Russia. They produced

---

* At 2 P.M., June 24, 1950, the Communist-trained forces of North Korea opened their military attack on the Republic of Korea, and thereby precipitated the Korean War.

the recognition of the Soviet in 1933. They produced the alliance with Russia in 1941. They produced the appeasement of Russia in Western Europe until its reversal by President Truman and Secretary Byrnes in 1945. I will not join in the explanations about China. Up to now there is agreement on only one point. We lost the game—400,000,000 to nothing.

Many of our left-wingers were not consciously doing all this. They were just trigger-happy to anything new in the ideological line.

Lest anyone think I am a recent convert in these views, I may cite that just nine years and 63 days ago in a public address I warned the American people that collaboration with Stalin to bring freedom to mankind was a gargantuan jest. I used the wrong adjective. I should have said tragic. For as a result, instead of the expansion of liberty, we witness a dozen nations and 600,000,000 human beings enslaved.

The fourth phase of this experience was that Soviet Russia has since our recognition violated more than 35 solemnly signed agreements.

The fifth phase of this experience has been with the Communists in the United Nations. That Charter for which we hoped so much contains lengthy pledges to the independence of nations, to human liberty and to non-aggression. About a dozen provisions of that Charter have been violated either in spirit or in letter by Soviet Russia. The Kremlin has reduced the United Nations to a propaganda forum for the smearing of free peoples. It has been defeated in its major purpose as a maker of peace and good will.

The sixth phase of this experience is that we now find ourselves in an expensive and dangerous cold war. We conduct the battle with subsidies to beguile peoples to rectitude from internal communism. A year ago we made the Atlantic Military Pact. The expressed hope was that although there was no commitment to go to war, these nations would build up their own arms to adequately defend their own rooms. In persistence to an old habit, we are taking up the check.

In the meantime we learn that our first defense—the atomic bomb—has been stolen from us.

The final phase of our experience with Russia is the belated realization that this is not one world. It is two worlds. The one-world idea seems to be lost in the secret files.

One world is militaristic, imperialistic, atheistic and without compassion. The other world still holds to belief in God, free nations, human dignity and peace.

Now to come to the point of all this. The American people ought to take a cold and objective look at this experience before we go any further.

This look should be directed to the fact that more and more the burdens of defending free men and nations are being thrust upon the American people, who are only six per cent of the population of the globe. We are becoming more and more isolated as the sole contender in this cold war. We are steadily losing ground because the non-Communist states are being picked off one by one or they are compromising with the Communists. Our countrymen are in a fog as to what, where and when all this leads to.

What the world needs today is a definite, spiritual mobilization of the nations who believe in God against this tide of Red agnosticism. It needs a moral mobilization against the hideous ideas of the police state and human slavery. The world needs mobilization against this creeping Red Imperialism. The United States needs to know who are with us in the cold war against these practices, and whom we can depend on.

Therefore, I have a proposal to make.

I suggest that the United Nations should be reorganized without the Communist nations in it. If that is impractical, then a definite New United Front should be organized of those peoples who disavow communism, who stand for morals and religion, and who love freedom.

This is specifically not a proposed extension of a military alliance or any color of it. It is a proposal based solely upon moral, spiritual and defense foundations. It is a proposal to redeem the concept of the United Nations to the high purpose for which it was created. It is a proposal for moral and spiritual cooperation of God-fearing free nations.

If the free nations join together, they have many potent moral, spiritual and even economic and military weapons at their disposal. They would unlikely ever need such weapons. Such a phalanx of free nations could come far nearer to making a workable relation with the other half of the two worlds than the United States can ever do alone.

By collective action we could much more effectively keep their conspiring agents and bribers out of all our borders and out of our laboratories.

It may be the non-Communist world is not willing to take such a vital stand. At least it would clarify what we have to do.

The test I propose is the logical and practical end of total diplomacy. It would make diplomacy dynamic and lessen the dangers of the American people. All this may give pain to some people. But by their cries ye shall know them.

My friends, I am not disheartened by all this recall of disturbing experience. We must retain our faith in Western civilization. In support of that faith we are perhaps a slow but a resolute and intelligent people. We have the greatest organ of education known to man—a free press. You can dissolve much of our confusions and frustrations.

And in rejecting an atheistic other world, I am confident that the Almighty God will be with us.

WILLIAM FAULKNER

"I decline to accept the end of man."

STOCKHOLM, Sweden, Dec. 10, 1950—William Faulkner, 53-year-old American author, reiterated his faith in man's eternal dominion over destiny as he accepted here tonight the award of the outstanding literary honor, the Nobel Prize for Literature.

Notable among the prize winner's works to date are *The Sound and the Fury,* and *As I Lay Dying.* Added to these are many other novels and essays.

Strangely enough, Mr. Faulkner's reputation has accorded him a reasonably wide but limited readership

in the United States, far short of the | has been reported as a "best seller"
material prosperity of many of his | in Western Europe in the recent post-
colleagues. On the other hand, he | war years.

I FEEL that this award was not made to me as a man, but to my work—a life's work in the agony and sweat of the human spirit, not for glory and least of all for profit, but to create out of the materials of the human spirit something which did not exist before. So this award is only mine in trust.

It will not be difficult to find a dedication for the money part of it commensurate with the purpose and significance of its origin. But I would like to do the same with the acclaim, too, by using this moment as a pinnacle from which I might be listened to by the young men and women already dedicated to the same anguish and travail, among whom is already that one who will some day stand where I am standing.

Our tragedy today is a general and universal physical fear so long sustained by now that we can even bear it. There are no longer problems of the spirit. There is only the question: When will I be blown up? Because of this, the young man or woman writing today has forgotten the problems of the human heart in conflict with itself which alone can make good writing because only that is worth writing about, worth the agony and the sweat.

He must learn them again. He must teach himself that the basest of all things is to be afraid: and, teaching himself that, forget it forever, leaving no room in his workshop for anything but the old verities and truths of the heart, the universal truths lacking which any story is ephemeral and doomed—love and honor and pity and pride and compassion and sacrifice. Until he does, he labors under a curse. He writes not of love but of lust, of defeats in which nobody loses anything of value, of victories without hope and, worst of all, without pity or compassion. His griefs grieve on no universal bones, leaving no scars. He writes not of the heart but of the glands.

Until he learns these things, he will write as though he stood among and watched the end of man. I decline to accept the end of man. It is easy enough to say that man is immortal simply because he will endure; that when the last ding-dong of doom has clanged and faded from the last worthless rock hanging tideless in the last red and dying evening, that even then there will still be one more sound; that of his puny inexhaustible voice, still talking. I refuse to accept this.

I believe that man will not merely endure; he will prevail. He is immortal, not because he alone among creatures has an inexhaustible voice, but because he has a soul, a spirit capable of compassion and sacrifice and endurance. The poet's, the writer's, duty is to write about these things. It is his privilege to help man endure by lifting his heart, by reminding him of the courage and honor and hope and pride and compassion and pity and sacrifice which have been the glory of his past. The poet's voice need not merely be the record of man, it can be one of the props, the pillars to help him endure and prevail.

DOUGLAS MACARTHUR

"Old soldiers never die; they just fade away."

WASHINGTON, D. C., April 19, 1951—General of the Army Douglas MacArthur, most picturesque of the commanders in World War II and virtual proconsul of the Western powers in the Pacific until stripped of his command in recent weeks by President Harry S. Truman, delivered his farewell to half a century of military life in an unprecedented setting, as the honored guest of a Joint Session of the Senate and House.

Never at a loss for eloquent expression, General MacArthur gracefully accepted his dismissal, but in this eulogy of his own career backed down not an inch from the stand which brought it about. He placed himself among the ageless line of old soldiers who "just fade away," but in his passing from the picture he cautioned that the halfway measures prescribed for the current war in Korea—confinement of action against the Communists to the small land mass of North Korea—would only encourage and perpetuate the determination of the Communists to continue their world-wide onslaught against the Western democracies.

The drama of General MacArthur's extraordinary appearance here was part of a political clash of forces that demonstrate how far the unanimity of views in World War II has deteriorated; some observers consider it a tragic example of the depths to which political intrigues can descend in the aftermath of great wars. And in this picture no single figure or group is singled out as being either wholly to blame or wholly blameless.

Many observers feel that President Truman, in upholding the authority of his office, had no choice, after General MacArthur's blunt but undiplomatic comments from his erstwhile headquarters in Tokyo, but to dismiss him from Supreme Command of United Nations Forces in the Far East. At the same time, the Congress, now controlled in both houses by Republican majorities, were given a new political issue.

It remained for General MacArthur to take simultaneous steps to preserve his reputation earned over half a century, to answer his critics, and yet to refrain from kindling further political fires.

I STAND on this rostrum with a sense of deep humility and great pride—humility in the wake of those great architects of our history who have stood here before me, pride in the reflection that this home of legislative debate represents human liberty in the purest form yet devised.

Here are centered the hopes and aspirations and faith of the entire human race.

I do not stand here as advocate for any partisan cause, for the issues are fundamental and reach quite beyond the realm of partisan considerations. They must be resolved on the highest plane of national interest if our course is to prove sound and our future protected.

I trust, therefore, that you will do me the justice of receiving that which I have to say as solely expressing the considered viewpoint of a fellow American.

I address you with neither rancor nor bitterness in the fading twilight of life, with but one purpose in mind: to serve my country.

The issues are global, and so interlocked that to consider the problems of one sector oblivious to those of another is to court disaster for the whole. While Asia is commonly referred to as the gateway to Europe, it is no less true that Europe is the gateway to Asia, and the broad influence of the one cannot fail to have its impact upon the other.

There are those who claim our strength is inadequate to protect on both fronts, that we cannot divide our effort. I can think of no greater expression of defeatism.

If a potential enemy can divide his strength on two fronts, it is for us to counter his efforts. The Communist threat is a global one. Its successful advance in one sector threatens the destruction of every other sector. You cannot appease or otherwise surrender to communism in Asia without simultaneously undermining our efforts to halt its advance in Europe.

I have from the beginning believed that the Chinese Communists' support of the North Koreans was the dominant one. Their interests are at present parallel with those recently displayed not only in Korea but also in Indo-China and Tibet and pointing potentially toward the South, reflecting predominantly the same lust for expansion of power which has animated every would-be conqueror since the beginning of time.

While I was not consulted prior to the President's decision to intervene in support of the republic of Korea, that decision, from a military standpoint, proved a sound one. As I say, it proved a sound one, as we hurled back the invader and decimated his forces. Our victory was complete, and our objectives within reach, when Red China intervened with ~~numerically~~ superior ground forces.

This created a new war and an entirely new situation, a situation not contemplated when our forces were committed against the North Korean invaders; a situation which called for new decisions in the diplomatic sphere to permit the realistic adjustment of military strategy. Such decisions have not been forthcoming.

While no man in his right mind would advocate sending our ground forces into continental China, and such was never given a thought, the new situation did urgently demand a drastic revision of ~~strategic~~ planning if our political aim was to defeat this new enemy as we had defeated the old. . . .

I have constantly called for the new political decisions essential to a solution.

Efforts have been made to distort my position. It has been said in effect that I was a warmonger. Nothing could be further from the truth.

I know war as few other men now living know it, and nothing to me is more revolting. I have long advocated its complete abolition, as its very destructiveness on both friend and foe has rendered it useless as a means of settling international disputes. . . .

But once war is forced upon us, there is no other alternative than to apply every available means to bring it to a swift end. War's very object is victory, not prolonged indecision.

In war, there is no substitute for victory.

The tragedy of Korea is further heightened by the fact that its military action is confined to its territorial limits: It condemns that nation, which it is our purpose to save, to suffer the devastating impact of full naval and air bombardment while the enemy's sanctuaries are fully protected from such attack and devastation.

Of the nations of the world, Korea alone, up to now, is the sole one which has risked its all against communism. The magnificence of the courage and fortitude of the Korean people defies description. They have chosen to risk death rather than slavery. Their last words to me were: "Don't scuttle the Pacific."

I am closing my fifty-two years of military service. When I joined the army, even before the turn of the century, it was the fulfillment of all my boyish hopes and dreams.

The world has turned over many times since I took the oath on the plain at West Point, and the hopes and dreams have long since vanished, but I still remember the refrain of one of the most popular barracks ballads of that day which proclaimed most proudly that old soldiers never die; they just fade away.

And like the old soldier of that ballad, I now close my military career and just fade away, an old soldier who tried to do his duty as God gave him the light to see that duty. Good-by.

The sequel:

There still remained years later sharp difference of opinion over the military events and decisions that brought about the historic clash be-tween President Truman and General MacArthur.

But the general, 71 years old when he took off his uniform, proved himself a true prophet in his famous quotation. Still active in 1959 as chairman of one of America's great corporations, he most certainly has not died, but as a military or political force he had discreetly faded out of public view.

MRS. FRANKLIN D. ROOSEVELT

"Without the United Nations our country would walk alone, ruled by fear, instead of confidence and hope."

CHICAGO, Ill., July 23, 1952—Speaking with the forceful conviction that has increasingly marked her public life since widowhood, Mrs. Franklin D. Roosevelt tonight declared that, despite the weaknesses of the United Nations, it must be supported because "the UN is the only machinery for the furtherance of peace that exists today."

Herself a delegate of this government to the United Nations, Mrs. Roosevelt spoke before the Democratic National Convention. Her words were addressed both to those within her late husband's political party who doubt the validity of the UN and to critics outside who consider it a political liability serving principally as a sounding board for Communist propaganda.

Mrs. Roosevelt recognized this criticism and met it in her usual forthright manner of speech. She cited the "torment and anguish" that has resulted from our heavy involvement in the Korean War, but she maintained that the United States had no choice but to take a stand, alongside other democratic members of the UN, against the expansion of communism by armed force. She quoted one famous ace in the Korean War as having stated the case quite clearly when he said in a public interview, "I fought in Korea so I would not have to fight on Main Street in Wichita."

This speech by Mrs. Roosevelt was considered an outstanding example of her public expression in the individual role which she has been permitted by the circumstances of widowhood to assume, and of the personal force of her own character —however controversial some of her remarks may be—as it has been exhibited since Mr. Roosevelt's death.

Now 67 years old, she has increased the tempo of her travels and writings, rather than diminished them. Her energy is so obvious that she could easily afford in the course of tonight's address to refer laughingly to "the old lady speaking to you now."

This and other speeches by Mrs. Roosevelt have been universally hailed as contributions to public thought about the long future of the UN, even by critics who take directly the opposite stand.

YOU ARE very kind to me and I am glad to have been asked to talk to you about the United Nations, about its past, about what it is doing today and more important, about its future.

I remember well, even though it seems a long time ago, hearing for the first time a statement and the reasons why, when the war ended, we must make another try to create another world organization to help us keep the peace of the world. This talk took place in my husband's study in the White House one evening during the bitter days of the last war when victory was not yet in sight.

My husband, discussing what would happen after the war, turned to a friend and said in effect "When this war is over and we have won it, as we will, we must apply the hard lessons learned in the war and in the failure of the League of Nations to the task of building a society of nations dedicated to enduring peace. There will be sacrifices and discouragements but we must not fail for we may never have another chance."

There have been sacrifices and discouragements, triumphs and set-backs. The United Nations is attempting to convert this last chance, carrying mankind's best hope, into an effective instrument that will enable our children and our children's children to maintain peace in their time. The path upon which we have set our course is not an easy one. The trail is often difficult to find. We must make our maps as we go along but we travel in good company with men and women of good-will in the free countries of the world.

Without the United Nations our country would walk alone, ruled by fear, instead of confidence and hope. To weaken or hamstring the United Nations now, through lack of faith and lack of vision, would be to condemn ourselves to endless struggle for survival in a jungle world.

In examining what the UN has done, and what it is striving to do, it must be remembered that peace, like freedom, is elusive, hard to come by, harder to keep. It cannot be put into a purse or a hip pocket and buttoned there to stay. To achieve peace we must recognize the historic truth that we can no longer live apart from the rest of the world. We must also recognize the fact that peace, like freedom, is not won once and for all. It is fought for daily, in many small acts, and is the result of many individual efforts.

These are days of shrinking horizons, a "neighborhood of nations though unhappily all of us are not as yet good neighbors."

We should remember that the UN is not a cure-all. It is only an instrument capable of effective action when its members have a will to make it work. It cannot be any better than the individual nations are. You often ask what can I, as an individual, do to help the US, to help in the struggle for a peaceful world.

I answer—Make your own country the best possible country for all its citizens to live in and it will become a valuable member of the Neighborhood of Nations. This can only be done with home, community, representatives.

The UN is the machinery through which peace may be achieved and it is the responsibility of 60 nations and their delegations to make that machinery work. Yet you and I may carry the greatest responsibility because our national strength has given us opportunities for leadership among the nations of the free world.

The UN is the only machinery for the furtherance of peace that exists today. There is a small articulate minority in this country which advocates changing our national symbol which is the eagle to that of the ostrich and withdrawing from the UN. This minority reminds me of a story of a short-sighted and selfish man who put green goggles on his cow and fed her sawdust. The cow became sick and died. I warn you against the short-sighted and selfish men who are trying to distort the vision of the American people. We must have eagle eyes. These men who lack vision are poor in hope. They turn their backs on the future and live in the past. They seek to weaken and destroy this world organization through their attacks on the UN. They are expressing a selfish, destructive approach which leads not to peace but to chaos and might eventually lead to World War Three. . . .

This brings us to the action taken by the UN which has brought sorrow into many American homes. The Communist attack on Korea and the brilliant fight put up by our armies is a matter of history. When the attack occurred we had two choices. We could meet it or let aggression triumph by default and thereby invite further piecemeal conquests all over the Globe. This inevitably would have led to World War Three just as the appeasement of Munich and the seizure of Czechoslovakia led to World War Two, the most destructive war in history.

Great sacrifices have been made in Korea by our soldiers, and at home by mothers, wives and sweethearts in support of this UN action. To a more limited extent the same sacrifices have been made by other member nations. There is torment and anguished waiting in many homes this very night but at the same time there must be gratitude that our own land has been preserved from attack and for all of us there must be pride in the proof of the staunchness and heroism of American men.

We pray for a just and lasting peace in Korea for the sake of the people of that land and for our own men and those soldiers of the United Nations fighting with them. We cannot hurry this peace until the Communists agree to honest terms. If you ask the reason why our men are in Korea I think it was perhaps best summed up by an American flying Ace, Major James Jabara, who upon returning to his home in Wichita, Kansas, in an interview was asked what his feelings were while fighting in Korea. Major Jabara said, "I fought in Korea so I would not have to fight on Main Street in Wichita."

Korea was not only the first successful application of collective security on the part of the UN to stop aggression, without provoking general war, but it has stimulated a free world to build up its defenses. It has not been as quick in the achievement of results as it would have been if the UN had been fully organized to put down any aggression. It has been impossible to organize that machinery as yet because two nations, the US and the USSR haven't been able to come to an agreement as to how this collective security within the UN may be organized. We think the fault lies with the USSR because she will not see that without a planned method of disarmament and control of all weapons, adequately verified through inspection, we and many other nations in the world cannot feel safe, but at least through the UN we can go on with negotiations and pray for a pure heart and clean hands which may eventually bring us the confidence even of the Soviet Union and lead us to the desired results.

In the UN we meet with the Communists and it is fortunate this meeting place exists. We know we can not relax our vigilance or stop our efforts to control the spread of communism. Their attacks on us in the UN have one great value—they keep us from forgetting our shortcomings or to become apathetic in our efforts to improve our democracy.

The UN has helped to keep the peace in many areas of the world, notably in Iran and Greece and Palestine and Indonesia, and Pakistan and India. These disputes might have spread into a general war and torn the free world apart and opened the way for Communist expansion and another world war.

While the UN came into being under the present Administration and President Truman has been steadfast in his support of the organization, the UN would not be in existence today if it were not for strong bi-partisan support in the very beginning.

. . . I beg you to keep an open mind, never to forget the interests of your own country but to remember your own country may be able to make a contribution which is valuable in the area of human rights and freedoms in joining with other nations not merely in a declaration but in covenants.

I returned not long ago from parts of the world where our attitude on human rights and freedoms affects greatly our leadership.

Some of you will probably be thinking that once upon a time the old lady speaking to you now, did a tremendous amount of traveling around the United States. In fact, you may remember a cartoon showing two men down in a coal mine, one man saying to the other: "Gosh, here comes Eleanor. Now what is she doing—traveling around the world just making more trouble?"

In World War Two when I visited so many hospitals in the Pacific I was glad I had traveled so much through my own country and could say to a lonely boy far from home: "You come from Lubbock, Texas?" The boy's face would light up. "Yes ma'am. I remember when you were there." I can only hope that in the future there may be some little unexpected values which will come out of these latest travels too.

I hope all our travels may serve the great common hope that through the United Nations peace may come to the world. . . .

ADLAI E. STEVENSON

"The ordeal of the twentieth century . . . is far from over."

CHICAGO, Ill., July 26, 1952—A balding man with twinkling eyes, scarcely known outside his native state of Illinois until a few months ago, tonight stood before the Democratic National Convention and exhibited the courage to inspire his party, and his country, with deeply convincing words on the eve of a race that hardly the most optimistic Democrat believes he can win.

The speaker, Adlai E. Stevenson, is his party's candidate for the Presidency in this election year. His certain opponent, to be named by the Republicans within a few weeks, is General of the Army Dwight D. Ei- senhower. Between the stature of General Eisenhower and the evident demand by the country for change in the White House after 20 years of Democratic control, there is little hope for Mr. Stevenson's election, as he well knows.

Hence his attitude, even more than his words, threw a new and refreshing ray of light on the idealized picture of American politics in action. His acceptance, although of necessity bristling with confidence, carried the deeper note of concern that the United States, regardless of the outcome of the election, stand fast on its high plateau of ideals.

I ACCEPT your nomination and your program.

I should have preferred to hear those words uttered by a stronger, a wiser, a better man than myself . . .

Now that you have made your decision, I will fight to win that office with all my heart and my soul. And with your help I have no doubt that we will win. . . .

And, my friends, even more important than winning the election is governing the nation. That is the test of a political party—

the acid, final test. When the tumult and the shouting die, when the bands are gone and the lights are dimmed, there is the stark responsibility in an hour of history haunted with those gaunt, grim specters of strife, dissension, and ruthless, inscrutable, and hostile power abroad.

The ordeal of the twentieth century—the bloodiest, most turbulent era of the Christian age—is far from over. Sacrifice, patience, understanding, and implacable purpose must be our lot for years to come.

Let's face it. Let's talk sense to the American people. Let's tell them the truth, that there are no gains without pains, that we are now on the eve of great decisions, not easy decisions, like resistance when you're attacked, but a long, patient, costly struggle which alone can assure triumph over the great enemies of man— war, poverty, and tyranny—and the assaults upon human dignity which are the most grievous consequences of each.

Let's tell them that the victory to be won in the twentieth century, this portal to the golden age, mocks the pretensions of individual acumen and ingenuity. For it is a citadel guarded by thick walls of ignorance and mistrust which do not fall before the trumpets' blast or the politicians' imprecations or even the generals' baton. They are, my friends, walls that must be directly stormed by the hosts of courage, morality, and of vision, standing shoulder to shoulder, unafraid of ugly truth, contemptuous of lies, half-truths, circuses, and demagoguery.

Help me to do the job this autumn of conflict and campaign; help me to do the job in these years of darkness, of doubt, and of crisis which stretch beyond the horizon of tonight's happy vision, and we will justify our glorious past and the loyalty of silent millions who look to us for compassion, for understanding, and for honest purpose. Thus we will serve our great tradition greatly.

I ask of you all you have; I will give to you all I have, even as he who came here tonight and honored me, as he has honored you—the Democratic party—by a lifetime of service and bravery that will find him an imperishable page in the history of the Republic and of the Democratic party—President Harry S. Truman.

And finally, my friends, in the staggering task that you have assigned me, I shall always try "to do justly, to love mercy, and walk humbly with God."

The sequel:

Mr. Stevenson went down to defeat. He ran and lost again in 1956. He accepted it without rancor. In subsequent years, still youthful and increasingly active in nonpolitical public affairs, he traveled at length and wrote prolifically.

While not seeking high public office actively, he remained in reserve as a younger "elder statesman," often compared in that respect to Thomas E. Dewey, the young and unsuccessful standard bearer of the Republican party in earlier years.

DWIGHT D. EISENHOWER

"History does not long entrust the care of freedom to the weak or the timid."

WASHINGTON, D. C., January 20, 1953—The third victorious general in a major war to be elected to the Presidency signalized his Inaugural here today with a warning to the country that the conflicts of this uneasy period of peace call for as much courage, stamina and united effort as were needed for victory in the war where he was Supreme Commander of all Allied forces in Europe.

Thus Dwight D. Eisenhower took his place in a line of succession following the two quite contrasting characters of George Washington and Ulysses S. Grant. Himself elected by the largest popular vote ever cast for a Presidential candidate, General Eisenhower offered no panaceas. Instead, he said that, "in the swift rush of great events we find ourselves groping to know the full sense and meaning of the times in which we live."

President Eisenhower takes office while the stalemate of the Korean War still hangs over the Pacific, and the full design behind the Communist program that has engulfed almost all of continental Asia raises the gravest unsolved questions.

In Europe, professed personal friendship for the wartime commander by high-ranking members of the Russian Government creates riddles as to the future, and possible pitfalls of involvement. In this atmosphere, interpretation of the President's Inaugural Address is meaningless. His own words are clear in their implications, making this an historic state paper.

THE WORLD and we have passed the midway point of a century of continuing challenge. We sense with all our faculties that forces of good and evil are massed and armed and opposed as rarely before in history.

This fact defines the meaning of this day. We are summoned, by this honored and historic ceremony, to witness more than the act of one citizen swearing his oath of service, in the presence of his God. We are called as a people, to give testimony, in the sight of the world, to our faith that the future shall belong to the free.

Since this century's beginning, a time of tempest has seemed to come upon the continents of the earth. Masses of Asia have wakened to strike off shackles of the past. Great nations of Europe have waged their bloodiest wars. Thrones have toppled and their vast empires have disappeared. New nations have been born.

For our own country, it has been a time of recurring trial. We have grown in power and in responsibility. We have passed through the anxieties of depression and of war to a summit unmatched in man's history. Seeking to secure peace in the world, we have had to fight through the forests of the Argonne, to the shores of Iwo Jima, and to the cold mountains of Korea.

In the swift rush of great events, we find ourselves groping to know the full sense and meaning of the times in which we live. In our quest of understanding, we beseech God's guidance. We summon all our knowledge of the past and we scan all signs of the future. We bring all our wit and will to meet the question: how far have we come in man's long pilgrimage from darkness toward light? Are we nearing the light—a day of freedom and of peace for all mankind? Or are the shadows of another night closing in upon us?

Great as are the preoccupations absorbing us at home, concerned as we are with matters that deeply affect our livelihood today and our vision of the future, each of these domestic problems is dwarfed by, and often even created by, this question that involves all human kind.

This trial comes at a moment when man's power to achieve good or to inflict evil surpasses the brightest hopes and the sharpest fears of all ages. We can turn rivers in their courses, level mountains to the plains. Ocean and land and sky are avenues for our colossal commerce. Disease diminishes and life lengthens.

Yet the promise of this life is imperiled by the very genius that has made it possible. Nations amass wealth. Labor sweats to create—and turns out devices to level not only mountains but also cities. Science seems ready to confer upon us, as its final gift, the power to erase human life from this planet.

At such a time in history, we, who are free, must proclaim anew our faith.

This faith is the abiding creed of our fathers. It is our faith in the deathless dignity of man, governed by eternal moral and natural laws.

This faith defines our full view of life. It establishes, beyond debate, those gifts of the Creator that are man's inalienable rights, and that make all men equal in his sight!

In the light of this equality, we know that the virtues most cherished by free peoples—love of truth, pride of work, devotion to country—all are treasures equally precious in the lives of the most humble and of the most exalted. The men who mine coal and fire furnaces and balance ledgers and turn lathes and pick cotton and heal the sick and plant corn—all serve as proudly, and as profitably, for America as the statesmen who draft treaties or the legislators who enact laws.

This faith rules our whole way of life. It decrees that we, the people, elect leaders not to rule but to serve. It asserts that we have the right to choice of our own work and to the reward of our own toil. It inspires the initiative that makes our productivity the wonder of the world. And it warns that any man who seeks to deny equality in all his brothers betrays the spirit of the free and invites the mockery of the tyrant.

It is because we, all of us, hold to these principles that the political changes accomplished this day do not imply turbulence, upheaval or disorder. Rather this change expresses a purpose of strengthening our dedication and devotion to the precepts of our founding documents, a conscious renewal of faith in our country and in the watchfulness of a divine Providence.

The enemies of this faith know no god but force, no devotion but its use. They tutor men in treason. They feed upon the hunger of others. Whatever defies them, they torture, especially the truth.

Here, then, is joined no pallid argument between slightly differing philosophies. This conflict strikes directly at the faith of our fathers and the lives of our sons. No principle or treasure that we hold, from the spiritual knowledge of our free schools and churches to the creative magic of free labor and capital, nothing lies safely beyond the reach of the struggle.

Freedom is pitted against slavery; light against dark.

The faith we hold belongs not to us alone but to the free of all the world. This common bond binds the grower of rice in Burma and the planter of wheat in Iowa, the shepherd in southern Italy and the mountaineer in the Andes. It confers a common dignity upon the French soldier who dies in Indo-China, the British soldier killed in Malaya, the American life given in Korea.

We know, beyond this, that we are linked to all free peoples not merely by a noble idea but by a simple need. No free people can for long cling to any privilege or enjoy any safety in economic solitude. For all our own material might, even we need markets in the world for the surpluses of our farms and of our factories. Equally, we need for these same farms and factories vital materials and products of distant lands. This basic law of interdependence, so manifest in the commerce of peace, applies with thousand-fold intensity in the event of war.

So are we persuaded by necessity and by belief that the strength of all free peoples lies in unity, their danger in discord.

To produce this unity, to meet the challenge of our time, destiny has laid upon our country the responsibility of the free world's leadership. So it is proper that we assure our friends once again that, in the discharge of this responsibility, we Americans know and observe the difference between world leadership and imperialism; between firmness and truculence; between a thoughtfully calculated goal and spasmodic reaction to the stimulus of emergencies.

We wish our friends the world over to know this above all: we face the threat—not with dread and confusion—but with confidence and conviction.

We feel this moral strength because we know that we are not helpless prisoners of history. We are free men. We shall remain free, never to be proven guilty of the one capital offense against freedom, a lack of staunch faith.

In pleading our just cause before the bar of history and in pressing our labor for world peace, we shall be guided by certain fixed principles.

These principles are:

(1) Abhorring war as a chosen way to balk the purposes of those who threaten us, we hold it to be the first task of statesmanship to develop the strength that will deter the forces of aggression and promote the conditions of peace. For, as it must be the supreme purpose of all free men, so it must be the dedication of their leaders, to save humanity from preying upon itself.

In the light of this principle, we stand ready to engage with any and all others in joint effort to remove the causes of mutual fear and distrust among nations, and so to make possible drastic reductions of armaments. The sole requisites for undertaking such effort are that—in their purpose—they be aimed logically and honestly toward secure peace for all; and that—in their result—they provide methods by which every participating nation will prove good faith in carrying out its pledge.

(2) Realizing that common sense and common decency alike dictate the futility of appeasement, we shall never try to placate an aggressor by the false and wicked bargain of trading honor for security. For in the final choice a soldier's pack is not so heavy a burden as a prisoner's chains.

(3) Knowing that only a United States that is strong and immensely productive can help defend freedom in our world, we view our nation's strength and security as a trust upon which rests the hope of free men everywhere. It is the firm duty of each of our free citizens and of every free citizen everywhere to place the cause of his country before the comfort and convenience of himself.

(4) Honoring the identity and heritage of each nation of the world, we shall never use our strength to try to impress upon another people our own cherished political and economic institutions.

(5) Assessing realistically the needs and capacities of proven friends of freedom, we shall strive to help them to achieve their own security and well-being. Likewise, we shall count upon them to assume, within the limits of their resources, their full and just burdens in the common defense of freedom.

(6) Recognizing economic health as an indispensable basis of military strength and the free world's peace, we shall strive to foster everywhere, and to practice ourselves, policies that encourage productivity and profitable trade. For the impoverishment of any single people in the world means danger to the well-being of all other peoples.

(7) Appreciating that economic need, military security, and political wisdom combine to suggest regional groupings of free peoples, we hope, within the framework of the United Nations, to help strengthen such special bonds the world over. The nature of these ties must vary with the different problems of different areas.

In the Western Hemisphere, we enthusiastically join with all our neighbors in the work of perfecting a community of fraternal trust and common purpose.

In Europe, we ask that enlightened and inspired leaders of the Western nations strive with renewed vigor to make the unity of their peoples a reality. Only as free Europe unitedly marshals its strength can it effectively safeguard, even with our help, its spiritual and cultural heritages.

(8) Conceiving the defense of freedom, like freedom itself, to be one and indivisible, we hold all continents and peoples in equal regard and honor. We reject any insinuation that one race or another, one people or another, is in any sense inferior or expendable.

(9) Respecting the United Nations as the living sign of all people's hope for peace, we shall strive to make it not merely an eloquent symbol but an effective force. And in our quest of honorable peace, we shall neither compromise, nor tire, nor ever cease.

By these rules of conduct, we hope to be known to all peoples.

By their observance, an earth of peace may become not a vision but a fact.

This hope—this supreme aspiration—must rule the way we live.

We must be ready to dare all for our country. For history does not long entrust the care of freedom to the weak or the timid. We must acquire proficiency in defense and display stamina in purpose.

We must be willing, individually and as a nation, to accept whatever sacrifices may be required of us. A people that values its privileges above its principles soon loses both.

These basic precepts are not lofty abstractions, far removed from matters of daily living. They are laws of spiritual strength that generate and define our material strength. Patriotism means equipped forces and prepared citizenry. Moral stamina means more energy and more productivity, on the farm and in the factory. Love of liberty means the guarding of every resource that makes freedom possible—from the sanctity of our families and the wealth of our soil to the genius of our scientists.

So each citizen plays an indispensable role. The productivity of our heads, our hands, and our hearts is the source of all the strength we can command for both the enrichment of our lives and the winning of peace.

No person, no home, no community can be beyond the reach of this call. We are summoned to act in wisdom and in conscience, to work with industry, to teach with persuasion, to preach with conviction, to weigh our every deed with care and with compassion. For this truth must be clear before us: whatever America hopes to bring to pass in the world must first come to pass in the heart of America.

The peace we seek, then, is nothing less than the practice and fulfillment of our whole faith, among ourselves and in our dealings with others. It signifies more than stilling the guns, easing the sorrow of war.

More than an escape from death, it is a way of life.

More than a haven for the weary, it is a hope for the brave.

This is the hope that beckons us onward in this century of trial. This is the work that awaits us all, to be done with bravery, with charity—and with prayer to Almighty God.

The sequel:

In the following years, President Eisenhower's thoughts expressed in his First Inaugural proved to be prophetic.

How he met the tests of his office were for others to determine in the long future, but his qualities of leadership in great periods of stress were notable.

CORNELIA OTIS SKINNER

*"A toast from the ladies of America . . .
BOTTOMS UP!"*

LAKE PLACID, N. Y., June, 1953 —Standing on a convention lecture platform instead of a stage, with the members of the American Gynecological Society assembled in annual convention as her audience, the celebrated monologist, Cornelia Otis Skinner delivered here a forthright commentary on the manner in which a woman and mother views the doctors in her life.

The organization of leading obstetricians switched from the usual routine of inviting an eminent colleague to address them and their wives. Despite her surprise upon receipt of the invitation, which she at first thought must be a joke, Miss Skinner came fully prepared to leave the doctors with a new perspective on the women who crowd their waiting rooms and who, as Miss Skinner reminded them, always shudder at the order to remove everything but their shoes and stockings.

For her part, Miss Skinner told them, she had carried rebellion to the point of invariably leaving on also her hat, for reasons duly explained.

LADIES AND gentlemen of the profession . . . if not the oldest in the world, at least one of the most time-honored. You find me in a more awkward position than any in which I have ever been placed by certain of your distinguished members. I am as bewildered by my presence here as you must be. In fact I feel as uncertain of the issue as I did on an occasion when, giving a monologue performance a number of years ago in a New England town, I started off under the handicap of a far from encouraging introduction. (I rather liked this introduction because it is such a fine example of New England's traditional thrift.) The lady of the organization which was . . . having me . . . (that highly obstetrical expression!) rose and with fluttering apology said "Ladies and gentlemen, owing to the high price of Rear Admiral Byrd, we have Miss Skinner with us this evening." Well, let's face it . . . you have Miss Skinner with you this evening and it's not owing to the high price of any of the fees you have charged me over the years.

As I understand it, the yearly address to this learned gathering should be of an instructive or enlightening nature. It is an odd and I must admit a somewhat pleasant sensation to be in the position of offering advice to the physician.

Well, whether or not you'll take mine, I think this is a golden opportunity for giving the medical profession a bit of the patient's point of view. In other words to hear from the person at the other end of the stethoscope or, in this case, the other end of the . . . shall we say the stereopticon? As the humble presenter of this angle . . . this seldom heard from point of view (I am referring to opinion, not position) I really feel, without undue modesty, that I am a good choice. Over the years I have had the privilege . . . or shall we call it the dubious pleasure . . . of considerable contact with your branch of the profession, due to the fact that my profession has obliged me to travel extensively throughout the length and breadth of the United States, and that the birth of a son, plus certain defects of my anatomy, have required frequent consultations, inspections and repairs to the extent that, in the words of Somerset Maugham, you have left me only the bare necessities of life. I have perhaps had more experience than most patients . . . (I'd rather say "clients" . . . the word "patient" immediately reduces me to a state of apprehension and general debility) . . . I have had more opportunities to see you at work . . . if see is what I mean . . . to compare your methods, your relationships with your clients . . . your manners . . . your bedside ones, your desk-side ones and your table-side ones. And I have also had occasion to speculate as to how much you know

. . . not of your science . . . but of the point of view of your clientele. . . .

For the nicely brought-up girl, there is something that is hard to reconcile with her genteel sensibilities about walking into the inner sanctum of a complete stranger, solemnly describing her symptoms and at the end of the recital hearing the stranger say "Will you please go into the next room and take off everything except your shoes and stockings?" It wouldn't seem so bad if it weren't for that shoes and stockings clause! To my impressionable mind it has always smacked of the more erotic refinements of Berlin during its decadence. Be it to the honor of my upbringing, I have always kept on not only my shoes and stockings, but also my hat! If a costume made up of a sheet and a John Fredericks model is not the smartest of attire, God knows it's the most respectable.

Now, Gentlemen (I say gentlemen because while I am well aware of the number of feminine members of the brotherhood-sisterhood there are, the harvest of my experience has been gleaned chiefly from the brothers), there is one aspect of your business of which you know nothing whatsoever and regarding which I believe it's high time you were made aware . . . of. And that is what goes on in your waiting-rooms . . . particularly when they are replete with women who in turn, are replete with child. Of course none of you ever pause to see . . . when occasionally you make an impressive dash from your outer door to your inner office— because you're late or because you couldn't face the prospect of looking at us all, or because you've an emergency phone-call, or because you're just plain late.

Women in the office of an obstetrician have a behavior all their own. It's a continuous scene of mutual inspection and speculation. One eventually gets accustomed every two weeks or so to seeing the same old familiar faces . . . but the old familiar contours are a constant source of interest far more fascinating than those old copies of *Life, Time* and the *New Yorker* which must have been read by all the members of a doctor's family, thumbed up, torn and jumped upon and eventually placed on the table of his waiting-rooms. The obstetrician's waiting-room is the one place of gathering where women inspect not each other's clothes . . . but each other's outlines. A newcomer enters, the eyes of the waiting sorority go straight to the midriff.

You know, you can do some pretty fancy calculating if you know how and what to observe. The beginner, as one might call her, comes blithely in, her hat at a smart angle, picks up one of those mangled periodicals, chooses either the sofa or an armchair, and relaxes into its depths. When her turn is called, she leaps nimbly to her feet, drops the periodical, picks it up with easy agility and skips in through the inner door. The more advanced . . . both in regard to condition and shape . . . say the 5 to 6 monthers, enter in slower motion. That same chic hat has gone further back on the head. She picks up a periodical (undoubtedly the same one as before) chooses a more upright chair, sits with less abandon and when her turn is called, rises slowly, drops the periodical, stoops to pick it up, but finding she can't reach it, bends her knees and retracts it, and with injured dignity plods through the inner door. Last scene of all that ends this strange, eventful history is Mother Nature-Ceres who waddles in, her hat, this time on the back of her head, as if to balance all that precedes her . . . picks up that same copy of *Life*, looks about for a place to sit down and finding no possible contour model, perches gingerly on the arm of the armchair, when her turn comes, again drops the magazine, again tries to pick it up forward, sideways, at an angle, even knee-bending, utters a mental "To hell with it!" and waddles majestically through that inner door.

Another aspect of the waiting-room I'd like to mention is the receptionist nurse. She has a cozy way of talking shop with the more loquacious clients . . . and she does so in a jargon that seems peculiar to the race of obstetrical nurses. "Mrs. Brown delivered last night," she'll tell someone brightly, or "We're expecting Mrs. White to deliver before tomorrow" . . . (that mail-carrier phraseology . . . "Neither rain nor heat," etc.) Then she uses another interesting term . . . she'll say "We've been having a run on girls lately" or "Better hurry, Mrs. Robinson, we're in the midst of a run on boys!" However, she is always a pleasant and sympathetic person . . . always most co-operative, especially when it comes to that sporadic little drama that is enacted at the beginning of these visits . . . when a patient comes in and, with arch discretion the receptionist asks "Mrs. Jones, have you something for me?" Sometimes a crisis arises when Mrs. Jones, in sudden panic, realizes she hasn't . . . but someone else may have . . . in which event, there is a whispered consultation between Mrs. Jones and the receptionist picking up the phone, dialing a number and an ensuing conversation which may go somewhat like this . . . "Hello? Schrafft's restaurant? I'm calling for Mrs. Cadwallader Jones. She was there for lunch today and she thinks she may have left a small parcel . . . second table to the left."

Of course, conditions may have changed. It was 23 years ago that I began these exhaustive researches . . . or rather they were begun on me. When I was in what is laughingly known as the state of expectant motherhood, I was also in the state of having to fulfill the obligations of a theatrical tour. (The actress' greatest difficulty is the acquiring of proper timing. Dramatic critics manage these things better. John Mason Brown's second son, he tells me, was born between CHARLEY's AUNT and GEORGE WASHINGTON SLEPT HERE.) For five months, I and little Nemo toured the Middle-West trailing clouds of sweetness, light and nausea. Being neither a pioneer woman nor a Mme. Schumann-Heink, for whom it was apparently nothing to be a Rhine maiden one evening and the next morning the mother of a new little Heink, I don't recommend a lyceum tour as the best of regimens.

All nonsense aside, I can't tell you how happy and proud I am that you should have chosen me to speak to you this evening. Surely yours must be the most rewarding of all the branches of medicine . . . the happiness you bring us, the health and new life you restore to us. As self appointed spokesman . . . spokeswoman . . . for my sisterhood, may I tell you of our gratitude and affection . . . I'll even say our love . . . (you know it is true that every new mother falls in love for a time with her obstetrician). May I herewith propose a toast from the ladies of America in words which are singularly apt . . . gentlemen of the profession, BOTTOMS UP!!!

HARRY S. TRUMAN

"Our government cannot function properly unless the President is master in his own house."

NEW YORK, N. Y., May 8, 1954—An angry voice was raised here tonight in the historically exceptional circumstance of a former and often-criticised President demanding greater power for the Presidency now held by the spokesman for the opposing political party.

Harry S. Truman, who personally led the campaign against President Dwight D. Eisenhower, lashed out at the broadened investigative activities by the Congress where the Republican leadership is, he said, embarrassing its own President by encroachment on the Executive establishment.

The argument is not a new one. This debate began in the first Administration of the American Government when President George Washington, angered by demands for information by a Senate Committee, refused thereafter to discuss his contemplated actions. He thereby established a precedent for Presidential right to act first in executive affairs and relegate Congressional action to review in connection with subsequent legislation.

As a natural sequel, President Truman had a hard tussle during two years of his own terms, when Republican control of Congress threw all the old debates between the two governing branches—President and Congress—into a turmoil. Yet today, it is not Democratic leadership but Republican in both Senate and House that is demanding continually broadened rights to subpoena members of the Executive Branch and their files, question them—particularly in the realms of foreign and military policy —and to make public as they desire the information so gathered.

Mr. Truman, in speaking as guest of honor at a dinner honoring his birthday anniversary, drew attention to a facet of his career that some observers believe will outlive the memory of his more direct actions as Senator, as Vice President and as President. This is his tireless study and frequently original presentation of new arguments interpreting the extraordinary form of government under which this country thrives.

It also is notable that while he often prefers the colloquial, and sometimes salty, brand of American speech to advance political arguments, he has the vocabulary and the power of language to discuss this classical question in the language befitting its dignity.

THERE'S NEVER been an office—an executive office—in all the history of the world with the responsibility and the power of the Presidency of the United States. That is the reason in this day and age that it must be run and respected as at no other time in the history of the world because it can mean the welfare of the world or its destruction.

When the founding fathers outlined the Presidency in Article II of the Constitution, they left a great many details out. I think they relied on the experience of the nation to fill in the outlines. The office of the chief executive has grown with the progress of this great republic. It has responded to the many demands that our complex society has made upon the Government. It has given our nation a means of meeting our greatest emergencies. Today, it is one of the most important factors in our leadership of the free world.

Many diverse elements entered into the creation of the office, springing, as it did, from the parent idea of the separation of powers.

In the first place, the President became the leader of a political party. The party under his leadership had to be dominant enough to put him in office. This political party leadership was the last thing the Constitution contemplated. The President's election was not intended to be mixed up in the hurly-burly of partisan politics.

I wish some of those old gentlemen could come back and see how it worked. The people were to choose wise and respected men who would meet in calm seclusion and choose a President and the runner-up would be Vice President.

All of this went by the board—though most of the original language remains in the Constitution. Out of the struggle and tumult of the political arena a new and different President emerged—the man who led a political party to victory and retained in his hand the power of party leadership. That is, he retained it, like the sword Excalibur, if he could wrest it from the scabbard and wield it.

Another development was connected with the first. As the President came to be elected by the whole people, he became responsible to the whole people. I used to say the only lobbyist the whole people had in Washington was the President of the United States. Our whole people looked to him for leadership, and not confined within the limits of written document. Every hope and every fear of his fellow citizens, almost every aspect of their welfare and activities, falls within the scope of his concern—indeed, it falls within the scope of his duty. Only one who has held that office can really appreciate that. It is the President's responsibility to look at all questions from the point of view of the whole people. His written and spoken word commands national and often international attention.

These powers which are not explicitly written into the Constitution are the powers which no President can pass on to his successor. They go only to him who can take and use them. However, it is these powers, quite as much as those enumerated in Article II of the Constitution, which make the Presidential system unique and which give the papers of Presidents their peculiarly revealing importance.

For it is through these great powers that leadership arises, events are molded and administrations take on their character. And so a successful administration is one of strong Presidential leadership. Weak leadership, or no leadership, produces failure and often disaster.

This does not come from the inherent incapacity of the people of the nation. It is inherent in the legislative government where there is no executive strong and able enough to rally the people to a sustained effort of will and prepared to use its power of party control to the fullest extent.

Again, we see today history repeating itself as the legislative branch of the Government, under the overshadowing fear of Communism, expands its functions and activities into the very center of the power of the executive branch.

The President is responsible for the Administration of his office. And that means for the administration of the entire executive branch. It is not the business of Congress to run the agencies of government for the President.

Unless this principle is observed, it is impossible to have orderly government. The legislative power will ooze into the executive offices. It will influence and corrupt the decisions of the executive branch. It will affect promotions and transfers. It will warp and twist policies. . . .

To this kind of encroachment it is the duty of the President to say firmly and flatly, "no, you can't do it." The investigative power of Congress is not limitless. . . . Today the tasks of leadership falling upon the President spring not only from our national problems but from those of the whole world. Today that leadership will determine whether our Government will function effectively, and upon its functioning depends the survival of each of us and also on that depends the survival of the free world, if I may be so bold as to say that.

And today our government cannot function properly unless it follows the provisions of the Constitution. Our government cannot function properly unless the President is master in his own house and unless the Executive departments and agencies of the Government, including the armed forces, are responsible only to the President.

J. ROBERT OPPENHEIMER

"We know too much for one man to know much."

NEW YORK, N. Y., Dec. 26, 1954 —J. Robert Oppenheimer, the noted American physicist, drew a dramatic picture tonight of modern man living in an eclectic world in which virtually all of the traditional theories have become outdated. He spoke at the closing session of the Columbia University Bicentennial Anniversary.

While his speech was dramatic in itself as a scholarly foray into a description of the unfolding pages of modern arts and sciences, Dr. Oppenheimer's appearance had the added edge of the peculiar position in which he stands today, at the age of 50, between greatness already earned to a large degree, and questions of character raised in political circles on the basis of records that may remain secret through his lifetime.

Earlier this year Dr. Oppenheimer was suspended as consultant to the Atomic Energy Commission for security reasons. Debate that attracted nationwide attention followed this peremptory act by the Commission, particularly since responsible officials reiterated that Dr. Oppenheimer's personal character is above reproach.

Dr. Oppenheimer also must be remembered as the "architect" of the work that developed the atomic bomb, for he was director of the laboratories in Los Alamos, N. M., where the bomb was perfected. He now holds the post of director of the Institute for Advanced Studies, Princeton, N. J., and by today's invitation the powers at Columbia University showed their opinion of him.

IN THE natural sciences these are, and have been, and are most surely likely to continue to be, heroic days. Discovery follows discovery, each both raising and answering questions, each ending a long search, and each providing the new instruments for new search.

There are radical ways of thinking unfamiliar to common sense, connected with it by decades or centuries of increasingly specialized and unfamiliar experience. There are lessons how limited, for all its variety, the common experience of man has been with regard to natural phenomenon, and hints and analogies as to how limited may be his experience with man.

Every new finding is a part of the instrument kit of the sciences for further investigation and for penetrating into new fields. Discoveries of knowledge fructify technology and the practical arts, and these in turn pay back refined techniques, new possibilities for observation and experiment.

In any science there is a harmony between practitioners. A man may work as an individual, learning of what his colleagues do through reading or conversation; or he may be working as a member of a group on problems whose technical equipment is too massive for individual effort. But whether he is part of a team or solitary in his own study, he, as a professional, is a member of a community.

His colleagues in his own branch of science will be grateful to him for the inventive or creative thoughts he has, will welcome his criticism. His world and work will be objectively communicable and he will be quite sure that, if there is error in it, that error will not be long undetected. In his own line of work he lives in a community where common understanding combines with common purpose and interest to bind men together both in freedom and in cooperation.

This experience will make him acutely aware of how limited, how precious is this condition of his life; for in his relations with a wider society there will be neither the sense of community nor of objective understanding.

The frontiers of science are separated now by long years of study, by specialized vocabularies, arts, techniques and knowledge from the common heritage even of a most civilized society, and anyone working at the frontier of such science is in that sense a very long way from home and a long way, too, from the practical arts that were its matrix and origin, as indeed they were of what we today call art.

The specialization of science is an inevitable accompaniment of progress; yet it is full of dangers, and it is cruelly wasteful, since so much that is beautiful and enlightening is cut off from most of the world. Thus it is proper to the role of the scientist that he not merely find new truth and communicate it to his fellows, but that he teach, that he try to bring the most honest and intelligible account of new knowledge to all who will try to learn.

This is one reason—it is the decisive organic reason—why scientists belong in universities. It is one reason why the patronage of science by and through universities is its most proper form; for it is here, in teaching, in the association of scholars, and in the friendships of teachers and taught, of men who by profession must themselves be both teachers and taught, that the narrowness of scientific life can best be moderated and that the analogies, insights and harmonies of scientific discovery can find their way into the wider life of man.

In the situation of the artist today there are both analogies and differences to that of the scientist; but it is the differences which are the most striking and which raise the problems that touch most on the evil of our day.

For the artist it is not enough that he communicate with others who are expert in his own art. Their fellowship, their understanding and their appreciation may encourage him; but that is not the end of his work, nor its nature.

The artist depends on a common sensibility and culture, on a common meaning of symbols, on a community of experience and common ways of describing and interpreting it. He need not write for everyone or paint or play for everyone. But his audience must be man, and not a specialized set of experts among his fellows.

Today that is very difficult. Often the artist has an aching sense of great loneliness, for the community to which he addresses himself is largely not there; the traditions and the history, the myths and the common experience, which it is his function to illuminate and to harmonize and to portray, have been dissolved in a changing world.

There is, it is true, an artificial audience maintained to moderate between the artist and the world for which he works: the audience of the professional critics, popularizers and advertisers of art. But though, as does the popularizer and promoter of science, the critic fulfills a necessary present function, and introduces some order and some communication between the artist and the world, he cannot add to the intimacy and the directness and the depth with which the artist addresses his fellow men.

To the artist's loneliness there is a complementary great and terrible barrenness in the lives of men. They are deprived of the illumination, the light and the tenderness and insight of an intelligible interpretation, in contemporary terms, of the sorrow and wonders and gaieties and follies of man's life. . . .

In an important sense, this world of ours is a new world, in which the unity of knowledge, the nature of human communities, the order of society, the order of ideas, the very notions of society and culture have changed and will not return to what they have been in the past. What is new is new not because it has never been there before, but because it has changed in quality.

One thing that is new is the prevalence of newness, the changing scale and scope of change itself, so that the world alters as we walk in it, so that the years of man's life measure not some small growth or rearrangement or moderation of what he learned in childhood, but a great upheaval.

What is new is that in one generation our knowledge of the natural world engulfs, upsets and complements all knowledge of the natural world before. The techniques, among which and by which we live, multiply and ramify, so that the whole world is bound together by communication, blocked here and there by the immense synopses of political tyranny.

The global quality of the world is new: our knowledge of and sympathy with remote and diverse peoples, our involvement with them in practical terms and our commitment to them in terms of brotherhood. What is new in the world is the massive character of the dissolution and corruption of authority, in belief, in ritual and in temporal order.

Yet this is the world that we have come to live in. The very difficulties which it presents derive from growth in understanding, in skill, in power. To assail the changes that have unmoored us from the past is futile, and, in a deep sense, I think it is wicked. We need to recognize the change and learn what resources we have. . . .

The truth is that this is indeed inevitably and increasingly an open, and inevitably and increasingly an eclectic world. We know too much for one man to know much, we live too variously to live as one. Our histories and traditions—the very means of interpreting life—are both bonds and barriers among us. Our knowledge separates as well as it unites; our orders disintegrate as well as bind; our art brings us together and sets us apart. The artist's loneliness, the scholar's despairing, because no one will any longer trouble to learn what he can teach, the narrowness of the scientist, these are not unnatural insignia in this great time of change.

This is a world in which each of us, knowing his limitations, knowing the evils of superficiality and the terrors of fatigue, will have to cling to what is close to him, to what he knows, to what he can do, to his friends and his tradition and his love, lest he be dissolved in a universal confusion and know nothing and love nothing.

Both the man of science and the man of art live always at the edge of mystery, surrounded by it; both always, as the measure of their creation, have had to do with the harmonization of what is new and what is familiar, with the balance between novelty and synthesis, with the struggle to make partial order in total chaos.

This cannot be an easy life. We shall have a rugged time of it to keep our minds open and to keep them deep, to keep our sense of beauty and our ability to make it, and our occasional ability to see it, in places remote and strange and unfamiliar.

But this is, as I see it, the condition of man; and in this condition we can help, because we can love one another.

JOHN FOSTER DULLES

"The fact is that today any problem in any part of the world ramifies into almost every part of the world."

WASHINGTON, D. C., April 11, 1955—American foreign policy, now and for the foreseeable future, must rest upon consideration of the effect of any action anywhere as it may be reflected throughout the rest of the world.

This interpretation was given by John Foster Dulles, Secretary of State and prior to his political honors a noted international lawyer, in a nonpolitical analysis of the background of his high office, before the Fifth Annual All-Jesuit Alumni Dinner. Mr. Dulles, a Protestant, accepted this invitation as an occasion to step aside from the controversies of foreign and domestic issues and to define, as a statesman who has served both Democratic and Republican Presidents, the high concept which scholars of worldwide experience see as the guide to the future place of the United States in a strife-torn world.*

The Secretary of State obviously was defending a course that has brought much criticism upon the Eisenhower Administration, both from the elements that consider American foreign policy to be vacillating and from other groups which feel, especially in viewing the onward march of communism in Asia, that insufficient risks have been taken.

NATIONAL ACTION should always reflect principles. Therefore, those who have responsibility for action have also a responsibility to assure that what they do represents something more than immediate political expediency.

* In a later press conference, Secretary Dulles emphasized that firm policies must be pursued even to "the brink of war."

However, the guides to conduct are not always clear and simple. Often, indeed, they seem to conflict. Perhaps it will be of interest if I indicate some of the problems which confront those who try to find, in morality and in reason, a compass to direct their course.

Let me mention, as a first problem, that of peace vs. liberty.

Peace is a goal which men have always sought. It is a goal which we particularly think of at this Easter Season when we commemorate the resurrection of the Prince of Peace.

It is difficult to exaggerate the horrors of war or the longing of humanity for peace. Wars used to be limited in their scope, and they were regulated so as to spare civilians from most of their dire consequences. I myself can think back to the days when private property was immune from seizure in time of war; when interruption of trade was limited to particular ports which were closely blockaded or closed to contraband of war, by which was meant the actual tools of war.

As a youth, I attended the second Hague Peace Conference of 1907, which drew up protocols designed to prevent the use in war of the new scientific developments of that time. It was, for example, sought to forbid the dropping of explosives from balloons.

The First and Second World Wars showed that modern war is "total" war and that it is whole peoples, rather than the military, who suffer its cruel effects. Furthermore, we know that war more than ever involves compulsory enmity, outrages against the human personality, cruelty, vengefulness, and wanton distortions of the truth.

Today throughout the world there is a rising demand for protection against the misery, the agony of body and of spirit, the massive destruction of life and of property which modern war wreaks upon man.

There is, however, another aspect of the matter. Peace can be a cover whereby evil men can perpetrate diabolical wrongs.

During recent years the Communist rulers, through their propaganda, have sought to capitalize on love of peace and horror of war as a means of extending their rule over all the human race. Through such propaganda efforts as the Stockholm "Peace" Appeal, they have tried to divert the peoples of the free world from necessary measures of defense and create throughout the free world a popular demand for peace at any price.

Crafty scheming underlies that planning. The Communist leaders know that, if pacifism becomes a prevalent mood among the free peoples, the Communists can easily conquer the world. Then they can confront the free peoples with successive choices between peace and surrender; and if peace is the absolute goal, then surrenders become inevitable.

In this connection we should remember that, while modern developments have made war more terrible, they have also made the consequences of retreat and surrender more terrible. Modern war could now destroy much of the life on this planet. But also it may be possible that craven purchase of peace at the expense of principle can result in destroying much of the human spirit on this planet. Peace, under certain conditions, could lead to a degradation of the human race and to subjecting human beings to a form of mental decay which obliterates the capacity for moral and intellectual judgment.

We know, in individual cases, the effects of brainwashing. It leads men to repudiate their cherished beliefs and accept as fact what, if they were sane, they would know to be false. Not infrequently those who have been brainwashed come sincerely to believe that they committed acts elsewhere than where they physically were at the time.

There are now techniques which make it possible to alter profoundly the human spirit. Furthermore, this can be done on a mass scale. Certain falsehoods are incessantly pounded, without respite, into the consciousness of those whose minds are terrorized, whose spirits are disheartened, and whose bodies are weakened from malnutrition. In the end the peoples become abnormal.

One cannot but shrink from buying peace at the price of extending over human beings the rule of those who believe that men are in fact nothing more than animated bits of matter and that, to insure harmony and conformity, they should be deprived of the capacity for moral and intellectual judgment. Man, we read in the Holy Scriptures, was made a little lower than the angels. Should man now be made little, if any, higher than domesticated animals which serve the purposes of their human masters?

So men face the great dilemma of when and whether to use force to resist aggression which imposes conditions which violate the moral law and the concept that man has his origin and his destiny in God.

Another dilemma which we face is that which I might call the dilemma of maps vs. people.

Maps have an extraordinary fascination and a profound influence. They provide a temptation to seize as solutions what are not real solutions.

Up until a few years ago, the American people were educated in terms of maps of Mercator's projection. They showed the North American Continent isolated from the rest of the world by the expanse of great oceans. George Washington, in his Farewell Address, spoke of "our detached and distant situation." That concept, originally valid, has dominated the greater part of our national life.

Now we face a world in which air is the means of communication. But air cannot be portrayed by maps alone. It is an invisible envelope that enfolds the earth without a break. So maps now need the supplement of an intelligent imagination. Some help can be got from polar maps. They help to teach that under modern conditions of communication areas which used to seem remote are in fact near.

Under present circumstances, divisions of land and water, of desert and mountain range, of river and of plain, have lost much of their significance. More than ever before, the human family has become one.

Nevertheless, it is still necessary to draw lines. There are national lines, which have a meaning. But even national lines do not have an unchanging meaning. That is well illustrated by Europe. A map of Europe today looks as it did a few weeks ago. But, in fact, in Western Europe an immense change is in process. It meant that, while nationalities will still exist, there will be cooperation so that the boundary lines will have lost much of their former forbidding significance. A new Western Europe is being born, and maps cannot reflect the ending of age-old rivalries.

In Korea the 38th parallel became famous as a line between the free and Communist-dominated parts of Korea. But the line did not demarcate the hopes and aspirations of the people. I recall being in Korea in June 1950 and addressing at Seoul a religious gathering of thousands of refugees. They had fled from the north and crossed the parallel to the south in the hope of finding the freedom of religion which they cherished.

In Viet-Nam a line was drawn at the 17th parallel. But hundreds of thousands of refugees have crossed it, fleeing to the south. Again the driving force was a longing for religious freedom.

And there is this to be remembered: For each person who succeeds in becoming a refugee from communism, there are many more who do not want to be contained by the lines which statesmen have drawn in the hope that that would solve their problems.

In the world today, with air the means of communication, with time and space almost annihilated, geography still remains a fact. But geographical solutions rarely coincide with human solutions. That is why we do not accept the finality of a divided world. . . .

Another dilemma that we face might be described as that of the part vs. the entire story.

It is almost always easy to find a solution if only part of a problem is known. It is my experience that those who are most positive about political problems are able to be positive only because they do not know all the relevant facts. Those who are most harsh in their judgments are able to be harsh for that same reason. When the whole of a problem is known, solutions become excessively difficult and judgments are not easily made. Tolerance has become a vital need.

There is hardly any international problem which lends itself to easy or sure solution. Those who principally know Europe readily judge that the problems of Asia are unimportant and that almost any solution will serve so long as it does not trouble Europe. Those who are principally concerned with Asia are sometimes annoyed if it is suggested that Asian problems cannot be solved without regard for Europe.

The fact is that today any problem in any part of the world ramifies into almost every part of the world. There are no longer any simple problems, nor any easy solutions. A course of action for Indochina may have to be judged in the light of its repercussions in Europe, the Middle East, or Moscow, and vice versa.

I have the impression that in the days before the world became so unified it was easier to make decisions. The issues were, or seemed to be, simple. Also, they could readily be explained. Today almost every problem has many complications, so that it is difficult adequately to explain the reasons for a decision and the multiple factors which go to make up that decision.

There is a habit of mind which is sometimes called "localitis." Those who are close to a problem, or those who only see part of a problem, quickly find a solution that seems obvious. Those who know more may find that the "obvious" solution is no solution at all. Balancing scales may, from one angle, seem clearly weighted on one side. But when seen in proper perspective, they may seem to be equally balanced, or weighted on the other side.

This need for balancing many factors has some undesirable consequences. I have already alluded to the fact that it makes adequate explanation difficult. Also, it often tends to deprive decisions of the dynamic quality which is needed to make them effective. Often the mainspring of action is a sense of certainty. Unhappily, those who are best informed are often deprived of that satisfaction.

The great deeds of history were wrought primarily by men with deep conviction and dynamic faith. They were sure that they were right.

It seems today that sureness can be dependably found only in the spiritual realm but that, when moral principles are sought to be practically applied, confidence tends to vanish. Certainty is not readily found in the mundane realm, at least where there is full knowledge of the facts. The yearning for more certainty and precision than is compatible with the complexity of affairs encourages only doctrinaire or fanatical attitudes and ultimate disillusionment. Perhaps it is good if fanaticism, in worldly terms, is on the way out. . . .

Then we have the dilemma which might be called that of the spiritual vs. the material.

There are some who believe that moral considerations ought not to influence the foreign policy of a nation, that moral considerations are all right for the individual but not for the collective unity. Corporate bodies, it is argued, should be directed only by material considerations.

It is, I suppose, always true that those who act in a representative and trustee capacity do not have the same freedom as is had by individuals in dealing with their own lives and the property they own. Thus, directors of a corporation are, in general, not free to use corporate assets for charitable purposes unconnected with the welfare of the corporation. To a degree, I suppose, the same principles apply to those who are trustees for a nation.

It is, indeed, generally the case that those who represent a government operate only for the immediate and direct self-interest of the nation they represent. That is why suspicion generally attaches to governmental grants. It is assumed that governments do not give away their taxpayers' money unless they see some specific quid pro quo.

The government of the United States has, I like to believe, a rather unique tradition in this respect. Our nation was founded as an experiment in human liberty. Our institutions reflect the belief of our founders that all men were endowed by their Creator with inalienable rights and had duties prescribed by moral law. They believed that human institutions ought primarily to help men develop their God-given possibilities and that our nation, by its conduct and example, could help men everywhere to find the way to a better and more abundant life.

Our nation realized that vision. There developed here an area of spiritual and economic vigor the like of which the world had never seen. It was no exclusive preserve; indeed, world mission was a central theme. Millions were welcomed from other lands, to share equally the opportunities of the founders and their heirs. We put our experiment on public exhibition so that all might see and follow if they would. Through the establishment of schools and hospitals, often under religious auspices, American ideals were carried throughout the world. We gave aid and comfort to those elsewhere who sought to follow in our way and to develop for themselves societies of greater human freedom.

These conditions prevailed for 100 years and more. Then, as our material power waxed, our spiritual power seemed to wane. We appeared to be less concerned with conducting a great experiment for the benefit of mankind and to be more concerned with piling up for ourselves material advantages. Our vision seemed to contract, and our sense of mission to lessen.

We had to meet the severest test that can come to a people, the test of prosperity.

It was said by Jesus that material things will be added unto those who seek first the Kingdom of God and His righteousness. But when that happens, then comes the great trial. For, as Jesus warned, those material things can readily become the rust that corrodes men's souls.

Thus there is a familiar pattern. Men who feel a sense of duty to some higher Being strive here to do His will. Because of their faith, they have power and virtue and simple wisdom. They build not only for the day, but for the morrow; not merely for themselves, but for mankind. A society so founded will, when nature favors, produce wealth and luxury for many. When those by-products come, they seem so good that they become promoted to be the all-sufficient end.

So there came a time when our people were drawn away from long-range creative effort and when they struggled to get and to hold material things. Practices originally designed to reflect a faith may not have been adequately vitalized by continuing faith. I believe, however, that it can fairly be said that, since the end of World War II, our nation has recaptured the faith in which it was founded and has resumed works such as those which in the past were called "The Great American Experiment."

With 60 other nations we have actively participated in the United Nations in its quest for peace. We have lent our moral, military, and material support to many free people. With more than 40 nations we have special mutual security arrangements. These measures are our contribution to the creation of a world which is safer and more secure for human freedom. This basic interest is the common bond between us and the other free nations.

We exert in every part of the world an influence—an influence which we try, as far as is humanly possible, to make an influence for justice and not an influence for self-aggrandizement.

No doubt we have made mistakes. But broadly speaking, our nation has played a role which I believe history will judge to have been honorable. It is a role which we could not have played unless those who exercised the power of government had believed that they were justified in putting moral considerations above material considerations. . . .

I have outlined some of the problems and perplexities which confront those who have political responsibility. I have deliberately tried to avoid being dogmatic. Rather I have sought to stimulate your own thinking. I will, however, close with this general observation:

It seems to me that a nation situated as is ours needs to follow a consistent and predictable course. We represent great power in the world—morally, intellectually, and materially. Other peoples and nations who are free and want to stay free usually want to coordinate their policies with our own. I do not speak now of coordination in detail. As to details, there are almost always differences. That is inevitable, because differences are the attribute of freedom. It is only despotism that produces conformity. I do, however, speak of such basic harmony as freely emerges from those who feel a sense of common destiny and who want to help, and be helped by, each other.

A measure of harmony exists today throughout much of the free world. It binds together, in a spirit of partnership, many of different races, creeds, and nationalities in many parts of the world. But the harmony for which many thus grope will never be perfected and preserved unless the United States pursues a dependable, consistent course.

There are many who, in particular cases, would like it if the United States would deviate from our basic principles to help them meet their particular problems. We rarely do so. That accounts for much of the superficial criticism we encounter abroad. But underlying these surface dissatisfactions lies, I feel, a deep, worldwide sense of respect for the United States because, even though we sometimes fall short, we do in general stand like a rock for certain principles and follow a course which, in its broad nature, is consistent and predictable. Without that, there can never be harmony and a sense of security as among the free peoples.

Obviously, a consistent and dependable national course must have a base broader than the particular beliefs of those who from time to time hold office. Our policies must, on the one hand, be dependably embraced by our own people and, on the other hand, reflect a decent respect for the opinions of mankind. It would seem that only principles which conform to moral law meet that specification. So not only the basic faith of our people, who are essentially religious, but also enlightened self-interest combine to urge that moral principle be a guide not merely to individual conduct but also the conduct of the nations.

The sequel:

Early on a Sunday morning in May, 1959, flags on all government buildings were ordered to half-mast, and the bell of famous Brick Presbyterian Church, in New York, tolled in tribute to the passing of its most distinguished member. John Foster Dulles had died of cancer in the Presidential suite of Walter Reed Hospital, at Washington, D. C., after several weeks of final confinement there.

In the manner of his death, following work up to the last moment his strength would permit, Secretary Dulles may have made as great a contribution to his country as in his seven arduous years in office. He had gone to the hospital to face his hopeless future only after laying the groundwork for the Conference of Foreign Ministers at Geneva in 1959, thus raising immeasurably the prestige of his office and of the cause for which he fought.

So dramatic was the impact of his death, only a few weeks after turning over his cares to Christian Herter, and continuing to the end as daily consultant with the President and the State Department, that the conferees at Geneva turned for a moment into unanimity of admiration. To his funeral flew the chief representatives of Britain, France and Soviet Russia, as well as Chancellor Adenauer of Germany. In Washington, the President was thus enabled to talk personally with all the Geneva conferees in an unprecedented manner of informality.

When taps were sounded at the Arlington Cemetery grave, to which Mr. Dulles' body was consigned as a veteran of military service in World War I, the notes of the bugle may have been also a trumpet call to a world in tension to move more positively toward the lasting cause of peace for free men to which the dead statesmen had given his last score of years.

ALFRED M. GRUENTHER

"The competition is very tough, and in this contest, there is no prize for second best."

NEW YORK, N. Y., December 7, 1956—General Alfred M. Gruenther, retiring Commander of the Allied Powers Europe, established under the North Atlantic Treaty Organization, gave an optimistic outlook on the ability of the West to maintain strength sufficient to deter Communist attack in the future, but pictured NATO as a continuing military and economic challenge for many years to come.

The soldier-statesman, successor to and intimate friend of President Dwight D. Eisenhower, is returning to civilian life after 38 years in military service, but his "retirement" promises to be a strenuous one as he has been chosen for the full-time post of President of The American Red Cross.

Tonight standing at the crossroads of these careers, he smiled wryly and began his speech by saying bluntly, "I feel that the title for this talk might well be: 'The throats that may be cut would be your own.'"

On that note he launched into a major address before the Sixty-first Congress of American Industry, exactly 15 years after the Japanese attack on Pearl Harbor precipitated American participation in World War II.

. . . THE PRODUCTIVITY of the United States is so high that it has become the envy of the entire world. In accomplishing this result, however, you have incurred the implacable hostility of the Soviets. They realize very clearly that if the system which you have worked so vigorously to establish can prevail—as I am certain it can—then their system with its sinister materialistic philosophy is doomed to failure. . . .

General Eisenhower arrived in Paris on the 7th of January 1951, to plan for the defense of Europe. It is well to recall the state of our defenses at that time. He found that our strength was at a low ebb, and morale even lower. The West had disarmed to a very considerable extent at the end of World War II, but the Soviets had not. Instead, they were using their greater strength to further their goal of world domination. Such events as the Czechoslovakian Coup, the Berlin Blockade, and, finally, the Korean invasion showed that Soviet imperialism was again on the march, and created an almost chaotic state in European morale.

As General Eisenhower studied this problem, he found that he was confronted by tremendous Soviet Bloc strength. On our side, there were distressingly few forces out of which to form a defense. Even more discouraging was the fact that the forces we *did* have could not be utilized effectively, for we had no unified command, no common strategic concept for defense, and inadequate communications even if we did have such a concept.

Now, almost six years later, that situation has improved very considerably. Our forces are four to five times as strong as they were then, and we have a common strategic concept. . . .

Such progress is very gratifying, but, of course, what people want to know is, do we yet have the strength to be certain of defending Western Europe? Could we give a guarantee that we could achieve our mission? Can we successfully defend *all* of NATO's territory? The answer is "No, not yet." We are still not that strong. When we have a German contribution, which will consist of some 12 divisions, some 1,300 tactical aircraft and a small naval force, we shall be able to give that assurance, assuming, of course, that we will use atomic weapons.

Our planning is based upon military realities. We formulate our defense concept on what the Red Bloc forces *could* do against us. We are not concerned with happy talk, with cocktail parties at the Kremlin, or with "cordial" visits, admirable though they may be. Our job is to assess the capabilities of the Soviet Bloc, and to keep them constantly in mind.

From a force standpoint the Soviets now have 175 well-trained divisions. They also have some 20,000 operational aircraft, about 80 per cent of which are jets. . . .

The Soviets have a relatively weak surface navy, but a very

powerful under-water fleet of more than 400 submarines. To compare that number, which has some significance, I need only recall to you that the Germans, when World War II started, had fewer than 75 submarines.

To Soviet military strength must be added the forces of the captive nations, which number some 75 divisions and air forces totaling about 2,500 planes. The Satellite forces are not nearly so well-trained as the Soviet forces, and their planes are not so modern. Furthermore, their reliability has always been a doubtful factor. . . .

You are aware, I am certain, that security involves, in addition to the military factor, the economic, political and psychological aspects. I propose now to discuss some of the economic factors.

Basically, the new Soviet 5-year plan emphasizes heavy industry, which greatly enhances the military capability. Take one critical item: steel. In 1928 the Soviets produced 5 million metric tons of steel. In 1955 they produced 45 million tons. The current 5-year plan calls for 68 million tons by 1960.

Their present capacity, 45 million tons, plus that of the Satellite areas, gives them a total for the Soviet Bloc of 60 million metric tons. The United States last year produced 106 million metric tons, and with the other NATO countries, the total is 180 million tons. Thus, we have a steel production advantage of three to one. Knowing this, we might be inclined to say: "Well, that gives us a tremendous advantage in industrial potential." That is true, but we must be careful in making such a statement. When you consider that out of U. S. steel production, there were 7½ million passenger cars produced last year, and in the Soviet Union, 95,000; when you consider 3½ million refrigerators produced in the U. S. last year, and only 150,000 in the Soviet Union—it is clear that their industrial war-making capacity is far greater than the one-third ratio which a superficial calculation might indicate.

It is well to remember that with the Soviet system—of being able to shift priorities readily, and their ability to concentrate on those elements which increase their war-making capacity—it would be dangerous to underestimate their strength. They are virtually operating at a war-time economy now.

At the same time, it must be borne in mind that they do have severe difficulties. For example, they have a great manpower problem. The number of young men available to their labor force has fallen to a new low because of the small number of births during the war. . . .

This brings us to the question: "Where do we stand as of now in the Alliance, since I stated earlier that we do not yet have sufficient military strength to give a positive guarantee that we could defend all of Europe against a full scale aggression?" I do not think there is any reason to be discouraged. We still maintain, as of today, an overwhelming capacity to retaliate with long-range air power if we should be attacked. As of today, that counter-attack would go through because of two factors: Offensive air power still has a big advantage over the defense. Secondly, because of our base system, which extends around the globe, our capacity to retaliate could not be destroyed even by another Pearl Harbor, although the likelihood of another one is very, very slight.

I want to make it unmistakably clear that the fundamental objective of NATO is to *prevent* another war from taking place. We can accomplish this by making an act of aggression so costly for a potential aggressor that it would never occur. That is why I have stressed the importance of our retaliatory capacity, which is a powerful one today, December 7, 1956. What it will be with respect to the defense five years hence it is not possible to say now. But I believe the west has it in its power to retain that capability.

However, it is not sufficient to have only a retaliatory capacity. We must also be able to defend Europe from invasion. Plans are being implemented to increase the strength of the NATO shield forces there to accomplish this purpose. It is essential to give the people of Europe a confidence that they cannot be overrun.

Since the NATO objective is to prevent war, it is well to recognize that a high degree of unity is required. Our people must have faith that the alliance is an effective instrument for preserving the peace. . . .

We now have 140 operational airfields which could be used this very night if necessary, with more in process of construction. This is an illustration of a problem that was met and solved, but required a high degree of understanding and patience. We must continue and increase this type of cooperation.

When Mr. Khrushchev delivered his speech at the 20th Party Congress last February—a very "short" speech of 7½ hours—he included a statement that they have in the Soviet Union 7,200,000 crusaders (by that he meant the membership of the Communist Party) in a population of 200,200,000.

And these men *are* crusaders. They believe in their sinister system with all of their heart and soul. Many of the people there probably do not, but under the leadership and discipline of that 7,200,000, they have developed a strong unity and a most effective military machine.

Our task is not only to provide military strength, but to match their fanatical zeal by our own sense of dedication. I can assure you that we have a problem ahead. The mantle of world leadership, whether we like it or not, has fallen upon the United States. Therefore, this alliance is going to thrive—is going to continue to be a factor for peace—in exactly the proportion to which the United States supports it.

That means that in the critical period ahead, our differences of opinion with our Allies—and those differences have been highlighted in the last few weeks in connection with the Middle East problem—will have to be settled, and our people will have to have a widespread understanding, and demonstrate leadership qualities more than ever before.

Make no mistake about it, we are in the big league now; the competition is very tough, and in this contest, there is no prize for second best. . . .

WILLIAM F. (BILLY) GRAHAM

"Learn the lesson of the worm."

NEW YORK, 1957—A new and internationally famous evangelist, "Billy" Graham, has emerged in the last decade as a leading force in religious work, by almost completely reversing the older "hellfire-and-brimstone" techniques of earlier evangelists epitomized by "Billy" Sunday.

A quiet and handsome young man, at this writing 39 years old, "Billy" Graham has been described as looking like a junior business executive and speaking like a college professor. Yet there is a fiery magnetism in his quiet delivery that has filled auditoriums including Madison Square Garden, attracted a sober crowd that jammed Wall Street when he spoke from the steps of the Federal Building, and found equal responses in foreign countries.

His constant theme is "humility," and his preaching is more in the nature of mass-counseling on that theme. His "crusades" are marvels of organization, with his appearances timed to coincide with detailed and specific follow-up work by local churches.

His words on "National Humility" are an oft-repeated text.

WHY IS there such a lack of grace today? There can only be one answer. The people have gotten away from humility. We must recognize it and face it. May God help us to be a humble people.

As God gives grace only to the humble, therefore, we need to study humility and learn what real humility is and then practice it daily. Practice it just as you would practice music if you wanted to be a musician. And above all things, do it right when pride is trying to manifest itself.

To humble yourself is to oppose self, to abase self, to break your stubborn will to do what self does not want to do, and to expose self by confessing faults and acknowledging wrongs. Nothing short of this is real humility. Humility is putting down pride. Smash pride, step on it, crush it, mash it, break it, and above all, expose it—not in the other fellow but in yourself.

You can break down and thresh out and destroy every mountain of self and every obstacle in your way, if you will just be a worm. Deny yourself if you want to be a worm. To deny self is to disown self.

Christ who was and is our example was the personification of humility. He came to demonstrate humility to us. And we get the secret of His success and victory when we hear Him cry out in Psalm 22:6, "But I am a worm and no man." In other words, Christ took the attitude of a worm.

A worm is perfectly helpless. It has no strength to fight or protect itself from danger. Whether food for birds or to be trampled underfoot by man, it resigns itself to sacrifice; but a worm is always busy. Hidden away out of sight, it gets little credit for what it does, yet it is the greatest blessing to plant life in the world. It lives entirely for others. A worm is of the earth earthly but it plows its way through the darkness, it feeds and thrives and grows fat on the very earth that brings such trials and headaches to others.

I beg of you, Christians, learn the lesson of the worm and humble yourself before God.

The sequel:

Billy Graham remains at this writing without a peer in the world of Protestant evangelism. Noted as a writer as well as preacher, a formal educator as well as evangelist, he traveled in 1959 to Australia in the most recent enlargement of his "crusade."

JOHN MASON BROWN

"I am sick and tired of the snivelers, the defeated and the whiners."

GROTON, Mass., 1958—John Mason Brown, noted critic and lecturer, consigned to a deserved ignominy the prophets of the "beat generation" in a talk to one of his favorite audiences, the "sixth form" and graduating class of the Groton School for Boys. He delivered the "Prize Day Address."

The subject is a favorite with Mr. Brown, and in language understandable to youth he paid his critical respects to two of the most pessimistic of the self-appointed "interpreters" of depressed youth—Jack Kerouac and John Osborne.

I MUST confess that I am deeply curious about the name with which your generation will be branded a decade hence. I claim no singularity in this. The qualities and the attitude towards life which that name reveals will be the nation's concern—and the world's. I make no pretense of being a prophet. I can speak only from my hopes. And my hopes for the name which your generation will merit are based upon my strong reactions to the various names currently applied to the generation ten years older than yours. You must know these names. In England, "The Angry Young Men"; in America, "The Beat Generation." I do not question the accuracy of these names, when it comes to revealing the attitudes and feelings of the authors associated with them or the small groups who are their devotees. But I am certain that these labels are no more than "coterie" tags which, since they speak only for a sector of a sector, are downright libelous when applied to a whole generation.

Your absorption with Caesar, Cicero or Catullus may have kept you strangers to the writings of Jack Kerouac. If so, do not count yourselves denied. And in your preoccupation with Milton—the Academy no less than the poet—and St. Mark as well as St. Mark's, you may not have seen John Osborne's play, *Look Back in Anger*. I single out these alleged spokesmen for their generation—the first in America, the second and more gifted writer in England—because they seem to me typically unrepresentative. The two men are brothers only in despair. Mr. Kerouac does not believe in reality; Mr. Osborne finds it unbearable. Mr. Kerouac has insisted that people are not people at all. "We are empty phantoms," he has said (and this may be superbly accurate as autobiography), "sitting here thinking we are human beings and worrying about civilization. We are just phantoms." Mr. Osborne is even more depressed by the mere thought of living. He has described his *Look Back in Anger* as a play about "two people who couldn't bear the pain of being human beings." Mr. Kerouac in his novel *On the Road* was the one to call his generation "beat." He does not mean that his characters, who are the Joads of delinquency, are bludgeoned, weary, or defeated. That would be too easy. By "beat" he means "beatific." As he soils the word, "beatific" stands not for blessedness but for happiness achieved through car-stealing, hot-rodding, dope-taking, industrious drinking, exchanging girls ("fetching hunks," he calls them), and the effortful avoidance of all kinds of gainful employment. Mr. Osborne's Britishers, though equally young, are more old-fashioned. They are just plain "beat." If I may say so, they are more "beat" by Mr. Osborne than by life. Mr. Osborne, supposedly the angry young man, is the victim of a sorry confusion. He is not really angry at all. He mistakes petulance for anger. I for one resent this bitterly. To me *anger* is a great and proud word, like *wrath* in the Bible. A tantrum is not anger. Anger, in the best sense, is a flexing of an aroused conscience. It is a big emotion which, I hope, the immorality of indifference will never keep you from summoning. I don't know about you, but I am sick and tired of the snivelers, the defeated, and the whiners. I am sick and tired of being expected to believe that ugliness is beauty, that melancholy is man's sole pleasure, that delinquency is delight, that disease is health, that laughter is something to be ashamed of, and that any denial is better than any affirmation.

Do not misunderstand me. When I attack negation, I do not want to sound like someone whose mother was frightened by a bluebird. I have lived long enough to be battered by the realities of life and too long to be downed by them. Many of us, if we have happy childhoods, are tempted when young to believe that life is a pony, beribboned and curried, which has been given to us as a present. With the passing years we, sooner or later, come to learn that, instead of being that pony, life is a mule which unfortunately has more than four legs. To the best of my knowledge, no one who lives long enough fails to be kicked, usually again and again, by that mule. Why this should surprise us or unnerve us, I as an older person have long since ceased to understand. This testing has been the eternal challenge. To live, men have had to live with this challenge through the ages but undaunted by it, even as they have had to live with the knowledge that death is the ultimate challenge of life. . . .

A generation is bound, in its major emphasis, to be a reflection of two things—the world it faces, and its response to that world. To say that the world at present stinks is to understate its fragrance. To say that is must stink forever is a lie, at least as I see it, and trust you see it too. To subscribe to that lie would be to invite the worst and to deserve it. You do not have to be told about the terrible threats of the present which could lead to mass annihilation and the savage end of civilization. But you, better than most, have been equipped to live not only with but above the appalling possibilities of our times. The world's new perils that you will face cannot change the enduring values and challenges of your individual living. As all aspiring men have done before you, you will have to fight a hard battle within yourselves. I have in mind the age-old conflict between the specialist, as we know him today, and that ideal of the whole man as it was realized by Jefferson, Hamilton, and Franklin after the Revolution. To succeed, you will now more than ever have to put on the blinders of the specialist. Even so, I trust that your specialization will not keep you from knowing the joy of hobbies and the enrichment that comes only from the fullest possible immersion in all the concerns and interests of life. I beg of you to live as participants rather than as spectators, unafraid of work and unafraid of play. . . .

HENRY CABOT LODGE, JR.

"Man can improve his material and physical lot
without sacrificing his civil rights."

CHICAGO, Ill., Sept. 2, 1958— "The great opportunity of the United States over the years ahead is to continue its leadership in proving that individual freedom and national prosperity, by contrast with the extinction of the former in an effort to create the latter, is man's best way of life."

So spoke Henry Cabot Lodge, Jr., United States Representative to the United Nations, in an address here before the annual convention of the American Legion.

Mr. Lodge, a former Senator and grandson of the famous exponent of "Americanism," thus helped to bring into focus one of the dominant values of the United Nations as a weapon for advancement of American ideals in the cold war with the forces and governments of communism.

In his talk, the youthful speaker reviewed many other facets of the problems of the world as they are seen from his vantage point, including those of statecraft in which he speaks personally for the President of the United States, and for the Secretary of State, from whom he receives his directions. But in what may be considered his own personal area of thought—in the delineation of the concepts to which his own service has brought him—he emphasized the continuity of thinking that marks the American approach to the future at a level somewhat higher than often appears in the daily hassle of debate.

. . . THE FINAL result of the United Nations' consideration of the Near East question came, as you know, about ten days ago when, instead of denouncing the United States or calling upon us to withdraw, or doing any of the things which the Soviet Union wanted, the United Nations adopted a resolution which embodies the kind of thing which we think should be done in the Near East. It contained a pledge of non-interference, and it in effect put the United Nations into Lebanon and Jordan. Both of these provisions, therefore, if lived up to, would make possible our withdrawal. Finally—and of great importance for the future, the resolution approved a long-range scheme for regional economic development along the lines proposed by President Eisenhower. . . .

Our future, in any event, is sure to be influenced by the current advances of science—and one of the most challenging new frontiers opened up by this advance is the vastness of outer space. The universe through which our world travels each day has no national boundaries. The scientists of the world have much to contribute to the peaceful exploration of outer space. All of us have much to lose if outer space is subjected to national rivalries. If nations can successfully cooperate in the study and exploration of outer space, new and brighter horizons may be opened up for all humanity.

It is good, therefore, to be able for the first time to announce here at the National Convention of the American Legion that President Eisenhower has instructed me to include the important and urgent subject of outer space at the next regular session of the General Assembly which meets in a few weeks. Specifically, the United States will propose a program for international cooperation in the field of outer space.

No matter what happens, study and exploration of outer space will go on and will take man where no human being has gone before. This will affect every man, woman and child in the world—and can be to their great benefit.

Our new space knowledge can be applied to medicine, communications, transportation and many other useful fields—including even our knowledge of the weather.

Progress in this field would be faster, cheaper, and more efficient if all the nations concerned agreed to work together.

Some practical program for international cooperation in the scientific and peaceful study and exploration of outer space must be set up.

We will continue our efforts to reach agreements, consistent with our national security, which will increase the prospects that outer space will not be used for military purposes.

But even as we work for such agreements, an important start must be made now in opening this new realm for the benefit of all mankind.

The United Nations, therefore, should immediately consider what it can do in this field; what outer space projects for peaceful purposes can be undertaken under United Nations auspices; and what sort of organization the United Nations can build so that the nations will work together in outer space.

The United States wants to see outer space used so as to enrich the lives of all people who live on this planet. We trust that our proposal will get the support of other nations and that, together, we can move forward toward this goal with the courage and vision of our early pioneers.

We must not get discouraged about the future. The Soviet communists today believe in a doctrine which is not peace and not war and which they have themselves described as "protracted conflict." We must accordingly be able to think of this struggle in terms of generations—a struggle which will span many elections, many fiscal years and many national conventions.

The Soviet Union is a big power and so are we. But the struggle in which we are engaged is no mere power struggle. For there is one element in the struggle which we *have* and which the Soviets have *not*. It is the element to which I referred at the beginning of this speech. It is the strength of our ideals—ideals for which the American Legion also stands.

From our Founding Fathers there have come down to us ideals which proclaim the dignity of man and the value and sanctity of the individual. The difference between our way of life and that of communism which has particularly vivid meaning for people in Asia, Africa and in every corner of the globe is our proposition proven by 180 years of actual experience: that man *can* improve his material and physical lot without sacrificing his civil rights. In fact, while his material lot improves, his freedom, his ability to think and to act for himself, to develop his personality—in the words of the Declaration of Independence, to pursue his happiness—all these things are enhanced.

There are, to be sure, many other differences which are apparent to us here in America. But the fact that we stand for material progress without sacrifice of freedom has particular meaning abroad.

One basic element in our way of thinking therefore is the right of every people in its internal affairs, to live its own life in its own way. As President Eisenhower said to the United Nations on August 13th:

"This world of individual nations is not going to be controlled by any one power or group of powers. This world is not going to be committed to any one ideology. The dream of world domination by one power or of world conformity is an impossible dream."

Comrade Commander and Fellow Legionnaires, let us in conclusion remember this: we must be strong in our military might, strong in the vitality of our economic life, strong in our national unity and strong in the vigor and skill of our diplomacy.

But underlying all these things is the struggle for the minds of men. We will win the struggle for the minds of men in so far as we make a reality, at home and abroad, of our humane ideals. In this, as in everything which pertains to the welfare of our country, the American Legion can and will make a priceless contribution.

CARL SANDBURG

"On occasions he was seen to weep in a way that made weeping decent, appropriate, and majestic."

WASHINGTON, D. C., Feb. 12, 1959—In simple prose reflecting the majesty of his greatest poetry, Carl Sandburg spoke today in tribute to Abraham Lincoln, to the study and interpretation of whose works he has devoted the greater portion of his 81 years.

The setting of the speech was part of a ceremony without precedent, as he stood upon the rostrum of the House of Representatives, addressing by invitation a Joint Session of the House and Senate, on the 150th anniversary of Lincoln's birth. Such sessions have been convened in the past century only to hear from dignitaries such as the President of the United States, heads of foreign governments or, in more recent times, generals home from the wars.

Mr. Sandburg walked with quiet dignity to the speaker's stand after Frederic March, the actor, had read

President Lincoln's Gettysburg Address. He talked for perhaps 12 minutes on the simple factors that have made the "Lincoln legend" a matter of documentation exceeding the literature written about any other American individual; yet all that he told in his brief speech seemed to be new in its meaning.

Unlike many of his auditors, trained to persuasive oratory, the elderly poet spoke in a hoarse and occasionally low voice. But a moment after he had finished, while he looked out over his audience, there came a thunder of applause. He bowed, and then moved with dignity from the platform.

NOT OFTEN in the story of mankind does a man arrive on earth who is both steel and velvet, who is as hard as rock and soft as drifting fog, who holds in his heart and mind the paradox of terrible storm and peace unspeakable and perfect. Here and there across centuries come reports of men alleged to have these contrasts. And the incomparable Abraham Lincoln, born 150 years ago this day, is an approach if not a perfect realization of this character.

In the time of the April lilacs in the year 1865, on his death, the casket with his body was carried north and west a thousand miles; and the American people wept as never before; bells sobbed, cities wore crepe; people stood in tears and with hats off as the railroad burial car paused in the leading cities of seven states, ending its journey at Springfield, Ill., the home town.

During the four years he was President he at times, especially in the first three months, took to himself the powers of a dictator; he commanded the most powerful armies till then assembled in modern warfare; he enforced conscription of soldiers for the first time in American history; under imperative necessity he abolished the right of habeas corpus; he directed politically and spiritually the wild, massive, turbulent forces let loose in civil war.

He argued and pleaded for compensated emancipation of the slaves. The slaves were property, they were on the tax books along with horses and cattle, the valuation of each slave next to his name on the tax assessor's books. Failing to get action on compensated emancipation, as a Chief Executive having war powers he issued the paper by which he declared the slaves to be free under "military necessity." In the end nearly $4,000,000 worth of property was taken away from those who were legal owners of it, property confiscated, wiped out as by fire and turned to ashes, at his instigation and executive direction. Chattel property recognized and lawful for 300 years was expropriated, seized without payment.

In the month the war began he told his secretary, John Hay, "My policy is to have no policy." Three years later in a letter to a Kentucky friend made public, he confessed plainly, "I have been controlled by events." His words at Gettysburg were sacred, yet strange with a color of the familiar: "We cannot consecrate—we cannot hallow—this ground. The brave men, living and dead, who struggled here, have consecrated it, far beyond our poor power to add or detract."

He could have said "the brave Union men." Did he have a purpose in omitting the word "Union"? Was he keeping himself and his utterance clear of the passion that would not be good to look at when the time came for peace and reconciliation? Did he mean to leave an implication that there were brave Union men, and brave Confederate men, living and dead, who had struggled there? We do not know, of a certainty.

Was he thinking of the Kentucky father whose two sons died in battle, one in Union blue, the other in Confederate gray, the father inscribing on the stone over their double grave, "God knows which was right"? We do not know.

Lincoln's changing policies from time to time aimed at saving the Union. In the end his armies won and his nation became a world power immersed in international politics. In August of 1864 he wrote a memorandum that he expected to lose the next November election; sudden military victory brought the tide his way; the vote was 2,200,000 for him and 1,800,000 against him.

Among his bitter opponents were such figures as Samuel F. B. Morse, inventor of the telegraph, and Cyrus H. McCormick, inventor of the farm reaper. In all its essential propositions the Southern Confederacy had the moral support of powerful, respectable elements throughout the North, probably more than a million voters believing in the justice of the Southern cause.

While the war winds howled he insisted that the Mississippi was one river meant to belong to one country, that railroad connection from coast to coast must be pushed through and the Union Pacific

Railroad made a reality. While the luck of war wavered and broke and came again, as generals failed and campaigns were lost, he held enough forces of the North together to raise new armies and supply them, until generals were found who made war as victorious war has always been made, with terror, frightfulness, destruction, and on both sides, North and South, valor and sacrifice past words of man to tell.

In the mixed shame and blame of the immense wrongs of two crashing civilizations, often with nothing to say, he said nothing, slept not at all, and on occasions he was seen to weep in a way that made weeping appropriate, decent, majestic.

As he rode alone on horseback near Soldiers' Home on the edge of Washington one night his hat was shot off; a son he loved died as he watched at the bed; his wife was accused of betraying information to the enemy, until denials from him were necessary.

An Indiana man at the White House heard him say, "Voorhees, don't it seem strange to you that I, who could never so much as cut off the head of a chicken, should be elected, or selected, into the midst of all this blood?"

He tried to guide Gen. Nathaniel Prentiss Banks, a Democrat, three times Governor of Massachusetts, in the governing of some seventeen of the forty-eight parishes of Louisiana controlled by the Union armies, an area holding a fourth of the slaves of Louisiana. He would like to see the state recognize the Emancipation Proclamation, "and while she is at it, I think it would not be objectionable for her to adopt some practical system by which the two races could gradually live themselves out of their old relation to each other, and both come out better prepared for the new. Education for the young blacks should be included in the plan."

To Gov. Michel Hahn elected in 1864 by a majority of the 11,000 white male voters who had taken the oath of allegiance to the Union, Lincoln wrote:

"Now you are about to have a convention which, among other things will probably define the elective franchise, I barely suggest for your private consideration, whether some of the colored people may not be let in—as for instance, the very intelligent and especially those who have fought gallantly in our ranks."

Among the million words in the Lincoln utterance record, he interprets himself with a more keen precision than someone else offering to explain him. His simple opening of the House Divided speech in 1858 serves for today:

"If we could first know where we are, and whither we are tending we could better judge what to do, and how to do it."

To his Kentucky friend, Joshua F. Speed, he wrote in 1855:

"Our progress in degeneracy appears to me to be pretty rapid. As a nation we began by declaring that 'all men are created equal, except Negroes.' When the Know-Nothings get control, it will read 'All men are created equal except Negroes and foreigners and Catholics.' When it comes to this, I shall prefer emigrating to some country where they make no pretense of loving liberty."

Infinitely tender was his word from a White House balcony to a crowd on the White House lawn, "I have not willingly planted a thorn in any man's bosom," or to a military governor, "I shall do nothing through malice; what I deal with is too vast for malice."

He wrote for Congress to read on Dec. 1, 1862:

"In times like the present men would utter nothing for which they would not willingly be responsible through time and eternity."

Like an ancient psalmist he warned Congress:

"Fellow citizens, we cannot escape history. We will be remembered in spite of ourselves. No personal significance or insignificance can spare one or another of us. The fiery trial through which we pass will light us down in honor or dishonor to the latest generation."

Wanting Congress to break and forget past traditions his words came keen and flashing. "The dogmas of the quiet past are inadequate for the stormy present. We must think anew, we must act anew, we must disenthrall ourselves." They are the sort of words that actuated the mind and will of the men who created and navigated that marvel of the sea, the Nautilus and her voyage from Pearl Harbor and under the North Pole icecap.

The people of many other countries take Lincoln now for their own. He belongs to them. He stands for decency, honest dealing, plain talk, and funny stories. "Look where he came from—don't he know all us strugglers and wasn't he a kind of tough struggler all his life right up to the finish?" Something like that you can hear in any near-by neighborhood and across the seas.

Millions there are who take him as a personal treasure. He had something they would like to see spread everywhere over the world. Democracy? We can't find words to say exactly what it is, but he had it. In his blood and bones he carried it. In the breath of his speeches and writings it is there. Popular government? Republican institution? Government where the people have the say-so, one way or another telling their elected leaders what they want? He had the idea. It's there in the lights and shadows of his personality, a mystery that can be lived but never fully spoken in words.

Our good friend the poet and playwright Mark Van Doren tells us:

"To me, Lincoln seems, in some ways, the most interesting man who ever lived. He was gentle, but his gentleness was combined with a terrific toughness, an iron strength."

How did Lincoln say he would like to be remembered? His beloved friend, Representative Owen Lovejoy of Illinois, had died in May of 1864 and friends wrote to Lincoln and he replied that the pressure of duties kept him from joining them in efforts for a marble monument to Lovejoy, the last sentence of his letter saying, "Let him have the marble monument along with the well-assured and more enduring one in the hearts of those who love liberty, unselfishly, for all men."

So perhaps we may say that the well assured and most enduring memorial to Lincoln is invisibly there, today, tomorrow and for a long time yet to come in the hearts of lovers of liberty, men and women who understand that wherever there is freedom there have been those who fought, toiled and sacrificed for it.

JOHN F. KENNEDY

". . . ask not what your country can do for you—ask what you can do for your country."

WASHINGTON, D. C., Jan. 20, 1961—The youngest man ever elected to the Presidency marked his Inaugural today, not with a promise of panaceas for the United States, but with a forthright challenge to its youth to seek new ways to advance the precepts of revolutionary social improvements.

Standing bareheaded in a wintry wind, he interpreted his election as the passing of "the torch" to a new generation, "born in this century, tempered by war, disciplined by a hard and bitter peace, proud of our ancient heritage."

This generation, he proclaimed, is "unwilling to witness or permit the slow undoing of those human rights to which this nation has always been committed, and to which we are committed today at home and around the world."

To the crowd of thousands that faced him from the grounds of the Capitol, and to scores of millions of television viewers, his words brought an undoubted sense of destiny; to some, also, a gnawing fear of what his interpretation of destiny might bring into national policies.

But one thing was certain: this handsome, intense young man, would bring to the Presidency a new, if controversial, national leadership. His address, in part, follows:

LET EVERY nation know, whether it wishes us well or ill, that we shall pay any price, bear any burden, meet any hardship, support any friend, oppose any foe to assure the survival and the success of liberty.

This much we pledge—and more. . . .

To that world assembly of sovereign states, the United Nations, our last best hope in an age where the instruments of war have far outpaced the instruments of peace, we renew our pledge of support—to prevent it from becoming merely a forum for invective—to strengthen its shield of the new and the weak and to enlarge the area in which its writ may run.

Finally, to those nations who would make themselves our adversary, we offer not a pledge but a request: that both sides begin anew the quest for peace, before the dark powers of destruction unleashed by science engulf all humanity in planned or accidental self-destruction.

We dare not tempt them with weakness. For only when our arms are sufficient beyond doubt can we be certain beyond doubt that they will never be employed. . . .

So let us begin anew—remembering on both sides that civility is not a sign of weakness, and sincerity is always subject to proof. Let us never negotiate out of fear. But let us never fear to negotiate.

Let both sides explore what problems unite us instead of laboring those problems which divide us. . . .

And if a beachhead of cooperation may push back the jungle of suspicion, let both sides join in creating a new endeavor—not a new balance of power, but a new world of law, where the strong are just and the weak secure and the peace preserved. . . .

In the long history of the world, only a few generations have been granted the role of defending freedom in its hour of maximum danger. I do not shrink from this responsibility—I welcome it. I do not believe that any of us would exchange places with any other people or any other generation. The energy, the faith, the devotion which we bring to this endeavor will light our country and all who serve it—and the glow from that fire can truly light the world.

And so, my fellow Americans: ask not what your country can do for you—ask what you can do for your country.

My fellow citizens of the world: ask not what America will do for you, but what together we can do for the freedom of man.

The sequel:

The Kennedy program, insofar as it could be assessed in the mid-1960's, came surprisingly close to meeting its main objectives of defending freedom abroad while extending it throughout the American social structure. His re-election in 1964 appeared certain. Then, on November 22, 1963, he was slain by an assassin's bullet.

ALPHABETICAL
LISTING OF SPEAKERS

SPEECHES BY CATEGORIES
(*In Chronological Order*)

I. INSPIRATION AND EXHORTATION

EDWARD RAWSON (1676) First Thanksgiving
JONATHAN EDWARDS (1741) Sinners and an Angry God
JOHN QUINCY ADAMS (1802) Plymouth Oration
DANIEL WEBSTER (1825) Bunker Hill Address
RALPH WALDO EMERSON (1859) Eulogy of Burns
HENRY WARD BEECHER (1869) Fellowship
CARL SCHURZ (1881) The Old World and the New
OLIVER WENDELL HOLMES SR. (1884) "Dorothy Q."
HENRY CABOT LODGE (1888) Our Forefathers
BOOKER T. WASHINGTON (1896) The American Standard
WILLIAM JENNINGS BRYAN (1896) The "Cross of Gold"
THEODORE ROOSEVELT (1899) The Strenuous Life
GEORGE C. VEST (1903) Tribute to a Dog
WILLIAM ASHLEY (BILLY) SUNDAY (1914) Evangelism
RUSSELL H. CONWELL (1925) Acres of Diamonds
ALFRED E. SMITH (1928) Religious Prejudice
OLIVER WENDELL HOLMES JR. (1931) "Live—I am Coming"
WILLIAM LYON PHELPS (1933) Owning Books
OWEN D. YOUNG (1934) Use of Knowledge
HERBERT HOOVER (1935) The Bill of Rights
WILLIAM ALLEN WHITE (1937) The Consumer
CHARLES EVANS HUGHES (1939) Meaning of Democracy
HAROLD L. ICKES (1941) Defining an American
FULTON J. SHEEN (1941) A Change of Hearts
WILLIAM FAULKNER (1950) Accepting Nobel Prize
WILLIAM F. (BILLY) GRAHAM (1957) National Humility
JOHN MASON BROWN (1958) The "Beat Generation"
CARL SANDBURG (1959) On Lincoln

II. HUMOR

CHAUNCEY M. DEPEW (1875) Woman
SAMUEL L. CLEMENS (Mark Twain) (1876) New England Weather
JOSEPH H. CHOATE (1880) The Bench and the Bar
WILL ROGERS (1924) Wealth and Education
ROBERT C. BENCHLEY (1930) "The Treasurer's Report"
IRVIN S. COBB (1941) Pretty Man With the Pink Clothes On

III. BY WOMEN

JULIA WARD HOWE (1870) To Oliver Wendell Holmes
SUSAN B. ANTHONY (1873) "Are Women Persons?"
JANE ADDAMS (1903) On George Washington
EMMA GOLDMAN (1910) Anarchy vs. Patriotism
ELEANOR ROOSEVELT (1952) The United Nations
CORNELIA OTIS SKINNER (1953) A Toast to Doctors

IV. EULOGIES

GOUVERNEUR MORRIS (1804) At Alexander Hamilton's Funeral
EDWARD EVERETT (1826) Adams and Jefferson
WENDELL PHILLIPS (1837) Murder of Elijah Lovejoy
RALPH WALDO EMERSON (1859) Robert Burns
WILLIAM LLOYD GARRISON (1859) John Brown
JAMES G. BLAINE (1882) President Garfield
OLIVER WENDELL HOLMES SR. (1884) "Dorothy Q."
RALPH G. INGERSOLL (1899) "Blaine, the Plumed Knight"
JANE ADDAMS (1903) George Washington
STEPHEN S. WISE (1914) Abraham Lincoln

V. ARTS AND SCIENCES

CHARLES W. ELIOT (1877) Education Is Nonsectarian
WILLIAM LYON PHELPS (1933) Owning Books
FRANK LLOYD WRIGHT (1939) Architects
J. ROBERT OPPENHEIMER (1954) On Knowledge

VI. PRESIDENTIAL SPEECHES (While in Office)

GEORGE WASHINGTON (1796) Farewell Address
THOMAS JEFFERSON (1801) First Inaugural
JAMES MONROE (1823) The Monroe Doctrine
ANDREW JACKSON (1833) Second Inaugural
ABRAHAM LINCOLN (1863) Gettysburg Address
  (1865) Second Inaugural

VII. INDEPENDENCE AND THE CONSTITUTION

VIII. SECESSION AND THE CIVIL WAR

IX. WORLD WAR I AND LEAGUE OF NATIONS

X. WORLD WAR II AND UNITED NATIONS

XI. MISCELLANEOUS

THE AUTHOR AND HIS BOOK

CHARLES HURD, *author, journalist and public relations consultant, was born on May 11, 1903, in Tonkawa, Oklahoma. He received his boyhood education from tutors and was an extension student at Northwestern University, Evanston, Ill., from 1918 to 1923. He began his writing career during his college years as a full-time reporter for The Associated Press in Chicago and then in New York City. He became an associate editor of Liberty magazine in 1926 and left three years later to join the staff of The New York Times in their Washington bureau. Until 1949 he remained there, having served as White House correspondent at various times and having been a London correspondent specializing in international politics during 1937 and 1938. He has since been actively engaged in the public relations field doing industrial promotion work through his own firm, Charles Hurd Associates. He was also a news commentator and has contributed to many magazines including Life, Reader's Digest, and American Magazine, wrote a regular feature on personalities for Redbook, and has had material published in anthologies. His books are* The White House (*Harper, 1940*); The Veterans Program (*Whittlesey House, 1946*); Washington Cavalcade (*Dutton, 1948*), *and* The Compact History of the American Red Cross (*Hawthorn, 1959*); A Treasury of Great American Speeches (*Hawthorn, 1959*); U.S. Mail, *in collaboration with Arthur E. Summerfield* (Holt, 1960); *Cavalcade of* Europe, *in collaboration with Lowell Thomas* (Doubleday, 1960); A Treasury of Great American Letters (*Hawthorn, 1961*) *and* A Treasury of Great American Quotations (*Hawthorn, 1964*). *He was married to the former Eleanor Branson of Washington, D. C., in 1934, and they make their home in New York City.*

A Treasury of Great American Speeches (*Hawthorn, 1959*) *was designed by Sidney Feinberg, and completely manufactured by American Book–Stratford Press, Inc. The body type was set on the Linotype in Times Roman, originally designed for use by* The Times *of London.*

A H A W T H O R N   B O O K